SOLIDARITY

SOLIDARITY

The Work of Recognition

ROWAN WILLIAMS

BLOOMSBURY CONTINUUM
LONDON · OXFORD · NEW YORK · NEW DELHI · SYDNEY

BLOOMSBURY CONTINUUM
Bloomsbury Publishing Plc

50 Bedford Square, London, WC1B 3DP, UK
Bloomsbury Publishing Ireland Limited,
29 Earlsfort Terrace, Dublin 2, D02 AY28, Ireland

BLOOMSBURY, BLOOMSBURY CONTINUUM
and the Diana logo are trademarks of Bloomsbury Publishing Plc

First published in Great Britain 2026

Copyright © Rowan Williams, 2026

Rowan Williams has asserted his right under the Copyright, Designs and Patents Act, 1988, to be identified as Author of this work

For legal purposes the Acknowledgements on pp. 259–60 constitute an extension of this copyright page

All rights reserved. No part of this publication may be: i) reproduced or transmitted in any form, electronic or mechanical, including photocopying, recording or by means of any information storage or retrieval system without prior permission in writing from the publishers; or ii) used or reproduced in any way for the training, development or operation of artificial intelligence (AI) technologies, including generative AI technologies. The rights holders expressly reserve this publication from the text and data mining exception as per Article 4(3) of the Digital Single Market Directive (EU) 2019/790

Bloomsbury Publishing Plc does not have any control over, or responsibility for, any third-party websites referred to or in this book. All internet addresses given in this book were correct at the time of going to press. The author and publisher regret any inconvenience caused if addresses have changed or sites have ceased to exist, but can accept no responsibility for any such changes

A catalogue record for this book is available from the British Library
Library of Congress Cataloguing-in-Publication data has been applied for

ISBN:	HB:	978-1-3994-3151-4
	EPDF:	978-1-3994-3149-1
	EPUB:	978-1-3994-3148-4

2 4 6 8 10 9 7 5 3 1

Typeset by Lumina Datamatics Ltd
Printed and bound in Great Britain by Clays Ltd, Elcograf S.p.A

To find out more about our authors and books visit www.bloomsbury.com
and sign up for our newsletters
For product safety related questions contact productsafety@bloomsbury.com

CONTENTS

	Prologue	1
	Introduction	9
1	Recognizing Strangers: Who Counts as Human?	23
2	Understanding Strangers: Empathy and Its Paradoxes	51
3	The Claims of Strangers: Debating Human Rights	75
4	Solidarity: the Making of a Discourse	101
5	The Solidarity of the Shaken: Jan Patočka and the Care of the Soul	129
6	Solidarity Without Enemies: Józef Tischner and the Conversation of Human Labour	155
7	Solidarity, Responsibility, Guilt: Dietrich Bonhoeffer's Helplessness	183
8	Solidarity, Co-inherence, Communion	209
	Conclusion	235
	Acknowledgements	259
	Endnotes	261
	Index	297

PROLOGUE

In the mid-1980s, my wife and I spent a couple of months working for the Anglican Church in South Africa, at a time of much tension and unrest in the country. Any hope of a future without deeper – probably violent – conflict seemed almost unimaginable. As we know, such conflict was avoided: figures – often unexpected figures – on both sides of the racial divide took considerable risks in opening up conversation and negotiation. They were acting out of a conviction that there had to be a future in which the different racial groups could recognize some common interest, rather than an endless stand-off, a zero-sum competition. In the years that followed the liberation of Nelson Mandela in 1990, that conviction was linked with increasing frequency to what was presented as a distinctively African form of humanism, crystallized in the IsiZulu word *ubuntu* – notionally the term for 'humanity' but routinely interpreted as designating a belief in mutuality and interdependence. It was often summed up in aphoristic form: 'I am because you are', or 'I am because we are' is probably the most commonly quoted of these, but many also refer to the IsiZulu maxim *umuntu ngumuntu ngabantu*, whose simplest rendering is something like, 'It is people that make people people.' The language of *ubuntu* is very closely associated with the late Archbishop Desmond Tutu[1] and thus with the work of the Truth and Reconciliation Commission in South Africa which Tutu chaired in the years of Mandela's presidency. *Ubuntu* was crucial for the ethos of the Commission, as Tutu's aim was to offer a vision of the future in which there could be some way forward through and beyond historic trauma and anger, however justified. The promise of the possibility of amnesty for the guilty was meant to enable a sharing of truths otherwise too shameful or traumatic to speak about, and so to offer the chance of another kind of relationship. And it is implicit in this discourse that liberation must be liberation for perpetrator as well as victim, oppressor as well as oppressed; the liberated victim is not wholly liberated until there is some sort of reconciliation with the perpetrator, because of the basic moral interdependence that constructs human identity. The final goal of the process is a restoration of, or witnessing to, *ubuntu* at the most fundamental level.

We were already fairly familiar with discussions around Latin American 'theologies of liberation' in this period, and with some of the debates about postcolonial religious and cultural identities in India, where my wife had grown up. But what seemed particularly sharp and complex in the discourse around what change might be possible in South Africa was something to do with the subject of this book – the question of the nature of 'solidarity' as an aspect of our humanity and a goal for a more humane society. Talking about *ubuntu* against the background of the brutal polarities of apartheid South Africa was, among other things, a way of talking about what it would mean to be conscious of at least some elements of a common agenda across deep divisions; about the search for some state of affairs that everyone involved might look at with hope; about something more and other than a simple reversal of power relations ('we are the masters now'). And it also entailed some serious self-questioning for those white activists who supported the struggle in various ways. I remember intense conversations about what it meant to act in 'solidarity' with people whose actual physical (and political) condition you simply didn't share; and some of those white activists tentatively exploring ideas about solidarity as seeking to some extent to share risks, and to keep asking oneself awkward questions about whether the privileged activist was simply replicating patterns of racially determined power (the critique of the 'white saviour' trope was not yet cast in the terms we have become familiar with in more recent years, but the substance of the issue was already being debated).

It is this moral hinterland that made the work of the Truth and Reconciliation Commission so profoundly hopeful for many inside and outside South Africa. Yet the Commission's legacy is more and more hotly debated and contested in South Africa today, in a society where historic injustices have not been definitively resolved by any means and where economic inequality, controversy over land ownership, and an array of other problems generated by the history of apartheid remain painfully visible. The 'truth' of the Commission's labours has not in itself brought reconciliation, or a sense of active mutuality; violent polarization is starkly (and increasingly) in evidence. There is a sense in some quarters that the language of *ubuntu* has confused rather than advanced a just and manageable future. Nyasha Mboti, in a lengthy and thoughtful article of 2015,[2] shows how the word has had to do far too much work for comfort. Definitions have been vague, specific application ambiguous, and, perhaps most concerningly, some proponents of the discourse (often sympathetically minded Europeans) have used it in a way that unwittingly reinforces an 'African essentialism', counterposing 'European' ideas of freedom and individual dignity to 'African' communalism and co-operation. Mboti in effect argues for something that we shall see championed by others in recent debate – a candid recognition that interdependence in and of itself is not the end of the moral story, since our 'making' of one another may be for good or ill; that incomplete and provisional endeavours at solidarity are not failures; and that we need to be very wary of erecting an idealized model of absolute mutual transparency as a goal in human affairs, in a way that elides the real, lasting, constructive difference that may act as a driver of innovation and self-critique.

But it is impossible to ignore the fact that the language of *ubuntu* represented, at a crucial moment of dangerous fragmentation, an alternative to a winner-takes-all conflict of mass bloodshed. In a sense, this book is written in the hope that there is something to be salvaged from that moment, and something to be learned if we want to make sense of solidarity as an ideal for – or indeed a fact about – human society. Granted, the language of *ubuntu* has been used loosely, sentimentally, even evasively by some; granted that the appeal to reconciliation can be experienced as a re-victimizing of victims, who are now expected to be the moral saviours of their abusers (talking about forgiveness in a Christian context can all too often sound like this). But what Mandela and Tutu and those whom they persuaded succeeded in doing was to make the case that mutual incompatibility and incomprehension did not constitute a necessary default position for human interaction; even that the struggle for hegemony and privilege was not the only conceivable pattern for political labour. Witnessing briefly at close quarters the arguments among Christian opponents of apartheid in the 1980s opened up for me a deeper awareness of how complex a business 'solidarity' might be against a background of massive, entrenched historical injustice and exploitation; but it also highlighted the fact that those at the receiving end of this injustice could still see that rectifying this situation could and should involve a betterment of life for all, not just themselves. It was and is a risky claim; but it was and is a necessary element in whatever prevents us from settling for a cyclical history of violently enforced control as the only possible future for the human race.

In other words, the *ubuntu* perspective, with all the questions that have to be asked about it, represented for me a theological and ethical challenge and a theological and ethical agenda. What it might mean to think through this discourse in our own context, where oppositions were often less clear-cut and political options more ambivalent, continued to be a matter of concern in writing and action in the years that followed. Some of that concern eventually found its way into a book called *Lost Icons: Reflections on Cultural Bereavement* in 1999,[3] where I attempted to analyse some aspects of the contemporary 'North Atlantic' cultural world in terms of what resources, narratives and paradigms for a robustly interactive form of social coexistence had been lost in modernity. The final chapter of this small work also began to address what it might mean in terms of individual psychology to believe that selves were constructed in relation, not 'given' as finished entities. Building to some extent on this, a 2012 collection of addresses mostly from the decade during which I worked as Archbishop of Canterbury[4] is an assortment of ad hoc essays on how the wider theoretical issues I had been thinking about might apply to various current social issues in the UK and elsewhere – human rights, environmental problems, the rule of law, the position of minorities and so on.

But underlying these brief interventions was an abiding interest in the exploration of what solidarity might mean; and this opened up for me two broader sets of questions related to such an exploration, and – as I saw it – not often enough connected with it in discussion. One was around our understanding of *empathy* – the claim or aspiration to be able to look at the world from another's standpoint, and with something of another's emotional and imaginative as well as intellectual resources. The other was how a philosophy (and theology) of human rights might be illuminated by a more consistently relational and embodied understanding of the supposed subject of rights. Invitations to lecture at the Moral Sciences Club at Cambridge and then at Harvard University in 2014, and at Fuller Divinity School in Pasadena in 2016 allowed me to develop some ideas on these matters, with very fruitful criticism and input from interlocutors in these institutions. Teaching at the Pontifical University of St Thomas Aquinas (the Angelicum) in Rome in the spring of 2022 provided the opportunity to begin connecting the themes of these earlier lectures with various authoritative texts on Catholic Social Teaching. Lectures on Gillian Rose (at the University of Kingston Upon Thames) and on aspects of the legacy of the 'Swansea school' of Wittgenstein interpretation, especially its engagement with society and the self (at the annual conference of the Welsh Philosophical society at Gregynog) pushed me to clarify some of the philosophical background to thinking about relationality. And a final stimulus was the chance to deliver two related short courses on solidarity at Yale Divinity School and Oxford University in early 2024.

So this book contains the substance of the Tanner Lectures at Harvard (2014), the Payton Lectures at Fuller in 2016, and the Taylor Lectures at Yale and Bampton Lectures at Oxford in 2024, as well as material from teaching or speaking in a variety of academic settings. But all these reflections can in some degree be traced back to the seminal problems that I first saw being engaged with in apartheid South Africa; hence, for me, the significance – even poignancy – of being able to have some of these ideas scrutinized in that country as the book neared completion. I had the privilege of sharing some of its ideas in seminars at the University of Stellenbosch, and absorbing something of the ongoing contemporary debates about justice, common good, racialized power, sanitized memories, unfinished moral business and a great deal more that run through the intellectual and political life of South Africa today. It is not that the foundational question behind the Truth and Reconciliation Commission is any less urgent: is there a way of engaging, speaking together, that does not presuppose an ultimate incommensurability in human goods, and thus an unavoidable contest about control? In a world where the stranger is not going to disappear overnight, can we do better than the denial of that stranger's right to some kind of partnership with us or the promise that some day the stranger will no longer be there – either because they have ceased to be strange or because they have literally ceased to be there?

If the language of *ubuntu*, as it is often used, is something of a shortcut (especially for those outside the South African situation with all its ongoing, unresolved conflicts), appealing to what is dangerously like a 'noble savage' mythology at times, it cannot simply be written off. It still embodies a crucial challenge to other even more problematic mythologies – myths of incompatible kinds of human subjectivity, of deep foreignness of feeling, myths of irreconcilable imperatives of self-protection, myths of insulation from mortality and from the shared condition of finitude and fragility, myths that have unquestionably shaped the collective psyche of 'modern' and 'Western' humanity. It is essential not to react to this recognition by idealizing the cultural other in a way that is in the long run as unconstructive as any crude prejudice or exclusion; but there is everything to be said for looking at what a consistently relational understanding of both subjectivity and society might deliver. An understanding of solidarity that involves the continuing work of recognition and self-questioning, the continuing labour of identifying possible shared discourses of value and hope, a continuing seriousness about difference and difficulty, and a persistent sense of the inexhaustibility of human worth seems at the moment a spectacularly counter-cultural position. Yet so much of the intellectual unease running through both our political and our philosophical language these days pushes us back to these questions about how we might imagine a solidarity that is critical and truthful. What is more, an understanding of solidarity that locates our human togetherness firmly within the context of a comprehensive interdependence – a 'conversation' with the non-human world that shows the same patience, respect and willingness to share and nourish life that ought to characterize our human interaction – is more and more clearly a matter of life and death for our planetary ecology.

One more prefatory thought: the experience of the Covid-19 pandemic, especially the dramatic lockdowns of 2020, briefly highlighted both the persistence and the fragility of solidarity language. The consciousness of shared jeopardy, shared frailty, could hardly have been more sharply experienced, and public rhetoric made much of our responsibilities to each other. We were exhorted to take care not to infect elderly relatives; we were told to sacrifice some of the instinctive rituals of solidarity – including family funerals – for the sake of a deeper solidarity, the saving of each other's lives. We fleetingly had a glimpse of what a society might be if those who most consistently and devotedly served the needs of the most vulnerable were valued according to their contribution to common safety and well-being. We were reminded forcefully that no one is safe unless everyone is safe. And we then very rapidly and efficiently began to forget all this, as global affairs returned to 'normal'. As if we had, in trying to imagine solidarity afresh, been drawing on a seriously depleted set of resources.

The pages that follow are an attempt to survey some of the resources we might turn to for rethinking and realizing solidarity, resources from a variety of cultural, intellectual and religious contexts – phenomenological philosophy, cultural theory, political protest, fiction and drama, theology. For the author, the focal and unifying point is the distinctive vision of law and common good that is rooted in the Jewish and Christian traditions. Readers may or may not share that vision or find it fully intelligible; but the themes that it touches on are no less worth exploring for all that. I hope this book will at least encourage the recognition that this vision can be used to think and imagine with, and that its challenges about what truth we might uncover and what untruth we might find courage to relinquish have (to put it mildly) a certain urgency.

INTRODUCTION

Just over ten years ago, in January 2015, 12 people were killed at the Paris offices of the French satirical periodical, *Charlie Hebdo*, an atrocity prompted by the journal having published a cartoon in which the Prophet Muhammad was depicted. Over the days and weeks following, the slogan, 'Je suis Charlie' went viral; groups and individuals displayed it endlessly on social media posts, on banners, T-shirts and buildings.

There was nothing new about the appeal to solidarity that this slogan so vividly implied; what was slightly different was the insistent foregrounding of *identification* with those who had been murdered. It was as if people were reaching for something that went further or deeper than 'support' and 'sympathy'. They wanted to announce that this was *their* issue, not simply a tragedy that had touched them or a cause with which they felt some affinity. And this in turn generated a sharp reaction – not just in those who proclaimed 'Je ne suis pas Charlie', for various ideological reasons, but those who were uneasy about co-opting a bloody and traumatic event into a dramatization of collective protest that could easily become simply 'performative', with the emphasis on the protester's moral orthodoxy rather than the specifics of the trauma. And there were those who noted with asperity that there had not been much sign of this style of solidarity with non-Western victims of atrocity; their sufferings remained remote and foreign.

This reproach could not be levelled against those who – as these words are being written – have been involved in a range of protest activities in response to the nightmare level of suffering and death in the Middle East. Once again, people have been reaching for the language of identification, not only support, but rather more obviously looking for ways of standing with those who are not culturally similar; the wearing of the Palestinian *keffiyeh* becomes a statement that the wearer aspires somehow to share the experience of the victims of bombardment in Gaza,[1] or at least to stand where they stand so far as this is possible, perhaps to take risks for their sake. On the other side of the ethical space, meanwhile, demonstrators in Israel gather to remind their government of the continuing plight of those taken hostage in the initial murderous attack by Hamas militants on 7 October 2023, making the same appeal to solidarity with named individuals brutalized by terroristic violence; while Jewish activists in Europe and North America also take to the streets in the name of solidarity with a whole nation faced by hostile neighbours whose aim is its annihilation, and in angry reaction to the resurgent and shameless antisemitism that they believe is being enabled by other demonstrators. In yet another twist of moral complexity in this language, Houthi militants from Yemen describe their attacks on Western shipping in the Red Sea as acts of 'solidarity' with Palestinians – not so much in this case an identification with victims as such, but still a declaration that the plight of Gaza's citizens is their business, in a very straightforward way that justifies acts of aggression against real or supposed allies of Palestine's chief enemy.

It is clear enough that the rhetoric of solidarity, especially in the age of mass online discourse, is a potent imaginative vehicle. It acts as a moral intensifier: it positions the activist or protester unequivocally alongside the victim of atrocity or injustice, and offers a straightforward way of distancing oneself absolutely from the perpetrator (the complementary and converse strategy is of course the use of 'not in my name' slogans in various contexts). The risk in such a context, though, is that appeals to solidarity become a way of simplifying a complex moral landscape. Online rallying cries for solidarity may be some distance from any detailed consideration of the possibilities of effective common action. The word itself – as we shall see in later chapters – has a rich and diverse history, much of which is deeply bound up with the labour movement; for many people, 'solidarity' will evoke the struggles not only of industrial workers over the last century and a half or so but most specifically of the Polish trade union of the 1980s. It will evoke a world of strike action and collaboration across different industries based on the recognition of common interests. It is not in that environment primarily about a *sense* of identification, but about specific areas of shared practical concern and the best ways of exerting pressure to deal with these. It is not primarily a marker of total and uncritical identification. But there is in contemporary discourse a yearning for some more dramatic way of articulating the passion to be visibly on the side of the victim of injustice or atrocity. Support or sympathy may be qualified, contextualized, developed; solidarity is a plain statement of belonging together without reserve, a commitment that defines exactly who you are with and who you are against. You can't be partly on the same ground; you are or you aren't. And if it's a question of whether you are or you aren't, clarifying where you stand may become more pressing than the labour needed to change a situation. The box can be ticked without much in the way of further action.

So, at least, critics of solidarity language will claim. Is all this not just theatrics, 'performativity', to use the fashionable word, a way of dramatizing one's own sense of moral intensity by appropriating the experience of others? The truth is that the wearing of an appropriately inscribed T-shirt or a *keffiyeh* by a demonstrator in London or Seattle won't alter the basic fact that the wearer may be protected in any number of ways from the acute, deadly vulnerability of those with whom they want to stand. Some demonstrators face disciplinary or legal sanctions, some students may be putting their academic careers at least temporarily at risk. But, the sceptic will say, in what sense is there any more going on than an intensification of expressions of rather distanced concerns? Beyond the mass demonstration, what particular commitments to ongoing action and change are emerging? It is easy enough to reach for the tired and cynical charge of 'virtue-signalling', and to see the language and symbolism of solidarity as another instance of that pervasive nostalgia for unqualified moral security that our very superficially secularized culture displays in so many forms.[2] The novelist Howard Jacobson wrote in the summer of 2024, in the wake of a series of protest actions associating a variety of tenuously related issues, that '"solidarity" is one of those come-ons that grab our consciences even when the conflation means little more than "here are a few of my least favourite things."'[3] And from a very different point of view, writers and commentators on racial conflict, especially those associated with the Black Lives Matter movement, have challenged what they see as self-deceiving, superficial, or merely gestural solidarity on the part of white anti-racists, who fail to grasp the ways in which their racial identity protects them from any real share in the precariousness of their non-white colleagues (in a demonstration, exactly who is more likely to be arrested or shot without question?).[4] Reni Eddo-Lodge's powerful and provocative *Why I'm No Longer Talking to White People About Race*[5] offers a particularly clear account of opportunistic or performative language and behaviour – a would-be solidarity that costs nothing, even when proclaimed as 'allyship' – while also outlining the kind of support that might count as effective solidarity.[6] 'I don't want white guilt'[7]; what is needed is intelligent collaborative action.

If there are questions about using solidarity language to effect a too facile or low-cost connection between different persons and communities, there is also a strong critique coming from a very different perspective, from those who see this language as always impregnated with attempts to withdraw and exclude. 'The twentieth century perverted cooperation in the name of solidarity', according to Richard Sennett in his brilliant study of the social and political significance of active and embodied co-operation, shared 'craft'.[8] Solidarity has been talked up as the proper response to the fragmentation produced by capitalism; but this strategy, according to Sennett, is a way of avoiding the real question. Fragmented social life needs for its healing a new set of practices, co-operative practices appropriate to a hugely changed world of work. Capitalism creates an environment of mobile, rootless

INTRODUCTION

and depersonalized labour, short-term and insecure employment, indifference to local culture and affiliations, sovereign disregard for the material surroundings and longer-term impacts of working practices. The difficult but necessary response is to clarify our understanding of the processes that lead to this and the slow work of thinking around the taken-for-granted habits that keep us enslaved to a poisonous working environment. The easy and tempting answer is to appeal nostalgically to a sense of simple belonging-together, which can be readily manipulated against 'alien' individuals and communities who are seen as undermining the timeless, natural togetherness of traditional working communities. Think of the repeated trope in – for example – Donald Trump's 2024 presidential campaign claiming that migrants from Latin America were taking 'Black jobs' in the USA: an attempt to woo African-American voters living with high levels of pressure and deprivation, including insecurity of employment. The same tactic has been deployed in Britain and in various continental European countries (including countries like Denmark and Sweden with their longstanding communitarian and co-operative traditions) against migrants from Eastern Europe, Western Asia and elsewhere. Solidarity without some kind of rethinking of the ethics of co-operation becomes an active enemy of social good in an increasingly diverse society. We have never, Sennett argues, effectively resolved the tension between two kinds of solidarity, 'the one emphasizing unity, the other inclusion',[9] the former seeing co-operation primarily as a tool for achieving collective ends determined by a top-down command structure, the latter more concerned with maximizing participation and retaining the ability to challenge forms of discipline and control that excluded certain categories of people. Sennett's implicit conclusion is that the former style has generally prevailed in our imaginations, and that it now exercises a 'perverse' power as a vehicle for consolidating exclusive identities. This – though Sennett doesn't explicitly develop the point – suits capitalist management well in some respects, even if not in others. As has often been pointed out, hyper-mobile labour resources are part of the programme of expansionist capitalism;

migrancy is good for a flexible economy that is not too closely tied to the specific good of a local environment. But at the same time, a nostalgic attachment to traditional forms of belonging, cultural, ethnic, religious or whatever, an attachment that can be weaponized against threatening strangers, can be an enormously useful distraction from asking where the real problem lies: resentment against migrants 'taking jobs' translates into hostility to migrants – not to the system that supports casualized and rootless work, emasculates workers' bargaining powers, and bypasses or overrides local democratic decision-making.

Solidarity, then, can have a bad name for diverse reasons – as a piece of performative and often self-indulgent borrowing of the stories and experiences of the vulnerable, and as an equally self-indulgent and 'perverse' response to the workings of power in global capitalism. These suspicious reactions are intelligible enough; and it is important in any honest treatment of the subject to address the risks of superficiality and exclusivism. But we are still left with the task of excavating the heart of the impulse that leads people to speak of solidarity rather than *merely* support or even sympathy, or of solidarity rather than *merely* inherited identity. As we'll see, the word itself has a tangled and remarkably varied history. As we have noted, the idea of acting as if someone else's suffering or constraint were your own is by no means the invention of sentimental twenty-first century activists. 'Solidarity forever' is a song from as long ago as 1913: 'When the union's inspiration through the workers' blood shall run', it begins, and the chorus ends, 'It's the union makes us strong.'[10] Solidarity in the context of the labour movement of the late nineteenth and early twentieth centuries meant that workers in different industries recognized that their interests were indivisible. 'One out, all out': to come out on strike in sympathy or solidarity was part of the strategy of building effective economic leverage to protect the rights of all working people in a context where the law offered little if any security. Solidarity did not mean *any* kind of appropriation of the plight of another, but something much closer to the recognition that structural injustices were inseparably part of a single interconnected system, so that the privation of one working community was an aspect of the challenge faced by all working communities, and an assault on one working community was an assault on all. The possibility of a general strike was in theory the ultimate sanction against employers picking off vulnerable groups of workers without challenge.

It is true that the word loses some of its freshness by the mid twentieth century; 'one out, all out' had become by the 1960s a comic trope rather than a revolutionary summons (as with the mythical union leader who calls his members to strike action when he overhears someone saying that the sun has come out). Arguably, it was the history of the Polish movement that restored its seriousness in the minds of many and gave the word an aura that felt less old-fashioned. But the term had already migrated to the world of labour relations from origins that were rather different. Although 'solidarity' was a word used here and there in European (especially French) discussion of law and economics before the middle of the nineteenth century, it was not in common usage before the later part of the century; and even then its context is mostly in the nascent discipline of social science, especially in the work of Fourier and Durkheim. For these early sociologists, its force is essentially descriptive; it has not yet acquired the powerful moral colouring that we hear in its use within the labour movement. It has not yet moved from being a *condition* to being a *virtue*, an imperative. And that dual resonance, descriptive and ethical, continues to complicate and sometimes to confuse the usage of the word. It can still have a primarily indicative sense: when the philosopher Richard Rorty contrasts two accounts of the basis of ethical judgement as 'objectivity' and 'solidarity', he has in mind first and foremost the sociological idea of solidarity as a fact about human social experience. He is distinguishing an ethic looking for external validation from one that is grounded simply in the accepted grammar of an identifiable and cohesive culture. But a potential reader approaching Rorty's work from a socialist background and engaged by the appearance of the word 'solidarity' in the title of one of his books, would be bewildered by a discussion that lacks any appeal to solidarity as a goal to be sought or a value to be nurtured. And their expectations would be rooted in a generally more familiar sense of the word, the sense with which we began, of the urge to take a particular kind of moral stance – one that is in some elusive way deeper than just declaring support for some human other, a stance deriving from the recognition of a crisis, a plight, that is shared.

The 'deeper' resonance has increasingly, in the last century, been amplified in a very different environment – within the official moral teaching of the Roman Catholic Church, which has identified the ideal of solidarity as a fundamental element in a just society. Pope John Paul II, in one of his most important pronouncements in this area, proposed in 1989 that the components of such a society were 'dignity, subsidiarity and solidarity'. But the use of solidarity as a category of specifically Catholic and Christian ethical thinking goes back to the first decades of the twentieth century, especially in the German-speaking world, where communitarian and anti-capitalist themes were explored in the context of a somewhat inchoate theory of solidarity. Developments in Eastern Europe in the post-war decades led to some very important refinements of the idea by writers like Józef Tischner in Poland and Jan Patočka in Czechoslovakia. That the radical Polish trades union movement of the 1980s should operate under the name of 'Solidarity' (*Solidarność*) was not accidental, given the importance of the categories of Catholic Social Teaching in the growing resistance to a corrupt, stale and oppressive official Marxism in the country; and equally, the heightened profile of the term in official Papal teaching from the 1980s onwards undoubtedly reflects the way in which the ideal of solidarity had, so to speak, won its spurs in the battle against the sclerotic social models of the old Communist bloc.

But the highlighting of solidarity in Catholic Social Teaching also chimed with a recovery of a more participatory understanding of the life of the Church itself and a sharpened critique of contemporary individualism from many theological voices. Fully to understand the appeal and the significance of solidarity in

INTRODUCTION

this context needs some attention to these theological trends; the distinction drawn by some theologians, especially those who had absorbed elements of modern Eastern Orthodox thinking, between the personal and the merely 'individual', provide one way in to this discussion, connected with the renewed emphasis on relationality as a key element in speaking about divine (trinitarian) life as well as finite existence. A more extreme reaction to classical individualism is perceptible in theories around the possibilities of modifying the organic subject by means of cybernetic intervention and enhancement; and some 'post-humanist' and 'trans-humanist' philosophies argue, among other things, for linking ideas about 'humanity' or human 'value' to patterns of hybrid cybernetic collaboration rather than to organic individuals.[11] All these trends prompt us to return to the question of what it is that makes sense of our assumption that certain organisms can be *conversed* with; that they each occupy a unique point of orientation analogous to our own, deserves exploring; and only in the context of such exploration will the idea/ideal of solidarity be fully intelligible. Identification with another implies the notion of identity in the first place, identity acknowledged in the world of symbolic exchange that is language and culture. And this in turn raises a set of issues to do with the reality and the limits of 'empathy', the degree to which we can claim to 'feel with' another human subject and the ambiguities and risks around such a claim.

In short, the complex of ideas around the word 'solidarity' opens up a dauntingly wide spectrum of conceptual questions, touching on issues in philosophy, psychology, legal theory and a good deal more. As we shall see in more detail,[12] talking about solidarity may settle on a number of different points along a spectrum from the descriptive to the normative.

Early uses in sociological analysis begin from a *descriptive* agenda: the word relates to something that is true of us whether we know it or not or want it or not. It is simply a factor of how social life is organized. To be in a relationship of solidarity is to be in a differentiated social reality in which complementary roles need to be exercised.

Moving on towards a slightly more 'normative' account, we can say, as with the classical uses of solidarity language in the context of industrial relations, that solidarity is a symmetrical relation between partners who share a common interest by way of common or interconnected work. The action that arises from this is grounded in that recognition of the interdependence of elements of the labour force, and, while language about this has a strong moral register, it remains close to the pragmatic acknowledgement of identifiably interlocking needs.

But this may also open out on to an *asymmetrical* relationship, a relationship between people who endure hardship, oppression and struggle in a situation that they have not chosen, and those outside that situation who decide to stand with them, for reasons of compassion or concern for justice or some such overtly moral reason. We are here very clearly in the realm of the normative.

But the fuller analysis of this in turn suggests another and more complex kind of symmetrical relation, in which there is a full recognition that the privation or suffering of another is in some way bound up with a *comprehensive* kind of dysfunction in a society. This will not be a simple matter of seeing the interdependence of functions in a social system but will take us to a deeper level at which it is possible to say both that the denial of another's human dignity is a diminution of my own human dignity (and vice versa), and that apparently very different kinds of suffering or privation need to be connected with one another and addressed together, so far as this is possible, if only to avoid an unhelpfully wooden disjunction between varieties of human deprivation, with the consequent problem of organizing them in a hierarchy of significance or seriousness. Prioritizing action in response to suffering of various kinds is an inevitable task; but it is important to remain alert to the risks of failing to imagine a future in which the resolution of one kind of privation has hopeful implications for resolving others – rather than thinking only in terms of a set of hermetically sealed issues. This is a notoriously difficult business these days, when the multiplication of questions connected with rectifying the persistence of aggression and discrimination against various human groups can appear as an endless catalogue of disconnected problems rather than suggesting how we might imagine some genuinely and deeply shared future to be hoped for.

This book will not attempt to discuss all these aspects of the history of 'solidarity' in equal detail; but I hope that it will succeed in identifying some connections worth developing – between the language and actions of contemporary political protest and the history of economic debates in and around the labour movement, for example; between ethics, epistemology and social theory; between theology and theories of human rights. The first part of the book offers a consideration of the issues we summarized a little earlier around what is involved in recognizing another human being: and we may learn something critical about solidarity by examining what an account of human interaction would look like in which full imaginative identification with another, or with certain others, is *not* strictly possible. This leads on to an extended examination of the meanings of 'empathy', as a concept or cluster of concepts clearly relevant to these questions, and of the use and abuse of the term in recent literature; and from there, we move to a treatment of some of the questions around human rights currently raised by various thinkers, religious and secular, with proposals for reimagining the discourse in a way informed by the models of imaginative mutuality emerging from the preceding discussion.

The second part of the book looks in more detail at the evolution of the idea of solidarity, from the nineteenth century onwards. We'll look briefly at the genesis of the term in legal and sociological usage, in writers like Fourier and Durkheim, at its adoption in the growing international labour movement and then at its migration into Catholic Social Teaching as articulated by successive popes, and other theological discourses, as well as its occurrence in some ostensibly more secular discussion, notably in the work of the Czech philosopher, Jan Patočka. We also consider the way in which solidarity can be 'weaponized' in a polarized and tribal political culture, or sentimentalized and domesticated in assorted performative habits.[13] How far is the appeal (articulated by the

Polish priest and philosopher, Jozef Tischner) for a 'solidarity without enemies' realistic in the existing climate of public discourse?

A final section moves towards a more synthetic view, negotiating the frontiers between theology and philosophy. Solidarity makes sense as a political and social virtue only when its anchorage in some consistent understanding of the human-as-such has been elucidated; without this, it becomes either a sentimental – and even self-serving – rhetoric or the affirmation of a group identity that stops short of suggesting anything about what is due to any and every human subject. Difficult as this idea may be to capture in ways that satisfy the stringencies of contemporary philosophy, a political ethic that has no way of tackling this is liable to decay into tribalism of one kind or another. As we shall see, there is a case to be made for approaching the question by way of addressing the crises (environmental or epidemiological, or a mixture of both, or those relating to the threat of nuclear war or diminishing food supplies or ageing populations) that presently confront humanity as a whole rather more nakedly than they have done in the past. Common vulnerability ought to be where a radical account of solidarity finds traction. And theological language proposes a further ground for this always 'given' level of connection through its various accounts of a persistent togetherness in 'sin' and in 'grace'.

But we shall also be looking at how this casts light on and extends the idea (sketched out by Tischner and Patočka in different ways) of solidarity as bound in with the ideas of common work and common language. For any thinker writing within the Jewish and Christian traditions, the shared labour of constructing a sustainable, equitable communal order in which each agent has a uniquely formative contribution to the agency and liberty of every other, is the ultimate key to understanding solidarity. The language of covenant and law in Judaism and the imagery of the 'body' of the community in Christianity both direct attention to this dimension of labour in the context of mutuality. It is certainly not that other traditions, secular or religious, are devoid of any resources for thinking about common work of this kind; but the thinkers dealt with here are consciously in conversation with Jewish and Christian insights, and help us grasp how these resources in practice inform political imagination.

Understanding solidarity in this way also has the capacity to open up some of our thinking about human rights to new dimensions. 'Right', understood as the apt or fitting response to the recognition of a universal human capacity for reshaping the world through the interaction of subjects, implies a larger and more positive framework than is normally allowed for in debates about itemized entitlements. If we want to see a refreshed discussion of human rights – for so many, the last embattled stronghold of some residual sense of the absolute in ethical discourse, yet woefully reduced, confusedly defined and even trivialized – there is a need to reframe the claim of rights in terms of the claim to have a role in the common work of 'world-making'. This is a claim that does not rest upon proven individual capacity to operate in prescribed and foreseen ways, but begins from the contentious but basic conviction that embodied presence itself prompts conscious relatedness, and that conscious relatedness, however inarticulately conceived or expressed, is the cornerstone of a genuinely co-operative social project. In such a project, my own (or our own) categories of the normatively and actively human are going to be consistently interrogated by other subjectivities and agencies that are radically different in varying degrees – from the relatively straightforward engagement demanded in the literal learning of a new language to the more demanding and long-term labour of coming to work and speak alongside those with different levels of mental or physical 'ability', of negotiating and renegotiating the risky waters of gender identity, of imagining the historic enemy as a subject with comparable levels of recognizable interest and 'investment' (Gillian Rose's term) to our own.

And what we are talking about here is in fact what 'solidarity' means in its most developed and comprehensive sense: the practice of a kind of identification, indeed, but an identification with whatever organic presence in the world shares the kind of exposure or vulnerability that is inseparable from my own organic presence in the world,[14] a solidarity that is bound up with embodiment.

Witnessing to – embodying more fully – such solidarity is a practice that has to be learned: it is in that sense a 'virtue'. But the learning of it is more than the acquiring of a cultural habit, since it is essentially a practice that works with the grain of what human experience/language presents as an unavoidable dimension of our very notions of selfhood: it is a 'condition' as well as an imperative. How far we can go with a robustly metaphysical account of this latter dimension will no doubt continue to be debated with energy. The Jewish–Christian theological tradition takes a view on this, largely in terms of its affirmation of the divine image in humanity, and this tradition informs what is written here in any number of respects. I do not assume that this particular perspective will be shared by all readers; but I hope that its insights will at the very least clarify the kind of questions that need tackling if we are to be delivered from the various forms of spiralling inwards and self-isolation, cultural and psychological, that are corrupting and paralysing more and more societies in our age. Luther could write of the human predicament as the subject being *incurvatus in se* – 'ingrowing', curled into itself; the monastic fathers of the Eastern Church identified *aftotes* and *philaftia*, literally 'selfness' and 'self-love', as the core of human degradation and unfreedom.[15] A fuller examination of what the language of solidarity has to teach us may contribute something to breaking this enslavement.

ONE

Recognizing Strangers: Who Counts as Human?

1.
At the beginning of the twentieth century, an Australian administrator defended the policy of forcibly removing children of mixed race from Aboriginal parents on the grounds that 'They [Aboriginal mothers] soon forget their offspring.'[1] The idea that some human beings simply do not share the primal emotions by which 'we' define ourselves as human – and 'humane' – is a frequent trope in racialized discourse (and it crops up rather strangely in some accounts of parental affection or its absence in pre-modern Western societies too; surely, with high rates of infant mortality, people could not have felt the deaths of children as *we* do?). 'They don't feel as we do' becomes part of our justification for denying a genuine human point of view to the cultural stranger. As Raimond Gaita puts it in discussing such denials, we are not dealing here with a straightforward anthropological observation but with a conviction that certain experiences simply cannot have for the cultural alien (past or present) the same depth and meaning they have for us. Even if some of 'us' prove deficient in our depth of response, that is a contingent misfortune rather than a congenital incapacity. He tells the story of a white Australian woman watching a documentary about the response of Vietnamese women losing their children in bombing attacks:

'At first she responded as though she and the Vietnamese women shared a common affliction. Within minutes, however, she drew back and said, "But it is different for them. They can always have more."'[2]

It is not as though the mass deaths of non-white and non-Western children have become any more morally troubling to a great many people since Gaita wrote this account. And it is part of a wider issue. In terms of solidarity, much depends on what we make of and how we interpret the apparently stubborn instinct to see the pain of other organisms like ourselves as being experienced in the way we might experience such pain – and thus as constituting some sort of moral appeal or challenge to us (the significant work of Axel Honneth on this acknowledgement as lying at the heart of any ethical approach to social struggle highlights this[3]). A remarkable amount of energy and ingenuity has, in the last few centuries, gone into the attempt to persuade us to be suspicious of our instinct to recognize genuine pain, sympathy, mental reflection and so on in other organisms – to make us suspicious, that is, of what we unreflectively take to be signs of a 'first-person perspective' equivalent to our own. Explaining that we are persistently likely to be deluded on this point – so that questions about solidarity need not arise – can be wonderfully reassuring. Dickens gives us a memorable exchange between Steerforth and Rosa Dartle on the subject in the 20th chapter of *David Copperfield*. Steerforth airily dismisses the capacity of the lower orders 'to be as sensitive as we are…[T]hey are not easily wounded'; and Rosa responds with acid sarcasm:

'I don't know, now, when I have been better pleased than to hear that…It's such a delight to know that when they suffer they don't feel! Sometimes I have been quite uneasy for that sort of people; but now I shall just dismiss the idea of them altogether.'

Joanna Bourke's brilliant 2011 study of this phenomenon[4] traces the ways in which the urge to clarify once and for all what it was that distinguished humans from the rest of the animal creation helped to consolidate hierarchies in 'what counts as human': once a set of satisfactory criteria had been established, it became possible to assess the relative claims of different ostensibly human agents to full recognition as normative humans. The seventeenth-century diarist and essayist John Evelyn concluded that, since authentic humanity was manifested in the practice of religion, apparently human agents like 'pigmies' who did not show signs of any awareness of God could not be counted as 'of the human race'.[5] Their external closeness to human form had to be delusory; any facts about speech or culture among such beings could not count as evidence for human status, since normative humanity had already been defined in terms of what these communities manifestly (to seventeenth-century eyes) lacked. In the nineteenth century, writers applied similar argumentation to the question of whether 'deaf-mutes' were capable of religious awareness, and more than one concluded that they could not be, since revelation depended on the transmission of ideas in language. Even if they could be trained to perform certain actions that might otherwise suggest piety, they could have no authentic inner knowledge of saving truth. In more secular terms (as in Kant's treatment of this question), they could produce only an 'analogue' of reasoning, a simulation of normative human behaviour. Even in physiognomy, the apparent humanness of a deaf-mute's face could only be a simulacrum of what would normally tell us to expect intelligent subjectivity.

The argument begins by stipulating what it is that makes some agent recognizable as human; and the effect, if not the aim, of stipulating such a condition for recognizing some other is necessarily to steer us away from a range of other possible criteria for recognition – including the most basic physical characteristics that might normally incline us to speak to such an agent in the expectation of a reply. We are being warned that in a case like *this*, we are not to expect a reply that will really 'count', even from an agent who is in physical terms recognizably similar. We might say that we are being encouraged not to trust our senses in these crucial moments of encounter. Bourke shows how similar argumentation persists into more recent times, not necessarily in connection with religious practice but often even more crudely on the basis of the sheer cultural or affective inaccessibility of certain other subjects. She traces at length[6] how a succession of white observers over several decades in the late nineteenth and early twentieth century created and maintained a set of stereotypes for describing the non-white population of Haiti; how the trope of soulless faces, 'incapable of expression' was established in accounts of non-white Haitian workers, who could then be assimilated to the zombies of Haitian folklore, and even, Bourke suggests, regarded implicitly as – like animals – appropriate subjects for vivisection. If, as she says, 'The face is not a universal given',[7] in the sense that the ideal or normative human face is always already culturally configured in ways that permit us not to recognize certain others that diverge dramatically from it, then we need to become a lot more sceptical about the facile humanism that takes for granted a universal human sympathy, an obviousness about human right or dignity.

Debates about the 'recognizability' of culturally strange humans had already been going on since the mid-sixteenth century especially as a result of the European encounter with cultural communities in the Americas. The famous Valladolid Disputation of 1550 in which senior Spanish theologians (including that uncompromising defender of the humanity of American indigenes, Bartolomé de Las Casas) debated the issue of whether indigenous peoples in the Americas were 'naturally' subordinate to Christian Europeans, being themselves 'naturally' incapable of self-governing.[8] There was discussion in seventeenth-century American Protestant circles as to whether indigenous and enslaved African people were capable of receiving baptism.[9] In such debates, there was a routine assumption by some that evidence of potential 'reasoning' capacity – such as would be required for baptism – could be judged solely by existing European and Christian standards. Towards the end of the century, John Locke, no less, was justifying the expropriation of the land of indigenous peoples on the grounds that they were incapable of extracting the optimum profit from it.[10]

This whole tradition amounts to a sophisticated attempt to provide grounds for scepticism about whether there is a 'real' subject, a fully intelligent first-person presence, behind appearances; and it is a tradition grounded in the need for some way of morally glossing the facts of oppression, enslavement and expropriation. From the more narrowly philosophical point of view, it is in its familiar and developed form a kind of mutation of the more general anxiety about the reality of 'other minds': what provides us with the resources we need to resist solipsism? But here it is directed against very specific categories of supposed other minds, minds that might be thought to operate in a non-standard or somehow deficient body, whose communicative capacities can be dismissed, and whose experiences therefore do not require or deserve understanding or representation. If you can't talk to others about what is happening to you in a way that can be recognized, you can't talk to yourself about it either; and if you can't talk to yourself about it, you are not experiencing it in a morally significant way – as the Aboriginal or Vietnamese mother is imagined as failing to experience the loss of a child in a morally significant way, in the Australian examples with which we began. You do not 'own' what happens to you – any more than you (literally) own the land on which you live, according to the determination of the philosophers. Joanna Bourke's work, to which we shall be returning more than once, makes it very clear that mutual human recognition is not self-evident and universal ('the face is not a universal given') – even though cultural history suggests that coming to see that it is not 'given' very often requires a kind of reverse 'sentimental education', breaking us of what the colonialist or racist authority would see as our lazy habit of taking the material signs of reflection or emotion to be reliable indicators of 'real' human sensibility.

Bourke's concluding argument is that we have to learn what she calls a 'negative zoelogy' – 'zoelogy' being a term formed on the analogy of 'theology'. What counts as life, including and especially human life, is going to resist conceptual capture. Just as God, in the classical structures of 'negative theology', cannot be identified as a self-contained item among other items, so a science of life needs to remind itself that every attempt to provide a decisive set of criteria for recognizing intelligent life, 'subjectivity', something like the personal, is fraught with risk. The object about which you are trying to speak is not really an 'object' at all, but a reality with which you cannot avoid engaging;[11] you are involved, invested (to use a term significant for Gillian Rose's philosophy, about which more later) before you open your mouth. You may develop criteria that work to distinguish humanity from the rest of the animal world, and find that you have in fact excluded some agents you have customarily acknowledged as humans, agents with whom you are already in some way engaged: do you then conclude that you were mistaken and these humans are only apparently human? Well, some have not hesitated to draw such a conclusion, as we have seen and still see.[12] But, whether with other putative humans or with animals, the strategy of trying to identify absolute and definitive (and hierarchized) difference is not the only option. We can instead acknowledge that we are living in a world of diverse languages and cultures – including the 'culture', the communicative universe of value and perception that is the world of an animal. Bourke has given us earlier in her book[13] a summary of some of the discussions in the nineteenth century of the anxieties generated by the idea of animal language: if animals could speak, what was left distinctive for humans to do? And she also notes the related attempts to locate some kind of 'primitive' human language within a scale of evolutionary advance towards the normative self-consciousness of the developed West. In contrast to such strategies, she argues, we need a model of 'alterity' that does not depend on imagining difference as *impenetrability*.[14] Recognition is not assimilation; the answer to our problems of non-communication is *neither* that there are uncrossable gulfs of difference between forms of life *nor* that we can ultimately assimilate otherness into our own categories in a 'flattening out of the contours of our world'.[15] We are always confronting the embodied specifics of difference and discovering the limits of sharing and understanding. Yet – paradoxically – it is in this discovering of limits, of real but imperfect solidarity, in the shifting frontiers between identity and otherness, that we discover the imaginative promise and the moral pressure of the longing for 'authenticity, certainty and community', even 'communion'.[16]

The 'communion' that Bourke so tantalizingly gestures to here is what is glimpsed and sporadically realized in the history of actual, enacted engagement. If 'communion' is (as I'll be suggesting later) a particularly intense version of solidarity, Bourke's choice of words in the specific context of her argument underlines the importance of actively negotiating with the other in shared action and the reciprocal labour of listening and making sense. In plain terms, we find out just how much we can understand of each other in and only in the specific work of coming to terms with the presence of the other here and now. But for the purposes of the present book's argument, two points are particularly worth underlining.

First: even if we give due weight to Bourke's (persuasive) argument that 'the face is not a universal given', the fact remains that the recognition of – or projection of – faces in the human environment is a pervasive phenomenon, apparently inseparable from the basic evolutionary need to be able to 'read' the intention of others from their physical comportment – posture, gesture and sound alike.[17] In mythology and poetic reflection, humans ascribe agency and what I have called 'first-person presence' to animals and indeed to features of landscapes (personified rivers or winds and the like in classical mythology). The need for people to construct elaborate arguments designed to undermine the humanity of a putatively human agent is grounded in the apparently strong human instinct to *expect* the possibility of intelligent interaction in the whole material environment. This impulse to recognize features of communicative habit and capacity in animals is, simply in anthropological terms, as widespread as any cultural trope. And while Bourke is surely right to observe that this routinely becomes a way of using animals to think with, or conscripting their behaviours into some version of human culture rather than attending to the 'cultures' that actual animals create, the impulse is nonetheless a revealing one. Much has been said about the anthropomorphizing habits of children as a phase in psychological development; and there have been some important recent studies[18] of the role of anthropomorphic thinking in relation to socialization and to issues around autism. It looks as though intensely 'socialized' experience, like that of the small child who is routinely at the centre of communicative initiative and effort by others, encourages the projection of agency and presence everywhere. And in later experience, the absence or withdrawal of social connection can increase the tendency to seek assurance in anthropomorphic projections of presences – with animals, in some instances, or in certain kinds of intense religious practice, or – very noticeably in contemporary culture – in relation to forms of artificial intelligence. Negotiating this successfully, understanding where recognition belongs and where it doesn't, is a key factor in mature socialization.

In short, we could say, while the face is not a given, the *expectation* of the face is: we look for what we can construe in this way, for a physical self-presentation that we can 'read'. And the difficulty of working out where recognition is appropriate, or what *kind* of recognition is appropriate is a major marker of individual maturation as well as a crucial cultural task. What Bourke is arguing, I think, is that we are consistently tempted by shortcuts in this task, shortcuts that try to consolidate abstract criteria of recognition rather than discover what as a matter of fact can be recognized. We may project personal presence on to a toy or a pet; after a while, we find that our routine practices of communication don't work with these partners. Where toys are concerned, we cannot ultimately identify an *initiative* coming from elsewhere as we can with human interlocutors. With due respect to Velveteen Rabbits and their kin, toys are bound to be seen in the long run as carriers of what we put into them (and none the worse for that). In the other instance (animals, especially pets), we have to come to terms with the fact that animals relate to us in terms that are largely – not wholly – inaccessible to us, and the role we play in *their* 'culture' is something we can only guess at. Ideally, we recognize something that is, as we say, 'deserving of recognition', even while we acknowledge that we have no technology for translation. We can say that an animal, or a community of animals, exhibits behaviour that we cannot but see as communicative, but we are not equipped to decipher its content in any satisfactory or comprehensive way (what exactly the dance language of bees is *saying* as opposed to the general drift of the information it transmits remains untranslatable[19]). To anticipate a discussion that will be pursued at greater length later on in this chapter, it is important that we begin with the expectation of interaction and communication, that we learn to discriminate what expectations are apt to the relation in hand, *and* that we retain a certain scepticism about our ability to draw absolute and fixed boundaries between kinds of living and communicative agents, let alone human living agents. One way of putting this (once again, a theme to which we'll be returning) is that we need to nurture the skill of seeing that there may be real communication and relation in which communication to or relation with *us* as the main focus of authenticity or intelligibility cannot be the last word.

And second, following from all this: recognition may be initially an unreflective response but its maintenance is a matter of *labour*, intellectual and imaginative work. It is, as we have seen, vulnerable to the assaults of a scepticism grounded in existing patterns of power or status; there will always be forces devoted to making problematic the 'expectation of the face', pressurizing us to doubt what physical signals would normally prompt us to assume. As the human psyche grows, it develops a highly complex set of protocols for recognition, screening out certain candidates (like toys), partly because it is absorbing the reality of social connection more fully and expansively. It is becoming used to the range of experience that routinely accompany social connection – reciprocity, deferral, the need to take time to decode signals, even things like humour and irony and wordplay. The growing psyche expects from an interlocutor at least some of this diverse filling-out of the primal fact of contact with another human organism. The challenge, in the light of our discussion so far, is to find the balance that allows appropriate and realistic habits of recognition, and resists the twin seductions of – on the one hand – selective epistemological scepticism (can these unfamiliar, non-normative candidates for subjectivity really produce the evidence that would make us recognize their interiority?) and – on the other – mythological credulity (there is first-person agency wherever we look, irrespective of the evidence of intelligible interaction). And this entails work, work for which (as we shall see) we need some thought-experiments to identify more clearly where problems of recognition actually arise, or where we encounter significant limits to what we can recognize and intelligently interact or speak with.

As contemporary philosophy insists (rather more than it tended to do fifty or sixty years ago, at least in the Anglo-American philosophical world), having a 'theory of mind' in our relation with other agents is not a matter of a solitary thinking ego judging whether assorted material objects possess a consciousness like its own. The self is constructed in relation, becomes what it is by being spoken to, acted upon, prompted to imitation; and its primordial state is one in which the boundaries of self and other in terms of consciousness are not resolved (we shall be returning to this theme later in this section[20]). To understand that I am a subject capable of symbolizing my history of response is always already bound up with understanding that I occupy a place that is materially distinct from other places inhabited by symbol-making subjects. That I am able to negotiate and share with them tells me that they are recognizable; that they remain materially and spatially distinct tells me that there are limits to what I know, as there are other locations than mine from which it is possible to act as a knowing and speaking subject.[21] As Bourke indicates, the difficult task is allowing this balance to shape our response not only to the non-'normative' human agent (developmentally challenged, neurodivergent, culturally alien, socially marginal) but to the communal intelligent life of non-humans as well – not with the goal of assimilating the human to the non-human in the 'flattening-out' move that she deplores, but in a readiness to test what involvement is in fact possible, what understanding might be created, in a range of encounters that we do not seek to script or control in advance.

If we think of the question, 'Can I be sure that it's possible for me to interact intelligently with this particular other? Can I know for certain that we share a world?' We may have to acknowledge that there is no abstract answer that we can shape ahead of the specific processes of encounter and exploration that we engage in. We have to see the oddity of the question when it is divorced from the actual business of an encounter over time. The absolutism that seeks to locate active substances on one or other side of a divide between conscious mental life, rigidly defined, and mechanical, 'subjectless' behaviour creates a host of problems, philosophical and practical. Most importantly, it creates an imaginative space into which I can withdraw from the relation actually presenting itself to me, a space in which I can determine in advance where I acknowledge and where I don't acknowledge a particular claim on my moral attention. As Joanna Bourke makes plain, the legacy of Descartes's conclusion that animals were essentially automata[22] has proved very long-lived, and has generated precisely the scepticism about the recognizability of certain human organisms that we have been examining here: this behaviour *looks* like the behaviour of a subject whose feelings must be comparable to mine, but I must learn to mistrust the instinct that leads me to assume there is a real subject there. Clarifying a little some of the new uncertainties and confusions about the digital simulation of intelligent human behaviour that arise in the context of debates about AI may turn out to be relevant in understanding the ways in which recognition becomes problematic if we try to tie it to a set of specific behavioural phenomena. More of this in the next section.

As we have seen, one of the most powerful tools of power in intellectual modernity has been a version of this inculcated suspicion which denies that this or that problematic other is truly capable of representing themselves to themselves, and so denies that there is a recognizable 'point of view' or 'point of orientation' there, so that there can be no question of giving serious intellectual or imaginative attention to such an other's account of their need, interest, pain or hope. Bourke chronicles the way in which even the subjectivity and interiority of human children could be assimilated by some writers to that of animals, given their supposedly deficient capacity for self-knowledge or self-representation;[23] not an academic point in the light of what continues to emerge about the pervasiveness of child abuse in churches and many other institutions, abuse that is characterized by a routine disparagement or ignoring of the child's first-person account of their trauma. And, to connect all this with the main theme of this study, this kind of stripping from the other of their freedom to articulate and narrate their own subjectivity necessarily confines 'solidarity' to those who share a set of characteristics that are not only determinable by some intellectual authority as human, but are also fully 'developed' according to that authority's standards. The distorted evolutionary mythology applied to the animal creation and then to the world's 'races', is here deployed to silence the pre-adult human – even in what would have been considered an advanced society.

2.
As we have noted, one factor that complicates our thinking about what it means to recognize another 'subjectivity', another actual and active point of view, is the bundle of anxieties and fantasies arising from our current slightly feverish obsession with artificial intelligence. We know that the 'determinable characteristics' of the behaviour we routinely reckon as likely to be human can, up to a point, be successfully simulated by mechanical means. But does the possibility of such simulation give us grounds for legitimate hesitation before we accept apparent signs of pain, self-reflection, intelligence, etc, for what we'd normally take them to be? Does it license us to take the kind of position that Dickens's Rosa Dartle parodies, a relief that we need not draw the obvious and potentially demanding conclusion that the signs of suffering mean what they seem to mean? Or should we start worrying, as some do, about what moral claims an artificial intelligence might have upon us? If indeed they can be said to *have* 'interests' in the way that we do, those interests are hardly comparable to our own; talk of solidarity here would be eccentric. But once we have granted that some behaviours that we instinctively take to be markers of internal experience can be convincingly represented by mechanical means without any 'internal' ground in a first-person perspective, we might seem to be faced with some possibly troubling consequences when thinking about non-mechanical systems. Do we end up ascribing 'personality' to advanced AI systems, on the principle that their simulation of subjectivity is no less morally compelling than that of animal life? Or are we bound to question the subject status, the 'first-person presence' of at least some of the organic presences with which we have to deal, since they are no more morally compelling than the AI simulation? If we want to avoid these uncomfortable options – if we are uneasy both with denying

subjectivity in this way and with treating AI systems as occupying a first-person position and so having a moral claim on us of the kind that organic agents do — what exactly is it that needs clarifying? In connection specifically with the concerns of this book, does a successful AI simulation of aspects of human behaviour mean we should think of ourselves as involved with an AI agent in something like the moral and imaginative solidarity we are supposed to acknowledge with other organisms? And conversely, more importantly, does a moral recognition of AI in this connection mean that our recognition of human subjects involves *no more than* what we accord to a digital simulation? What would be the long-term ethical and imaginative implications of this?

The ever-increasing convincingness of AI simulation of human responses is a fairly familiar trope in recent fiction and film — stepping up the level of successful simulation involved so as to push the reader to interrogate further and further the limits of identification with a non-human and non-organic agent.[24] The question is complicated by the way in which the success of advanced forms of simulation can be used to argue a strong behaviourist approach to organic life itself: if we can produce simulations of what seems to be meaningful behaviour that in fact have no 'inside' dimension, how do we know that *any* supposedly meaningful behaviour — even our own — has an actual inside to it? In more technical terms, how do we know that consciousness is not an epiphenomenon, a by-product of mechanical process, devoid of any truth-content?

A discussion of this problem in its widest ramifications would require a book several times the size of this.[25] But it is worth spending some time looking at how the problem is posed in a fictional context. Terrel Miedaner's novella of 1977, *The Soul of Anna Klane*,[26] includes — in a somewhat ragged longer narrative — a couple of shorter pieces designed to provoke thinking about consciousness and mechanism. One of these, 'The Soul of the Mark III Beast,'[27] begins precisely with the identification of a character as someone who 'considers biological life as a complex form of machinery'.[28] The brief narrative then introduces us to 'Mark III Beast', a toy designed to simulate various features of familiar organic behaviour.

When it is plugged in to an electrical circuit, for example, it emits a sound like the purring of a cat; when threatened by a human wielding a hammer, it makes 'a shrill noise like a cry of fright'.[29] The maker of the toy has invited a colleague who defends the idea of respect for living organisms to destroy this charming device, in order to demonstrate that our hesitation in the face of evidence for animal suffering is a simple prejudice of the mind, unconnected with any genuine physical sense of solidarity ('it is your mind', he says, '...not your biological body, that hears an animal's plea'[30]). The point is that, *ex hypothesi*, the Mark III Beast has no interiority; to understand that its behaviour licenses no ontological conclusions about a first-person presence is to understand that what we take to be our instinctive response is in fact a cultural prejudice.

The process of 'killing' the device turns out to be more protracted and difficult than anticipated. It appears to demonstrate fear and panic, it glows and purrs when picked up by a human (being 'programmed to trust unarmed protoplasm'[31]), it emits sounds of 'distress' when assaulted:

'Dirksen pressed her lips together tightly, raised the hammer for a final blow. But as she started to bring it down there came from within the beast a sound, a soft crying wail that rose and fell like a baby whimpering. Dirksen dropped the hammer and stepped back, her eyes on the blood-red pool of lubricating fluid forming on the table beneath the creature...'[32]

Douglas Hofstadter in his comments on this piece concludes that the idea of 'soul', the idea of an integral responsive subject capable of telling itself the story of itself, is 'a function of our own ability to project'.[33] But this is an analytically thin account of what might be read in the narrative; and, more importantly, it is still wedded to the highly problematic philosophical model of an isolated consciousness forming theories about what is happening 'outside' it—as if we first had knowledge of our own inner processes and then projected them on to other organisms whose external behaviour mirrored our own. This picture looks increasingly inadequate and misleading: it fails to reckon with the ways in which the subject's discursive awareness of itself is always already grounded in what it absorbs from a communicative environment; the idea of being a 'self' we can scrutinize and engage with emerges in the practice of structured communication, language in the widest sense, including gesture and facial expression. Mimetic theory has insisted that the very phenomenon of desire is learned: identity emerges, not as a primordial assertion of a pre-existing ego but as the possibility of inhabiting a temporally extended, increasingly complex process of goal-setting which is given constantly developing structure by the temporally extended processes in which the nascent self is already embedded. In broad evolutionary terms, 'more capable and conscious animal kinds are interwoven in deeper articulation with the multifarious forms of an evolving ecological whole'; in the human context, imitation allows for information to be acquired without immediate risk and maximizes the speed of collective adaptation to changing environments, as well as securing the possibility of durable social interaction.[34] In short, it will not quite do to imagine the solitary creative self forming hypotheses about objects in its field of sense experience; it is co-produced with the complex of social stimuli it receives. The clear gulf that Miedaner's mechanistic scientist assumes between the body's reactions and the mind's projections is a fiction.

But there is more to be said here about the nature of Dirksen's emotive response to the behaviour of the zoomorphic toy, a response that is presented in the story as confused, troubling or embarrassed, a response that is both instinctual and apparently rationally indefensible. Our response to the pain-like behaviour of the mechanism makes sense only because we are already formed by the habit of 'reading' certain material behaviours as connected with felt states. That is to say, we are moved to feel for the 'distress' of the mechanical device because we have learned how to acknowledge and respond appropriately to pain in organic life. We learn that certain physical signs we make are rightly read by others as *meaning* pain or need, and our own cultural induction entails the reading of the signs that others make.[35] We do not 'project' in a vacuum, any more than we weigh the pros and cons of deciding that this behaviour justifies the conclusion that someone is feeling pain.[36] Response to pain is an element in the coherent set of policies for living that we take for granted in human interaction. Those who do not exhibit these responses are judged to be in some way deficient in social intelligence or relational capacity. Our response is bound up with a whole cluster of related imaginings and actions: we interrogate in words ('where does it hurt?') or activity (probing an injured limb, listening for the heartbeat), and we routinely ask what might alleviate the situation. Such consequential behaviour starts from but does not stop with the recognition of behaviours as pain-related; and if Miedaner's story had been extended to include these typical elements in our response, we should see that the credibility of the simulation would begin to break down. We should simply not know how to go on if we could not probe an organic system, by way of act or speech, to discover what exactly was wrong. If this were happening in a context in which we were faced with a putative human subject, we should not just be baffled by the impossibility of extracting some kind of first-person account of what the matter was (this is after all not an unusual element in dealing with serious injuries and unconscious patients); we'd be more fundamentally frustrated by the impossibility of grasping in a non-organic system how this or that piece of damage or malfunction related to anything comparable to the carriers in organic systems of the neural information involved in feeling pain. We should in short be brought up against the fact that the behaviour was indeed a *simulation*: this *looks* like pain because the designer of the device has observed the physical behaviour that we count as pain and reproduced it; but he has not reproduced the processes connecting behaviour with neural pathways, for the simple reason that there are no such pathways in a non-organic system. Once we understand the practice in which the scientist is engaged, we understand that any question about neural pathways, as much as any question about alleviation of pain, is misplaced; just as in the case of an actor representing pain on stage, the question 'where does it hurt?' would be misplaced if we understand the practice of theatre.

In other words, in any situation like that described in Miedaner's fiction, we should very quickly realize that the device in front of us was *designed to simulate* pain (and pleasure). Yes, we reactively and unthinkingly project an interiority on to it; but we do so simply because recognizing signs of pain is culturally familiar and embedded in practices of apt or suitable response and further questioning and exploration. In the Wittgensteinian phrase, we know 'how to go on'; at a certain point with the electronic device, we don't. We can see that we have been led to an assumption that fails to establish itself once we ask the next obvious question, as we would in routine responses to this behaviour. And from this point of view, the issue is not that unique or novel: we are culturally familiar with the simulation of feeling, painful or joyful, in theatrical performance. If we go backstage after a performance of – say – *Titus Andronicus* to congratulate the actor playing Lavinia, we do not approach her or question her as we would an actual survivor of rape and mutilation; we know that, were we to speak to her as if she had actually endured the horrific experience whose external markers she has just been reproducing, we should be met with incomprehension. We might well respond with a certain sensitivity to the possible psychological strain involved just in *simulating* such extremity; we might hesitate to be too jocular too quickly. But we should not consider ferrying our actor friend to a hospital or police station.

Putting it a bit differently, the point is that we are able to speak about simulation precisely because we know in a general way what *non*-simulated pain or trauma is like. We know that it is manifested, made knowable in a variety of ways, of which someone's or something's physical behaviour is a normal part but not the whole. A successful simulation provokes a temporary shock, stirs something of the response we should habitually give – as with Dirksen in the story; and just as the skilful inventor knows what behavioural phenomena prompt distressed response in the observer, so the great actor will prompt us to feel at least something of the sensations of desperate compassion, anguished concern, rage at the horrors of violence, that we should feel in 'real life'. But our human practice already has resources to cope with the difference between this and the actual crises of extreme violence. One of the most intellectually lazy aspects of the way some writers experiment with the notion that we live in a 'Matrix'-style simulation is the failure to notice that the grammar of 'simulation' depends on criteria for acknowledging what is *not* a simulation. To say that everything is a simulation is plain nonsense. You can, if you want, suppose an endless regress of simulation levels, such that within one simulation universe you might have criteria for discerning representations of what would count as fiction *in that universe*; but you could not dispense with the basic disjunction itself between fact and simulation. In the terms of an older metaphysical anxiety, we should stop worrying that 'everything is a dream', since the grammar of 'dreaming' involves criteria to distinguish it from waking experience.

Thus in the case of wondering about whether a robot is 'conscious', endowed with a first-person presence, we need to pause and consider where and how exactly the question arises. It is a question that emerges – as in the films and fictions mentioned – when a programme is devised that represents more successfully than ever before a range of behaviours that have been observed in the organic world. And if this is combined with the exceptionally rapid processing of data now normal in computing systems, it may give the appearance of the kind of responsiveness that we associate with organic, and more specifically, human, activity. But, as some commentators have observed,[37] the human self-correction of errors in information transmission regularly depends on *concepts*, and the technology of data processing does not create concepts but only algorithms. Both concept and algorithm select from an informational field, but the latter has to fix on what units it will recognize for the purpose of counting, while the former identifies formal features of diverse substances and practices that allow them to be linked together and to remain open to an indefinite number of candidates for the same formal recognition. That is to say that the concept is flexible in ways that the algorithm is not. And the use of the concept is, it seems, linked to the embodied processes of negotiating an unpredictable material environment, in which it is evolutionarily important that the accumulating of information has this kind of flexibility; a new challenge or threat can be 'formally' analysed to establish what it has in common with what is already familiar, where algorithmic processing struggles with unpredicted input.

Two pertinent points emerge from this discussion. First, we need to be very sceptical about the language of 'projection' as sometimes used in this context. It is easy to slip into the fiction that each of us is primitively a self-sufficient consciousness that has to make educated guesses about the behaviour – and so the 'subject' status – of our neighbours in the world. Second, the practice of simulation depends upon a clear set of habitual and taken-for-granted protocols in routine linguistic and cultural life for disentangling deliberate representation, however advanced and lifelike, from actual encounters with living reality, remembering that the latter includes our capacity to imagine a future that we as organisms can only *experience* as an indeterminate, 'unprogrammed' horizon. As we return to the main theme of our discussion, it will help to bear in mind this second point in particular. The sense in which we can identify with another putative subject in the light of a shared 'plight', a common materially conditioned situation with challenges that are specific to organisms, is a significant element in making sense of what we say about solidarity; and we shall be returning later in this book to the idea that solidarity comes most clearly into focus when we can see it as a situation of shared *exposure* to what we do not control. Solidarity as a moral response rather than just a given fact begins from the acknowledgement of a common vulnerability. If we think back to the situation described by Rai Gaita, what we see is an initial, pre-reflective recognition of this shared plight; it is a movement of the imagination that brings home to us a vulnerability in our own situation that is made more vivid by the immediacy of another's pain. Some of the unwelcomeness of acknowledging that other's pain, and the attractiveness of the various strategies for minimizing or denying it, has to do with how hard it is to be truthful about my fragility as an organic subject exposed to the passage of time and the advent of change. And in connection with what we have just been exploring in relation to simulated pain behaviours and the like, it is by no means clear what could be meant by imagining our ordinary physical vulnerability to be somehow in 'solidarity' with the condition of a machine intelligence. But we shall be returning later on to the question of solidarity as shared vulnerability.

3.

Inducing scepticism about what another feels is a by-product of an assortment of historical and political anxieties. As Joanna Bourke observes, these are anxieties inseparable from issues around power and entitlement: with whom must I share my supposed privilege? If the starting point is the entitlement of the male, the European, the 'rational' subject, and so on, what is sought is some kind of grounds for refusing to share the territory of privilege. There is what Bourke calls a 'limited economy of sympathy' depending on a 'hierarchy of sentience'.[38] And so the defender of this privileged territory will seize on the philosophical destabilizing of the union between sign and substance, will deploy that early modern strain of scepticism about appearances, to cast doubt on the possible claims of certain others. The irony comes in as this strain of philosophical scepticism exhibits its potential as a 'universal acid', casting doubt on the self-evident clarity of the rational subject's account of their (his) own interiority; anxiety about the alien other's intrusion into the space of normal and normative rational humanity opens out into a much wider anxiety about subjectivity itself. That is why Miedaner's story begins with a scientist trying to persuade colleagues that interiority must be a myth if its supposed evidential signs are so easily capable of being replicated in mindless mechanical operations.

Ultimately, of course, a consistent self-directed scepticism is paralysing; speech itself becomes impossible if one suspects that not only the sounds made by another but the sounds made by oneself have no connection with what I understand to be my intention. It is in this context that Stanley Cavell, that most sophisticated analyst of scepticism among recent philosophers, describes scepticism as an element in our aspiration towards 'non-humanity'[39] – yet at the same time an inescapable factor in humanity itself. It is intrinsic, Cavell argues, to our identification as human speakers that in our speech we work with a paradoxical imperative towards an ideal 'sublimity' of utterance in which mediation or indirection is no longer to be found and there is only transparency. Language can seem to be never good enough, always demanding recursive attention, ceaseless scrutiny about its fidelity and aptness to what it is not. In this lies the tragic possibility that haunts all our human relationships. We are embedded in location, materiality, linguistic and symbolic difference that has arisen over time (whether we are talking about individuals or societies), in the mutual impenetrability of what we call selfhood and diverse identities. We cannot talk without acknowledging our separateness. Yet that insuperable separateness tantalizes us with the vision of a clarity we cannot attain. 'Human contact is to be read', as Cavell puts it, gnomically as ever:[40] speech entails labour and time, and therefore to some extent entails doubt and error and starting all over again. The tension between the hope for some definitive transparency and the immediate and unyielding pressure for expanding imaginative work is the life of language itself, and so constitutive of 'the human'. Language strains against itself, says Cavell,[41] and it is here that scepticism and Romanticism improbably converge: any practice that we see as human incorporates this strain, this temporally extended business of enlarging what is communicated. We return from the nausea or vertigo induced by the aspiration to post-human transparency and the abyssal suspicion that there is nothing there if we cannot get past the mediating signs; we return into the material and time-taking labour of making sense as best we can. And for Cavell this also means resisting the temptation of absolutizing, not scepticism, but the embrace by philosophers like Richard Rorty of the 'groundlessness' of our language,[42] the idea that what we say depends entirely on cultural consensus rather than on any processes of strict verification. For Cavell, the simple 'mobility' of language, its actual stresses, doublings-back, self-corrections and strugglings with the frustration of communicating all indicate that any idea of both language and value depending on decisions about *agreement* is seriously inadequate. If our confidence about truth depended on agreement, how should we understand the irreducible *difficulty* of speaking the truth, our anxieties about error and miscommunication? And – although Cavell makes less of this – the political implication of privileging agreement in this way is that any moral critique of consensus becomes simply another 'groundless' move in what can finally be no more than a bare contest for majority-based power.[43] We could on this basis have no coherent narratives of how different sorts of attitude or behaviour are learned and unlearned beyond this record of contest.

In relation to our concerns here, what springs out in Cavell's discussions is the refusal to define the human by consulting the listed capacities of a physical individual and assessing whether there are enough 'positives' to allow some other the full status of a human partner. We are indirectly steered back to Joanna Bourke's point about the face not being a given – and the counter-point that we *expect* a 'face' where we recognize ongoing patterns of behaviour. When acute communicative barriers are encountered, we do not habitually say that the impenetrable other is not human. We may conclude, even if we don't put it quite like this, that their and/or our existing linguistic practice alike are not adequate to what is needed. We may or may not pursue the question of how our practices may be improved or extended; we may or may not pay intensified attention to the practice or culture of those we don't manage to speak with.[44] Heightened sensitivity in recent decades to the cultural habits of speakers who have historically been regarded simply as deficient (hearing- or speech-impaired, neurodivergent in various ways) or disabled (those who have lost certain motor functions) has meant a greater readiness to engage in this way – though the depressing levels of ignorance and negativity around people with Down's Syndrome, evidenced in the uncritical readiness of so many to treat the condition as automatic grounds for abortion, suggest that we have some way to go yet. Cavell's framework makes some sense of the idea that the physically/biologically familiar form we encounter has a prima facie claim to be regarded as a partner in speech, even when we are in practice at a loss to know how that claim may be met.

A number of philosophers – some directly influenced or provoked by Cavell – have argued that the facts of language as such steer us towards an ethical perspective that – whether or not they use the word – has something to do with solidarity as we have been considering it. Cora Diamond, for example, in an influential essay of 1988,[45] links the concept of the 'human' with what is exchanged in a 'humanizing' glance between two persons in a situation of potentially dehumanizing alienation or cruelty (echoes of Bourke's discussion of the givenness or otherwise of the 'face'), and, in a way congruent with much of our discussion here, resists any separation between the recognition of 'a member of the species *homo sapiens*' and the bundle of responses involved in the exchange of human glances. She sees this as grounding a sense of what the 'form of human life' as such might be, so that a solidaristic ethic is built in to the shared practice of our relations. D. Z. Phillips criticizes this position as 'Romantic',[46] observing that the evaluative responses we make to the face of the other are not uniformly or automatically solidaristic: we may 'acknowledge' the humanity of the other, their first-person presence, precisely by a more deliberate act of humiliation or rejection (a point we shall return to in discussing the ambivalence of 'empathy' as a moral panacea[47]).

But Diamond and her fellow 'Romantics' have a point. Phillips is importantly right to challenge any notion that there is invariably a solid core of humanitarian identification with the suffering other that mandates a response of compassionate engagement; this would be an ethical shortcut, ignoring what we have already noted about the *labour* of recognition and the non-givenness of the human face. But it is also right to note that any disjunction between simply assigning an object to the species *homo sapiens* on the one hand and acting in expectation of a conversational interaction with them on the other requires a heavy load of intellectual and imaginative effort. As Raimond Gaita puts it: 'If "human being" meant only *homo sapiens*, then the term could play no interesting moral role.'[48] How that moral role actually works itself out is indeed not immediately prescribed by the facts of recognition as such, but what is going on in the actual encounters under discussion is a process distinct from *assigning* a phenomenon to a category. To embark on a process of 'assignation' is a step back from something: remember

Gaita's description of the Australian woman's initial response to the Vietnamese mothers, followed rapidly by her 'drawing back'.

This particular kind of retreat is a reversion to stereotypes that have been learned in a complex cultural experience that takes time to be internalized with any fullness. Identifying and assessing a set of abstract capacities to be checked out before we commit to 'routine' conversational engagement is hard work because it demands a quite sophisticated set of protocols for questioning or suspecting what our senses deliver (our 'senses', not with the crude meaning of bare sense data, but as the habitual forms of material recognition and negotiation that we have learned as growing organisms) in encounters that we have not planned or scripted in any way. Our engagement may, as Phillips reasonably observes, be something other than benign, but it is not helpfully thought of as the end point of a process of *assessment* (and Phillips, of course, would not think this for a moment). We can say that the expectation involved in the exchange of a 'human' look – while it does not deliver a single and substantive ethical programme – entails the possibility of some degree of 'mutual exposure', distinct from the way we observe an inanimate object or even (generally) a live animal, though that would need some more exploration. We are still entangled in recognition, in reading and being read. In this sense at least we can speak of a shared world, and even of a kind of shared labour being embodied in such a moment. Particular attempts at converse and exchange may fail; some may be shaped by the negative side of recognition that understands all too well how cruelty or neglect may be experienced by another. But we should think it unusual to conclude from this that recognizability itself was no longer an issue; we might think it inaccessible, or we might resist any sense of mutual claim, but it would be a major conceptual shift to say that there was no perspective there that was capable of being communicated, no 'inner lives of any depth'.[49] Hence the busy anxiety of those forms especially of early modern anthropology determined to delegitimize the alien mind or the alien look, determined to deny the claims of others to recognition. Embarking on this task requires an unusual level of withdrawal from the ordinary intelligent life of embodied speakers; which does not mean that it has not turned out to be a popular intellectual game...

4.

This chapter has aimed to explore some of the ways in which ideals of human solidarity that are grounded in mutual recognition and shared language may be and have been complicated – or aborted – by various pressures to deny or minimize the scope of recognition. It has also set out to show how the assumptions often at work in discussion of the supposed 'subjective' aspect of artificial intelligence reveal an unsettling tendency further to confuse the issue by intensifying the suspicion that 'recognizable' behaviour may not be a reliable sign of what we have traditionally called subjectivity.

A wide range of cultural strategies for consolidating and retaining power over various kinds of 'other' has – in recent centuries – drawn on a developing strand in philosophy that cast doubt on any immediate or instinctive acknowledgement of another's 'inner' world on the basis of our recognition of their material performance. The problem has been posed of how we can be certain that material signs of feeling or intelligence in another embodied agent are grounded in a 'real' interior life, or at least in an interior life strictly comparable to our own felt experience. Arguments and assumptions – like those of Descartes – about the absence of anything like intelligent sentience in the animal world have been extended, by way of supposedly scientific anthropology, to forms of biologically human life that were in one way or another patently divergent from the imagined norm, with the goal of denying their claim to be attended to in the same way as the behaviour of 'normative' humans. While it was rare to find a full-scale denial of recognizable human sentience, clear hierarchies were established, both of intelligence and of emotional complexity and sensitivity: 'They soon forget their offspring.' And the ultimate result is an intellectual and political framework in which a first-person perspective is in practice consistently denied to certain agents and communities of agents. They are dispossessed of the freedom to name, narrate, locate themselves in the same way and on the same literal and metaphorical territory as we do.

As we've noted, it is not that 'scepticism' as such is the problem. Cavell explains how and why the recurrence of radical doubt, the suspicion that I am fundamentally deceived about the world I inhabit, is a regular element in the life of human intelligence, something that characterizes our life as more or less reflective subjects who are repeatedly challenged/invited to connect one set of impressions to another, and to make judgements about their relationships. It is an aspect of the active, critical character of our engagement with the environment. The difficulty comes when, faced with the threat of total not-knowing about ourselves and our world, we posit – so Cavell argues – an 'ideal' state of total transparency, unmediated access to one another's insides, that we think ought to be possible, and start measuring our actual *practices* of learning and understanding by the standards of this ideal. Cavell's brilliant reading of Shakespeare's *Othello* spells out the risk of searching for absolute assurance of what is going on in another's mind and heart, to the extent that ordinary certainty, the ordinary trust that makes mutual relation possible, is undermined by the obsessive search for absolute and incontrovertible certainty about another. What happens is that a vicious circle is initiated if we end up judging the ordinary practices by which we assure ourselves when in doubt (our routine standards of comprehensible conversation and consistent action) by the standard of this imagined absolute clarity and openness. The bar for certainty is raised to a non-human (superhuman) level. Understand the symbiosis between scepticism and Romanticism, says Cavell, between radical doubt and the vision of manifest presence all around us, and you may understand something crucial about what a human form of life looks like; reduce this to the obsessive search for assurance, the denial of interiority in the other, or the dissolution of the very idea of the first-person perspective, and you will be trapped in one or another kind of 'non-human' practice.

And in the context of our enquiry here, this hints at a point that will become more significant as we go on: paradoxical as it may sound, the recognition of difference and difficulty in our conversations is an essential strand in the understanding of solidarity as a moral phenomenon. We do not have unmediated access to others. If we think this is a *problem*, if we imagine that there might be a better option than language (including in 'language' the whole range of body-based symbolic activities), we condemn ourselves to the dangerous frustrations that Cavell discusses: we set up an unattainable standard of certainty and punish ourselves and others because it is never realized. We can trap ourselves in a situation where nothing can be taken as proven because it can't be proved beyond doubt. Language is what we imitate and appropriate as we are socialized; it is what we learn as we learn how to move around in the physical and relational world. As we have noted already, the more complex that world discloses itself to be, the more our linguistic repertoire extends; and the more variety we encounter in the ways others make sense and represent themselves, the more we are driven to refine, interrogate, rethink that repertoire of ours, finding out how to make sense of the experiences of *not* making sense of and with each other, how to find a way through difficulty. Ideals of solidarity and mutuality in human social practice do not do away with the need for what I have been calling 'labour' in managing the diversities of response and learning required of us, even in the most routine engagements, let alone the creative work of building conversational relationships with radically unfamiliar equipment and habit.

Emphasizing the need for labour in this way is one thing that prevents talk about solidarity dissolving into the sentimentality with which it is often associated by unsympathetic commentators (remember Howard Jacobson's waspish remark[50] about solidarity as a 'conscience-grab' that elides diverse issues in a welter of self-congratulatory feeling). It remains crucial to discuss the topic with attention both to the underlying philosophical questions we have touched on, questions about the formation of the speaking self, and to the processes and practices that illustrate the challenges and the temptations of the discourse. It is also, of course, necessary to disentangle a number of very different ways in which the word can be and has been used in its (relatively recent) history as a more or less technical term. It has, as we noted in the Introduction, hovered between purely descriptive and strongly normative usages, and we shall be returning to some of the attempts in twentieth-century social thinking to map more fully and connect more intelligibly these various elements.

But in order to grasp more fully some of the themes that have emerged in the discussion of this chapter, it may be helpful to look in more detail at the question of *empathy*. When people talk about solidarity as in some way involving the feeling or sensing of the experience of another as connected to our own experience, to the point of talking about 'identifying' with it, what exactly is going on? Is this fundamentally the same as solidarity, or does solidarity have a wider reference? The next chapter will examine some of the ways in which empathy has been deployed in recent discussion of personal and social ethics as a key moral concept; we shall see, I hope, that while it will not function in this role as neatly as some would like, it is still a central component in thinking through what solidarity means.

TWO

Understanding Strangers: Empathy and Its Paradoxes

1.
'Any problem immersed in empathy becomes soluble.' This is the resonant conclusion of Simon Baron-Cohen's book, *Zero Degrees of Empathy*,[1] which argues eloquently for regarding empathy as a fundamental building block for any ethical stance towards the world, and as a response that makes it possible to overcome profound hostility and incomprehension. He offers an account of the neural patterns in the brain that normally constitute an 'empathy mechanism' or 'empathy circuit'; a typology of low- or zero-empathy responses; an account of various negative effects of such responses; some speculative suggestions about genetic factors in such cases; and a careful distinction between those who live with primarily cognitive empathic loss and those who manifest an absence of emotional affect. The whole analysis allows him to identify deficiencies in empathy as underlying all kinds of aberrant human behaviour. To lack empathy is *'turning another person into (no more than) an object'*.[2] Empathy itself can be defined as adopting what he calls 'a double-minded focus of attention' (i.e. attending to something other than the contents of one's own psyche), identifying with the thoughts and feelings of another, and responding 'with an appropriate emotion'.[3] Baron-Cohen – who has written in detail about the neuroscience of autistic conditions – carefully draws a distinction between individuals with no awareness of the subjectivity of others (whose behaviour is cruel or randomly destructive) and those who, like many persons with Asperger's Syndrome, cope with overload in the 'systemizing'

(pattern-recognizing) areas of the brain by screening out certain kinds of informational input. Baron-Cohen describes this as a 'positive' variety of zero empathy, in the sense that it is a necessary defence mechanism that can routinely coexist with strong moral sensibilities. Even if a person functioning with more severe symptoms of an autistic condition can sometimes act in ways that we should usually think of as violent, this is not to be confused with the cruelty of the psychopath, knowingly inflicting pain on someone acknowledged as a subject.

Baron-Cohen charts intriguingly[4] the ways in which the neural patterns associated with empathic response appear to connect with the activation of regions of the brain involved with the registering of our own experiences (and vice versa). Relatively recent research on the activity of 'mirror neurons' in the brain, reproducing the patterns activated in what the brain is actually engaging with (even to the extent of prompting me to gaze in the same direction as another person whom I casually observe[5]) has attracted a good deal of attention – though Baron-Cohen himself warns against too facile an assimilation of this activity to empathy as such, and Susan Lanzoni, in her magisterial survey of the topic,[6] insists on the riskiness of reducing a complex cultural and linguistic phenomenon to raw processes of simulation in the brain; although she also underlines the utility of evidence from such sources for thinking – for example – about ways of educating people to modify some kinds of prejudice.

But the difficulty that arises for Baron-Cohen's account of the nature of 'empathic erosion', as he calls it, is that the association of cruel and inhuman actions with some sort of deficiency or malfunction in the 'empathy circuit' has to do too much work, and lands us with some conceptual confusions. It is clear that there is evidence for psychopathic subjects exhibiting abnormalities in the workings of the amygdala and lowered activity in the temporoparietal junction, where judgements are made about the intentions and meanings of others – both of these non-standard patterns of activity being the opposite of what is normally involved in the 'empathy circuit' identified in the brain.[7] But this in itself must qualify the sweeping statement at the beginning of the book that inhumane behaviour means treating another person as an object, and that it can therefore be assimilated to lack of empathy. The excitation of certain brain functions in response to images of the suffering of others might suggest that, so far from this meaning the reduction of an other to an object, there is a real apprehension of the other as subject *because* they are understood as undergoing pain. To broaden this out further, we might look more carefully at Baron-Cohen's account[8] of a particularly appalling atrocity in Uganda in 2002, where a female commander of rebel militia ordered a group of mothers in a subjugated village to kill their own children. This is the very opposite of treating another as an object; it is a conscious intensification of psychological violence, and for many if not most readers the intensification will be sharper as coming from a woman who might know from inside what emotions she is working on. The commander is very well aware of exactly what maximizes the pain of the other women and in that sense grasps their status as subjects all too clearly. As Baron-Cohen seems to grant at one or two points, the problem is not that the person inflicting unspeakable suffering does not know what they are doing – quite the contrary; the problem is that they know all too well, and that their response to this knowledge is 'inappropriate'.

Those who have clinically examined or imaginatively reconstructed the minds of torturers have been familiar with the way in which a skilful torturer will 'identify' with the fears, obsessions, phobias and longings of the victim (Orwell's *1984* lays this out pretty clearly). That is to say, the torturer will to some significant extent be able to predict the effect of threat or pain; they will to some extent 'inhabit' the space of the victim's experience. We may understandably hesitate to call this 'empathy', but it is certainly not a refusal to see the victim as a subject. It is a form of 'empathic' knowledge deployed to reinforce a certain kind of power. And one of the lacunae in Baron-Cohen's discussion is how dealing with, responding to, imagining or identifying with the experience of another subject is entangled with questions about power. This is not only an issue in the case of the torturer; it can be an unsettling dimension in the response of a well-meaning ally. Think back to the discussion above[9] of the ambivalence of some attempts at 'allyship' on the part of white people trying to express solidarity with those who suffer racist exclusion or oppression. A claim to empathic understanding, even one made with generous and unselfconscious intention, can in practice be a claim to power: it can be an appropriation of the experience of another, an assimilation of otherness to my own identity, and so a denial to the other of the liberty to 'own' and to narrate their own identity – the sort of denial that we noted in the last chapter as typical of most deeply ingrained forms of oppression and enslavement. When Baron-Cohen says, at the end of his book, that 'Any problem immersed in empathy becomes soluble',[10] the reader may well want to interrogate such a bland formulation. It follows closely on Baron-Cohen's moving account of listening to two people, an Israeli and a Palestinian, both of whom have lost a son in the murderous conflicts of the region, speaking together as advocates for reconciliation. Surely this is an instance of how empathy works for the transformation of intractable conflict? And I want to say yes and no. Without some such mutual exposure, without the recognition of a solidarity in trauma, nothing much shifts; yet the conflict that has taken the lives of the young men whose fathers are standing together is the result of a compacted legacy of violence extending far beyond the Middle East of the last seventy-five years, and rooted in some formidably complex issues about power, security and identity. 'Empathy' is hardly a solvent of all this; even in the encounter of two bereaved fathers, there will be asymmetries of power and privilege, and indeed of risk; there will be the danger of expecting the less powerful or privileged to do a disproportionate amount of the work needed to create or restore a 'felt' connection, a recognition. This is not in the least to minimize the significance of attempts to do what Baron-Cohen is talking about. It is hard to overstate the importance of such courageous acts of witness and of the ongoing (and at the moment deeply vulnerable) work of the Bereaved Families' Forum in the context of Israel-Palestine.

They are indeed potentially transformative; but they are fully and actually so only when they open the door to deeper and more radical transformations in social attitudes and political agendas; when they expose the power relations that have to be named and changed in the situation.

'Solidarity in trauma': the point is that empathy in Baron-Cohen's sense and solidarity do not simply coincide. I may recognize the suffering of the other for what it is, but my 'identification' with it may be wholly instrumental to my own purposes; my goal is to reinforce the advantage I have. This is, at its most dramatic, the torturer's agenda. But it is also all too often the submerged and unacknowledged agenda of the well-intentioned would-be ally. I know how you are feeling; so I don't need to learn from you. I know how you are feeling because I know that I suffer exactly as you do. I know how you are feeling, and so absorb your story seamlessly into mine. As we shall see later in this chapter, the moral paradoxes of claims to empathy are multiple and subtle. And when we speak about solidarity in such a context, it ought to be clear that the identity or identification we are hoping to realize is precisely *not* instrumental in this way, if only because some kind of genuinely convergent interest is being presupposed – not an interest that is going to be defined unilaterally by one of the parties involved. If we are in this way pointed to a future beyond the dominance of either party, we are beginning to look beyond any sentimental ignoring of imbalances of power, any unthinking denial of the existing asymmetries.

The danger of *trying to make empathic identification do the work of solidarity* is increasingly clear in the prevalence of primarily performative acts of supposed solidarity, declarations of common concern that do not change toxic relations and power imbalances but in effect reinforce them. But it can also be seen in a phenomenon analysed acutely by Aruna D'Souza in a recent essay[11] and echoing a theme discussed in our previous chapter – the assumption that the other is or should be transparent to me, so that I have access to their inner lives in a way that allows me to assimilate or appropriate them.[12] She notes how various artists and writers have contested this assumption by weaving a dimension of 'opacity' into their work: for example, by reproducing some classic photographic images of indigenous peoples but obscuring their faces, re-photographing them with protective hands covering the heads and some of the bodies of the subjects;[13] or, still more challengingly (in a work by Dylan Robinson, a critic of Canadian First Nation origin[14]) including a passage addressed to indigenous persons only, asking non-indigenous readers to stop reading and start again with the chapter following. D'Souza contrasts the aspiration to comprehensive empathy, which conceals the aspiration to erode actual otherness, with the 'imperfect solidarity' of her title – the pragmatic search for what we might call, with a nod to Donald Winnicott, 'good enough' solidarity, thoughtful, tactical collaboration, based on the continuing risks of communicating across genuine difference. 'Communication through the thicket of mistranslation is an act of generosity. To be able to act together without full comprehension, to be able[15] to float on the seas of change: What would a politics based on that capacity look like?' She also contrasts 'love' with 'care': 'love', as she uses the word, is essentially a matter of felt attachment, the sort of thing that routinely belongs with recognition of affinities, while 'care' is a more universal and radical affair. There is, for her, no 'unconditional love';[16] love is always invested in the ego at some level. Care, on the other hand, is 'outward-directed', capable of being exercised towards those who do not have to prove their likeness to us before we give them respect, manifest in the ability to 'sit with the unknowability of the other and still care for and with them'.[17]

The distinction is one about which we might argue; love may be a more capacious word than this implies, care may turn out to have implications for the ego. To grow into a habit of care is also to grow into a disposition of feeling, not simply a determined mental policy – as D'Souza makes abundantly clear with her examples. But the main point of her essay is to remind us of the groundedness of solidarity in the always 'imperfect' work of language and embodied encounter, and so to dismantle the edifice of potentially sentimental appeals to empathic identification.

That there is a claim by the other that is independent of my immediate recognition of another as like me, or my ability to absorb and encompass the emotional state of such another, is an essential aspect of D'Souza's case. And it needs to be read against the background of the growing cultural valuation of empathy that we have already noted. Susan Lanzoni's overview of the development of the language of empathy in post-Second World War North America[18] spells out how the term – until then largely the preserve of psychological specialists – rapidly became 'an aspirational value'[19] and a tool both for explaining familiar phenomena and for predicting successful connection-making in the worlds of advertising and entertainment. In other words, it became culturally normal to think of empathy in an *instrumental* way, as a tool to overcome estrangement in order to facilitate one or another kind of effective exchange, personal, social, financial. At its most simplistic, this has led to a style of talking about empathy as a sort of enhancement of individual experience: the empathic person has a more fulfilled life,[20] becomes a more effective agent in the business of social (including economic) interaction. But as in the case of solidarity language more generally, there is a fundamental problem about empathy when it is effectively configured as the *absorption* of another's experience into my narrative, a means of challenging someone else's ownership of their distinctive story. In this kind of would-be empathic identification, I am assuring myself that there is no territory where I cannot go, no barrier of otherness that I cannot overcome (D'Souza's appeal for 'imperfect' solidarity has no role in this kind of framework). Or perhaps, picking up an insight from Leslie Jamison's haunting collection of essays, *The Empathy Exams*,[21] I am making a bid for safety from the risk that I may not be acceptable to some other: '*I care about your pain* is another way to say *I care if you like me*'.[22] Or perhaps, by assimilating the pain of another into my own narrative, I am reaffirming my presumptive right to be the object of any compassion that is going: 'I wonder if my empathy has always been this, in every case: just a bout of hypothetical self-pity projected on to someone else.'[23] In all these interpretations, empathy serves the need not of a stranger but of a self that cannot bear the idea of a real stranger, and is compelled to deny the ultimate strangeness, the inaccessibility, of what it encounters and steer attention back to the clamorous self. Part of Jamison's goal in these essays, and in the experiences they explore, is to push back against this compulsion, to find situations where identification is brutally difficult, where it is so obviously problematic that it turns back in self-interrogation. She points[24] to the work of James Agee as an example of what she is feeling her way towards, a writing that consciously invites a *failure* in interpretation and understanding; and by returning to the 'opacity at the core of bodily experience'[25] she also suggests that what lies on the far side of empathy (as conventionally and sentimentally thought about) is an awareness in which my own pain as well as that of the other is made strange to me, made to be something other than a thing I definitively 'own' and know.

Out of that moment of self-estrangement may come something significantly new – perhaps something like the transition from empathic identification to compassion described by the French Buddhist writer, Matthieu Ricard.[26] Empathy, as Ricard understands it, is still stuck in an entanglement with the self's sensations, an entanglement with the unchallenged ego (the same point as Aruna D'Souza makes in her critique of empathic 'love') that blocks off a truthful attention to the other and thus inhibits loving compassion. We are all too readily seduced by the promise of new *experiences*; but what if the point is not the acquiring or absorbing of new experiences (new narratives that become part of the story we tell ourselves about ourselves), but a different kind of clarity involving the acceptance of the 'opacity' Jamison directs us towards? And clarity of this kind might be able to embrace not only the phenomena of another's suffering but also the web of conditions, including the distribution of power, in which that specificity of suffering belongs and in which my own responses are also located and shaped.

The relevance of all this for thinking about solidarity is evident. The whole question about the recognition of the subjective state of another agent is given a further dimension of complexity by the sophisticated work done in mapping neural patterns of connection that occur when we are confronted by the evidence of pain in another (the mirror neuron phenomenon). It seems that there is a traceable physical basis for our instinctive acknowledgement of such distress. But – as writers like Lanzoni and Jamison stress – this in itself tells us relatively little; how we go on to deal with this acknowledgement is a cultural matter, not simply a biological one.[27] And once we have granted this, we have to face the work that has to be done. The idea that 'empathy circuits' in the brain somehow do the substantive moral labour for us is clearly empty; but what sort of labour are we now thinking about? Leslie Jamison writes about the choice to pay attention, committing ourselves 'to a set of behaviours greater than the sum of our individual inclinations';[28] in more teasing vein, she argues for the importance of 'interrogated sentimentality',[29] the willingness to take risks by inviting people to take seriously some of their embarrassingly 'obvious' emotional reactions and let go of a comforting and superior habit of irony – but without falling prey to corrosive and untruthful simplicities, facile and unquestioned emotion. Lanzoni concludes her study by insisting, with Ricard, that empathic engagement in its most constructive form is 'an ability we can educate',[30] and that what she has been discussing is a habit that 'draws us into what can be known in others and in things, but also into what cannot be known'.[31] We are repeatedly brought up against the 'opacity' Jamison writes about. And one of the themes to which we shall be returning in this discussion is the significance, odd as it may sound, of such 'opacity' for understanding what it means to realize solidarity in our common action: the importance for solidarity of discovering the unsurpassable distance between agents.

2.

To make fuller sense of this, I want to turn to what remains one of the most fertile early philosophical treatments of empathy, from an era when the word's usage was still being established, and its meaning was not yet tied to emotional identification. Edith

Stein, Jewish by birth and eventually Catholic by profession (and a Carmelite sister, killed in Auschwitz as a Jew and declared a saint by the Catholic Church in 1998), studied with Edmund Husserl, the founder of modern phenomenological philosophy, and played a key role in the editing, completing and publication of his work (as we shall see, Husserl's influence will recur time and again in the twentieth-century discussions that frame so many questions about solidarity). Her doctoral dissertation of 1916[32] addressed the question of how empathy (*Einfühlung*) was to be defined – not, as she insists,[33] as an answer to the question of how we as a matter of fact arrive at knowledge of another's state of mind, but an attempt to grasp what is constitutive of the condition we think of as 'knowing another's state of mind'.

This groundbreaking discussion anticipates some of the most significant phenomenological work of the mid-century, especially that of Maurice Merleau-Ponty (who is explicit about his debt to her), and provides in its exceptionally dense pages one of the most painstaking philosophical accounts of what is being claimed when we say that we in some sense know what someone else is experiencing.[34] We clearly do not know this as a 'thing', an object that impinges on our external world as physical objects do; but there is nothing abnormal about this, as such knowledge is familiar in other contexts. We do not have direct sense-based knowledge of those elements of a physical object that are beyond our immediate sensorium, but we can properly say that we know they are there; more interestingly still, we can say that in memory we *know* what we experienced at some point in the past. We don't infer it, we do not work it out from evidence; but at the same time, it is not what Stein calls 'primordial', like our routine experience of objects. Knowledge of another's state of mind is, she argues, a 'secondary primordiality' – that is, it is an awareness of what is present to another, not by some mystical process by which we replace the other who is experiencing the world, but by projecting ourselves into the location of another subject, being, as she says, 'at', but not 'in' the place of another.[35] We have the capacity to put ourselves at a point of orientation that is not ours. There is no dissolving of the self in the other – or dissolving of the other as if replaced by the self; what is involved is the conviction that what the other sees, senses, experiences, is available to me, in addition to and in distinction from what I myself 'primordially' see, sense, experience.

Stein goes on to connect this with the basic and irreducible fact of my material location as a body. I cannot withdraw from this location *in* or *as* a body, I cannot – say – test out my visual perception of my own bodily organs as I might test the accuracy of my perception of some other material object, my knowledge of the body's movement is radically unlike my knowledge of any other object's movement; and so on.[36] I am where my body is, and that bodily location is a 'zero point of orientation'[37] – though this does not mean that the 'I', the ultimate terminus of experience, is simply identical with this, as 'I' have experience of my own physicality and of parts of my body. That is why Stein can say – in what is at first a tantalizingly odd phrase – that we can imagine an 'I' without a body more readily than a body without an 'I'.[38] We could not form the concept of a body without registering that the body just *is* what a subject is aware of as its locus (there is a crucial difference between a body in the fullest sense and a cadaver). And once we have clarified this dual focus of 'orientation' (the body, and the terminus of experience that allows me to say that 'I' perceive or fail to perceive that body from 'within') we may begin to grasp what is involved in seeing another body for what it is, a parallel 'zero point', incapable, as I am incapable, of seeing itself as a physical whole, occupying a perspective that cannot be identical with mine and so seeing a world that is not mine and is at one level radically inaccessible to me. But this recognition of another physical object as a *body* tells me that the world I inhabit is not simply the world that I am experiencing through the senses at any one moment. Indeed, the world I happen to experience at any one moment literally could not be a 'world'. My own awareness of space itself involves the acknowledgement of a perspective that is 'foreign'. In this sense, empathy is a central and constitutive element in the construction of the very idea of a world, and so of the very idea of *my* body as defining a specific orientation within a world of bodies, conscious and non-conscious.[39] Alasdair MacIntyre sums this up lucidly: 'In my empathetic awareness of others I move from taking my own standpoint as *the* "zero point of orientation" to considering it as *a* spatial point among many.... [T]hrough reiterated empathy I become aware of myself as others are aware of me and so understand my physical body as one and the same as the living body of my lived experience.... My awareness of myself as embodied mind, which is itself integral to my being an embodied mind, is constituted through interaction with others.'[40] Seeing things in a world is seeing things that are always in some significant dimension hidden from me as an atomized consciousness. As a major American poet has observed,[41] Stein in this respect lays the foundations for a certain kind of poetics; but that is another story.

The empathic perspective means that I come *to see myself as seen.*[42] And this is fundamental for seeing myself as belonging in a world, a world not only of material objects to be negotiated but, more crucially and problematically, a world of alien motivation and volition.[43] To inhabit a world is to know oneself acted upon as well as acting, and thus to know oneself as never the sole independent source from which order and meaning proceed. To use an idiom cited earlier that is not extensively used by Stein but is clearly congruent with her argument, to inhabit a world is a matter of 'reading and being read'.[44] We cannot negotiate our physical life without reading our environment in terms of other agencies in general (whose workings are immediately perceived but not immediately understood) and other 'intentionalities' in particular (whose workings are equally data that require time to map and analyse so as to develop policies of coping or interacting with them). As Stein emphasizes more than once,[45] it is not quite that we make analogical inferences from our experience of our own selves to those of others ('When I do this physically, it expresses such-and-such an internal state; so when I see the same physical behaviour in another, I conclude to the same inner reality'). Analogy is indeed at work, but in a different way: as I learn in my own self-perception to see myself as an active respondent to the unpredictable environment in which I occupy a single and unrepeatable position, so the routine negotiation of this position with other agencies consolidates the picture of other 'zero points' acting out of comparable self-understanding and self-locating. I don't look for 'evidence' of other minds; but the notion of what a mind might *be* (mine or an other's) is constructed in the exchanges of 'reading and being read', in the ultimate givenness of language itself in all its forms. It is in this way that Merleau-Ponty fills out Stein's very schematic thoughts, describing language as 'the subject's taking up of a position in the world of his meanings'.[46] My self-perception and 'self-appropriation' as a body, my awareness that I am reflectively charting a path in a world that is not under my control, by way of assorted and instinctive habits of 'reading' (including what Stein sees as the not-quite-primordial but always given awareness of the unseen or 'averted' hinterland of what I immediately sense in my material environment) – all this entails the recognition of comparably intelligent subjects of perception; without this, I cannot coherently think either a self or a world. And, as Stein notes tantalizingly,[47] this includes some degree of recognition for animal 'subjectivity', the recognition that the animal's presence as an intelligently responsive body implies recognition of something like a point of view.[48]

But what remains distinctive for Stein about human understanding is that the other emerges irresistibly as an agent whose gestural and verbal behaviour is the tangible form of purpose and desire. Intelligent and intelligible action is motivated action; motivation is to do with what is wanted, desired; wanting, desiring, is a matter of *valuation*.[49] To put it slightly differently, the idea of a zero point of orientation opens out into a zero point of purpose, a *direction* of will, within a 'range of experienceable values'. My negotiation with other subjects or agents has to be worked out in the context of potentially diverse goals and wants, of other motivated agents negotiating their own desires; and in this process, my own assessment of my goals and wants is to some extent placed in question. There is no absolutely protected status for the rightness or naturalness of what I want. So in this process, the 'deficiency or devalue' of my purposes has to be confronted at least as a possibility; and in this sense, says Stein, the exercise of empathy tells us both what we are and what we are not.[50] Once again broadening out a little from her own vocabulary, we could say that the point being made is that my 'reading' of myself and my history is 'ventured', risked, in the processes of meaning-laden exchange. In the terminology of a very different but far from antithetical philosopher, I learn how the other is 'invested' in their position in the social and political nexus we together inhabit, how their 'self-mediation' and mine are both parallel and interwoven in the processes of speech and intelligent action.[51] As *speakers*, both I and other agents become questionable to ourselves, and in that 'becoming questionable' we continue to develop as fully linguistic agents.

Stein concludes her thesis with a number of tantalizing remarks about what a purely *geistlich* ('intellectual', 'spiritual', 'mind-based', 'immaterial'...the term is proverbially hard to render) relationship between conscious agents might be. Her translator notes in her introductory comments that she has opted for 'spiritual' as the rendering for *geistlich*, but (despite Stein's own references right at the end of her discussion to the need for a fuller examination of the religious consciousness) this imports a rather misleading set of associations. Stein's concern is not primarily the nature of religious experience – she explicitly leaves this to others – but a rather wider issue. She is interested in the extent to which we are able to think of the kind of complex interrelation with other selves that she has been analysing as somehow extending beyond the psycho-physical co-presence of embodied agents and their artefacts (and once again, as at the beginning of her thesis, she considers relation with the human past as in important ways analogous to the knowledge of other selves/motivational complexes in the present). She has already noted[52] that the psycho-physical organism does not, in the world as it actually is, guarantee the realization of the capacities of persons, and she seems to want to entertain the possibility that the contingencies of embodied history do not evacuate or negate the real givenness of those aspects of human identity that are frustrated (by premature death or serious disability, for example). The closing comments on what is purely *geistlich* might then relate to an underlying question about what it is in human identity that depends on relation with what is *not* vulnerable to contingency. And this – fleetingly – opens the door from the discussion of empathy as she conceives it into the larger matter of the transcendent ground of human value or dignity as such. We are, she implies, perhaps grounded as subjects, as spirit (*Geist*) in more than *just* embodied relationships; but what that might mean in detail is not the focus of her work at this point. It is something to which she returns much later in her explicitly Christian writing.[53]

It may be helpful at this point to sum up a few of the points in Stein's discussion that bear most directly on the central issues of this book. Her account of empathy is most markedly distinctive in its consideration of what we could call the reflexive and recursive aspects of our response to other subjects: I learn what it is to be a body (not just a piece of flesh) in interaction with other purposively acting bodies, just as I learn to be a speaker by being spoken to in the interactions of speech. I do not and cannot begin as a ready-made subject advancing into the field to defend my territory; I am already located in a world that I must learn to chart and negotiate in and through sharing in the common work of charting and negotiating that is going on around me. I have to *learn* where I am, to learn that I am a 'body'. To think of a world at all, Stein insists, is to think of what precedes and exceeds my sense of myself, what is always already given to me as the reality of what I don't and can't see/sense as an individual but is able to be seen/ sensed from perspectives that are not directly ('primordially', in Stein's terminology) mine. The empathic sense of that which I do not directly sense, the imaginative standing 'at' the point of another's perspective on the world, is far more fundamental than any kind of supposed identification with the emotion of another; although Stein is quite clear that empathy does involve elements of emotion, empathic awareness is not for her the appropriating of another's feeling, not a 'feeling of identification'. As she notes very briefly,[54] empathy is distinct from 'sympathy' as she defines it. Sympathy is unequivocally a matter of *my* emotion generated by someone else's emotional state: I feel x for myself because I observe the signs that you are feeling x; but this does not translate into any claim about privileged knowledge of your feelings, a sharing of your 'introspection'. Empathy on the other hand is the imaginative sharing of another's field of perception, in the broadest sense: I see imaginatively the field in which you are operating, including the emotional state with which you respond to it; but this is a more complex matter than certain emotional phenomena appearing in me because of what you present to me.[55] This 'broadest sense' of sharing a field of perception is what is addressed in the final sections of her book in relation to the recognition of the other's perspective as that of a zero point of valuation and desire, not only of immediate physical perceiving; the 'world' we are being inducted into as we grow as linguistic beings is a world of value and physical coping strategies inseparably interwoven. With a nod to Girard, we can acknowledge the mimetic impulse as much more than the imitation of physical behaviour.

This has two very important implications. First, there is the fact that the phenomenon of empathy, by involving us in a collectively generated world of perception and meaning, holds open for us the perennial possibility of error; empathy means that our stance is corrigible.[56] Gillian Rose's reflections on the dialogic formation of consciousness, the 'staking' of a position that has then to be seen afresh as a misrecognition of the self by the self in the light of engagement with another 'misrecognizing' subject[57] represent a parallel move to what Stein outlines so very sparely. But the second aspect of her account is perhaps still more pertinent here. As Stein emphasizes in several places, empathy is never the dissolution of self in other or other in self; its entire function in the economy of the embodied psyche is to embed in thinking and speaking the fact that the inhabitable and intelligible world depends for its appearance in speech and thought upon perspectives that remain irreducibly diverse. Empathic awareness is always of a point of view that *I do not and cannot occupy*; if it were otherwise, I could not have a coherent account of what it is for me to occupy a point of view at all; I would not inhabit a world. The question sometimes raised about whether empathy is a bid to absorb otherness into sameness ('I know exactly how you feel'; so you no longer own or occupy your own perspective) is dealt with here by Stein's clear insistence on the distinction between standing 'at' and standing 'in' the place of the other. So standing 'at' this place takes for granted that I remain aware that this place is not my own; its distance from my own is precisely part of how I make sense of occupying a point of view as such, a 'zero point', both a physical point of view and an 'axiological' perspective (a set of intentional and value-based habits).

3.

If in the light of this we turn back to some of the discourse around empathy that was discussed earlier in this chapter, it is clear that Stein's 'empathy' is something quite other than an occult way of getting from where I am to where the other is and having the same feelings, or even having a correct knowledge of those feelings.[58] Stein, as we have seen, allows that empathic awareness includes emotion of some sort, but resists the reduction of such awareness to a matter primarily of feeling or even of knowing about feeling. It is to do with seeing imaginatively what the other sees; but this necessarily remains *my* seeing (and so, as a supposed version of what the other sees, a highly fallible set of imagined perceptions). This resonates to some extent with the eloquent assault on empathy as a factor in moral decision-making developed by Paul Bloom.[59] For Bloom, the problems with the messianic claims for empathy made by some – and with the identification of evil itself with deficient empathy – are manifold. They include the fact that empathy in an emotion-focused sense can facilitate ingeniously cruel acts,[60] and also the way in which appeals to empathic identification in responding to the urgent needs of other persons or communities can restrict our effective response to those causes that most immediately resonate with our urge both to feel better and to make those with whom we already at some level identify feel better — i.e. empathic identification may be the kind of sentimentally biased response that turns out to be a very poor guide to what is actually most morally urgent. 'Empathy is driven by immediate considerations, making us too-permissive parents and too-clingy friends',[61] and it skews our priorities to what touches our emotions most directly rather than to what most needs attention in a rational calculus of human suffering. In terms of charity campaigning, appeals to save the lives of poignantly photographed babies and children will be likely to attract more donors than a programme looking to establish a women's co-operative or a water-desalination project in an environmentally-threatened river delta. But in cold fact, both of the latter might save more lives (of babies and adults).[62] Bloom's concern, not unlike Aruna D'Souza's, though with a more overtly rationalist emphasis, is to encourage the development of an ethical culture in which reasoned compassion is more important than 'empathy' in the popular sense (and he alludes approvingly[63] to Matthieu Ricard's disentangling, mentioned above, of empathy and compassion).

But Bloom's implied disjunction of empathy and reason has its own problems. By focusing on the problems around privileging unexamined feelings of emotional resonance or familiarity, he screens out the wider metaphysical discussion that Stein and others like Stanley Cavell invite us into. This is not surprising, of course, as Bloom does not set out to offer a philosophical analysis, but it leads to some over-narrow conclusions. The wider philosophical frame suggests that we need to take account not only of 'emotional attunement' or emotional 'congruence' in thinking about empathy,[64] but of what Stein thinks of as 'orientation' — the point of view from which an environment is perceived and evaluated. As she argues, this emphatically doesn't exclude emotion, but it also takes in what we could call a complete attitudinal positioning, so that empathy is seen as an attunement to a broad and differentiated state of awareness, which I recognize as other to my own yet capable of intelligent interaction with it. It is this fuller sense of empathic awareness, taking in perception and intention, that introduces into the discussion of empathy the idea not so much of sharing – let alone appropriating – another's interiority, but of attending to it with respect for its difference, its history and hinterland, its dimensional depth – and also reckoning with its perspective on oneself. For Stein, to experience or exhibit empathy is to acknowledge the debt of my own labour of self-making to the agency of what is not inside me; to be immediately aware of possibilities that are not mine, as also of values that may not be mine, and so to grow in a capacity to imagine another perspective without an instant negative and threatened judgement. This motif of 'respect' is something we shall return to in the context of discussing what we might make of human rights discourse within a more consistently solidarity-based ethical language. Stein's approach also has some resonance with the very differently impressive analysis of Rae Langton,[65] who sees the imagining of the 'foreign' point of orientation as, importantly, an aspect of our recognition of the *contingency* of our own identity in the world. From both perspectives (Stein's and Langton's), empathic awareness plays a role in de-centring the selfhood we take for granted, and its pre-critical or pre-'conversational' account of its needs, claims and agendas.

As we have noted, there is a paradox at the heart of all this discussion of empathy. Stein's model, along with some aspects of the approaches of others like Jamison and Langton, makes us think of empathy as something other than a way of crossing the gulf between one subject and another and reducing or abolishing the strangeness of another's experience. It is the means by which I acquire and maintain the idea of a world in which I am object as well as subject, 'read' as well as 'reading'; and so it is also how I am kept familiar with my own strangeness to myself. The sense of our contingency (in Langton's language), or of our involvement in misrecognizing and being misrecognized (in Gillian Rose's scheme) is bound up with an empathic sense that delivers a constant, interrogative pressure to recognize the irreducible strangeness of the world around – 'the depth of the mystery of human separateness', as Cavell puts it.[66] The empathic response, or rather the empathic element in our whole apprehension of the world, is to understand that things and people are strange; that the 'analogy' with our own experience is not about concluding that they are Just Like Us but grasping that they are *themselves*, that they stand at a distance from us that cannot be abolished – and indeed at a distance from themselves, learning, as we learn, what we are doing or saying by being objects as well as subjects, having a role in a narrative we do not script. And this is of course not unrelated to the significance of the body in this discussion: we have already seen how understanding oneself as a body rather than a piece of raw flesh, so to speak, is understanding that one occupies a world, in which the space where a person lives (while not identical with the actual room that the body happens to take up) is not transferable, and so always involved in negotiation with the space of others. The entire repertoire of meaningful behaviour that we develop as we grow through infancy is brought into being in this negotiating of space – from the primal gestures of reaching for or pushing away to the codes of bodily sound and movement, language and communicative gesture, that 'offer themselves' or 'bid' for reading, for interpretation.

This may be the point to revert briefly to the continuing discussion of the relation between talking about empathy and current research in neuroscience. While – as we have seen – it is risky to speak too simply of 'empathy genes' and 'empathy circuits' in the brain,[67] it seems to be the case that lesions in particular areas of the brain (the orbitofrontal cortex especially) result in a family of effects that all involve some sort of deficiency in the capacity to 'read' the physical behaviour of others. The person so affected experiences difficulties in interpreting facial expressions, in recognizing irony or jokes, in picking up social cues and so on, and, in extreme cases, in grasping anyone else's emotional state at all. What is interesting in the context of the discussion here is that this account of certain neural patterns resonates with a picture of empathy as not so much a capacity to *feel* what someone else is feeling as to decode or interpret their 'world'. The normally developing and uninjured brain acquires the routine ability to 'read' expressions and gestures, tones of voice and different 'registers' of utterance, the ability to picture and imaginatively enter other practices of negotiating with the environment and of representing one's selfhood, as well as to monitor and reflect on our reception of such picturing and imagining on the part of others ('being read').[68]

The point made in this connection by some researchers – and in Iain McGilchrist's monumental and polymathic writings about the hemispheres of the brain[69] – is that the neglect or undervaluation of these forms of knowledge and skill, both in individual development and in the cultural preferences of modernity, has a far-reaching negative effect on human intelligence overall, and so on human 'flourishing'. An account of the brain's activity that concentrates simply on granular problem-solving produces a serious and damaging imbalance in that it sidelines the activities that relate to a more comprehensive patterning of experience both in time and in space.[70]

Very striking in all this is the convergence with discussions like those of Stein and Cavell: the ability to imagine oneself 'at the point of' the other's experience is connected with the ability to imagine one's own past experience; and both are in turn connected with seeing/experiencing one's body and the bodies of other agents as a whole. The complex relation between the 'zero point of orientation' as Stein understands it and the physical locality of the material body finds an echo in the perceptual capacity of the inhibited or damaged brain where there is a separation between the perceiving self and the parts of the body that are routinely experienced as 'my own'. Touching one hand with the other is not the same kind of experience as touching another's hand, despite the obvious similarities; the nature of the malfunction in the right-brain-inhibited subject is that the subject experiences touching their own body in the same way as touching any other material object.[71] Without wanting to assume a simple correlation here between the radically different worlds of phenomenological analysis and neuroscientific research, it is surely significant that both are able to trace some continuity in the mental activities of conceiving oneself as a body, recognizing coherent and unifying patterns in the appearance and behaviour of others, and narrating a continuous past. In other words, the realm of the 'empathic', as it emerges in the phenomenological tradition, becomes something very much more than a curious, if morally weighty, capacity to share the emotions of another: it is the focal element in developing a working understanding of the subject in time, space and intersubjective relation.

And this points us finally back to the themes of recognition and solidarity with which we began. In the first chapter of this book, we looked at the various ways in which the recognition of other human organisms as speakers, owners of their own perspective, subjects with experiences comparable to our own, could be and have been derailed by the creative appropriation of mechanistic interpretations for organic behaviour, and of some kinds of philosophical scepticism. We noted how the yearning for some kind of absolute transparency between speakers or agents sets an impossibly high bar for mutual communication, indirectly encouraging a sceptical response when these standards cannot be met. And against this unhelpful binary of scepticism on the one hand and assured transparency on the other, we discussed the ways in which viable discourse about solidarity needed to incorporate those elements of labour, misrecognition and self-scrutiny that emerge in the actual business of human language.

All of this naturally leads into the questions addressed in this second chapter, about 'empathy' as a means of access to other subjectivities, the 'introspection' of other agents/speakers. Given that empathy has become a popular term in treatments of ethical behaviour in recent decades, it is important, as with the language of solidarity more broadly, to interrogate versions of empathy that offer some sort of shortcut in the processes of learning about the perspective of others – notably in the idea that empathy can be thought of primarily as a 'double-focused' action of the brain (Baron-Cohen's adjective), in which I am aware of two affective responses to my environment, my own and that of the other. This model will take us only so far, and it will not in itself provide an ethical panacea; however correctly we may know another's mind and sensibility, the question remains of how we use such knowledge.

So it is important to take a step back and scrutinize a bit more closely the idea of empathy itself, asking how a clarification of this may help us in refining the notion of solidarity in ways that are less likely to be kidnapped by considerations of 'fellow-feeling' alone (as we'll see, this point has been of some importance in the development of ideas about solidarity in Catholic Social Teaching in the last half-century). Edith Stein's phenomenological analysis shifts the emphasis away from sharing feelings to grasping the existence and to some extent the 'shape' of a perspective that is not mine – and she is clear, like others discussed here, that this perspective is only properly grasped as still *other* to me. It has often been said that, in a situation where I am trying to give comfort and support to a suffering person, it may be more helpful to say, 'I have no idea how you must be feeling' than to say 'I know what it must be like for you'; the empathic understanding of the seriousness of the other's perspective is one that takes it seriously *as* other and so as necessarily, crucially, 'opaque' to me. In such a perspective, solidarity becomes – ironically – inseparable from a consistent concern and respect for difference. We shall be coming back to the sort of picture of humanity that might make sense of this, but the recognition of how much of our sense of ourselves, our narrative practices, our awareness of our embodiedness and much more is involved with the irreducible strangeness of the world is a crucial corrective to any mythology that begins from a monadic consciousness whose operations are always infallibly transparent to itself.

Several significant modern reflections on solidarity, secular and religious, move in this direction, and we shall be looking at these in more depth in the second section of this book. Before opening this discussion, however, I shall be spending some time on a topic that, while in fact closely related, is not always treated in direct connection with these issues around solidarity, empathic awareness, and action for the sake of the stranger. 'The human face is not a given,' to cite once again Joanna Bourke's analysis of the evasions of solidarity and recognition that have characterized so much of European modernity; but that is a way of saying that *the claims associated with the human face* are not a given. Bourke deliberately (if also critically) evokes the language of Emmanuel Levinas, for whom 'the human is the being that possesses a "face" and all ethics is a response to face-to-face contacts'.[72] Recognizing the face is recognizing a claim – i.e. recognizing a *right*.

Rights language is a contested area in all kinds of ways. It has become a flashpoint for political controversy, with mounting pressure, for example, in some conservative circles in the UK for a withdrawal from various international rights-related agreements and from the jurisdiction of the European Court of Human Rights. It has also become an issue in philosophical and theological discussion especially among post-liberal writers of one kind or another. As we shall see in the next chapter, there are real questions about the individualistic and abstract models of rights taken for granted by both critics and defenders of the language in recent years. But it is difficult to conceive of an ethic or politics of solidarity without some account of human rights; my hope is that by approaching this question by way of what we have already discussed in relation to recognition and the empathic awareness of the other's point of orientation, it may be possible to re-locate the discourse of rights to some extent, and recover some of its potential to unsettle the myths of human selfhood that continue to distort or undermine that hope for 'communion' that Joanna Bourke so tantalizingly hints at.

THREE

The Claims of Strangers: Debating Human Rights

1.

'Bearer of no personality, no social identity, no aspirations above those of fulfilling the most basic needs, [the modern individual] encounters us simply as the bearer of "human rights", that tide of undifferentiated demands that relentlessly erodes the coasts of our social institutions.'[1] This description of the contemporary Western mind and myth by a senior moral theologian sums up a number of concerns about what 'rights' language has done to our collective imagination that are shared by both religious and secular thinkers. Does modern 'rights discourse' canonize the idea of single individuals born with a set of abstract entitlements? Does it condemn us to an endless round of circle-squaring attempts to adjudicate warring claims based on this conviction of unchallengeable entitlements? It is an unease as eloquently expressed on the left as on the right. One of the most searching collections of essays in recent years on the philosophical grounding of rights discourse,[2] most of whose contributors share a radical political perspective, reiterates the point. The individual subject of human rights is an abstraction – and precisely and paradoxically *because* of this is also in practice a very specific kind of human subject, the sovereign possessor of unconstrained will, unfettered negotiating power, and the secure certainty of self-transparency (and thus capable of adjudicating the moral status and subjective depth of other putative subjects in the way we have already discussed). Costas Douzinas, one of the editors of this collection, has developed in several major studies[3] the argument that the development of modern human rights language is inseparably bound up with the modern notion of sovereignty in the nation state: the sovereign state is what defends 'natural right', the routine expectations of human social agents as such, and so is the authority that determines what counts as natural right – in the first place for its own citizens, then in contest with other sovereign states (what Douzinas calls 'the competitive solidarity of sovereign governments'[4]). This allows the 'moralizing' of geopolitical conflicts, so that the securing of a convergent global market system can be reimagined as the securing of natural rights – but with little or no perceptible effect in terms of the actual agency of persons and communities whose dignity is denied by violence or inequality. Developments in the last couple of decades, with the growing use of the concept of a right to intervene in states failing in their delivery of 'natural right' – a notion commonly invoked when geopolitical interest and economic benefit are at stake (most notably in Iraq) – will illustrate the point. But behind this lies a dangerous vagueness about the 'human' in 'human rights'. It is, says Douzinas, a 'floating signifier', a term in search of an elusive essence of the human; that is to say, it is a term in search of criteria for inclusion and exclusion, in search of a standard that will clarify who in fact has the right to claim a right, who has proper legal subjecthood. As a floating signifier, it is easily conscripted into the ongoing effort to deny claims of solidarity on the part of those who lack the necessary criteria. 'A human being is someone who can successfully claim human rights,' in Douzinas's summary formulation. And the circularity of this delivers human rights discourse into the hands of competitors for global domination; the supposed 'universality' of the language of human rights becomes a tool for the levering of geopolitical advantage, in the interest of a unified system of market exchange.[5]

A parallel critique of the register of modern human rights language comes from John Milbank, whose historical survey of the medieval origins of the discourse spells out the growing association of 'right' (*ius*) with property or possession in the later Middle Ages and in early modernity.[6] The language of *ius* originally belongs with the theology of *iustitia*, 'justice', defined as the highest of the cardinal virtues because it is not simply a state of the individual soul, but is a condition in which a shared good is more important than the good of any one individual, and is also a virtue irreducibly bound up with willing the good of the other.[7] The transferral of the terminology of *ius* to the territory of atomized agents disputing enforceable claims is a major and catastrophic change. In the earlier context, there could be no 'just' claim for an individual agent or substance that was not always already embedded in a convergent cosmic order: justice is, to quote Milbank, himself summarizing the work of Michel Villey,[8] 'an objective ideality that could be *participated* in', a situation of appropriate interrelation (appropriate 'intervals') between persons or things or both persons and things.

One clear implication of this is that a 'right' in the medieval framework is not something that can be absolutely possessed, since it is always conceived as a proper relation between two or more subjects. In the terminology of the scholarly debate about this history, we cannot find in the earlier medieval discussion any ground for speaking of 'subjective' right, an abstract entitlement belonging inalienably to this or that individual – the 'atomocentric' model of rights, as Douzinas calls it.[9] But equally, 'right' is not simply a function of some conventional collective discipline, a claim that has been created simply by widespread agreement; it looks to the idea of a proper 'fit' between things and/or persons that is independent of any human consensus or any executive coercion. If – to borrow a phrase from the Roman Catholic scholar, Roger Ruston – 'relationships are not added on, as it were, after creation, but belong to what it means to be human, to have a human nature',[10] then there is something always standing in the way of any political claim to control every aspect of its citizens' lives – a prior locatedness or embeddedness in a given order of interconnection that cannot be negated in the name of executive convenience. Our 'right' is not primarily a claim for entitlements as individuals of a certain kind ('human'), but the bare fact that we occupy a certain place in the network of created relations, and are – in virtue of this fact – both subjects and objects of appropriate expectations. The language of 'inalienable' right is at best unhelpful here, Milbank argues:[11] an inalienable possession is still by definition something that is *distinct* from the subject as such – one among a category of possessions some of which can as a matter of fact be divorced from the particular person's ownership and some of which may be treated as for practical purposes intrinsic to the person. But if we ask about what is not 'fungible', not up for negotiation and exchange, the answer is increasingly (in late medieval and early modern thinking) an abstraction – sometimes expressed as 'self-ownership' or self-mastery, or the right of self-protection or innate freedom of will (whether or not actually realized). And this, says Milbank, is of course 'compatible with more or less any actual bondage'.[12] By reducing right to a matter of self-relation ('the mind is its own place', in the words of Milton's Satan), we risk colluding with the selling-off of any and all specific political and social freedoms, while paying lip-service to inalienable dignities. And we thus sacrifice once and for all the critical and revolutionary force of the original idea of natural right as something not vulnerable to the determinations of this or that actually existing socio-political power system. Milbank here echoes not only Douzinas but also Illan Rua Wall's reflections[13] on the role of what he calls 'de-propriation' in the struggle for rights. A model of human rights that works with a sort of catalogue of legally recognizable entitlements needs, according to Wall, to give way to a politics directed towards creating a pattern of social interdependence that does not have to negotiate with the power of a homogenizing state apparatus for the recognition of entitlements. The idea of enumerating the things that are 'proper' to a human subject takes us back again to the problematic logic of possession and the dangers of dealing only with an abstract human subject who may possess more or less of a list of possible 'rights' – as well as raising the spectre already discussed in our first chapter of who determines whether a putative agent/subject satisfies the conditions for recognition in virtue of possessing certain attributes.

There will be more to say about some of these themes later on, but it may help at this stage to add some nuance to the argument, so strongly made by Milbank in particular, for a drastic discontinuity between the high medieval and the modern senses of rights. From the side of the medieval discussion, it is important to understand that Aquinas's ideas of *ius* and *iustitia*, while focusing on the notion of a *right place* to occupy within rightly proportioned or distanced relations with others, also see this as grounding a proper freedom to exercise the particular kind of action appropriate to that place – or indeed a freedom to rectify a situation where such freedom is blocked. Aquinas can say, for example,[14] that it is a matter of *ius naturale*, natural right, that the superabundance of the rich is 'owed' to the poor for their support and well-being. Remember that *iustitia* is the supreme cardinal virtue because it is directed towards something other than the individual self: the appeal to right may be an appeal to *rectification*, to something like what Douzinas and Rua Wall call 'right-ing', the active creating of new relations beyond existing legal categories (Aquinas argues in the same section of the *Summa* that a starving person stealing food from the overabundance of another is not guilty of theft). In other words, we can say that a person has a 'right' to action of the kind that will secure their ability to guarantee their survival as a living participant in the universal network of relation. Talking about 'right' only in terms of cosmic order can give the impression that there is no ground in this classical model for action to defend one's rights and those of others, especially when the definition of cosmic order is assigned to a visible system of control and authority that denies any right of appeal because of its claimed sacred character. But the full outworking of something like Aquinas's theory takes us in another direction. The tension set up between natural right and positive human law is one of the foundational elements in the gradual emergence by the eighteenth century of a doctrine of rights as *liberties* that might need to be forced from the hand of a recalcitrant and unaccountable human authority (in Church or state). Douzinas argues[15] that this longstanding and indeed pre-medieval theme of 'natural right' being affirmed in the face of what he calls 'ancestral' custom and legitimation means that the notion of the 'natural' here is intrinsically an 'act of rebellion' against tribal or patriarchal authority, but that Christianity's use of the category of natural law damagingly obscured this in certain respects until the Enlightenment produced its own curious blend of Christian universalism (as St Paul says, 'in Christ' there are no distinctions between categories of human individuals) and classical appeals to nature over ancestry or sacred communality.

In fact, a close consideration of what Aquinas's account of *ius* is doing would have to qualify Douzinas's narrative substantially; the potential of seeing 'right' as 'rebellious' is emphatically not absent from Aquinas's frame of reference, even though he would not use precisely this vocabulary. But the point here is that speaking about *ius* does involve ascribing *something* to the individual – a proper claim to be able to appeal to the supposed cosmic order as a justification for particular actions of protest or disruption to affirm the freedom to exercise one's appropriate role in the social and cosmic complex. It is Boethius in the sixth century CE who speaks about the status of the person as *sui iuris et alteri incommunicabilis* – ['existing in its own right and not communicable to another'].[16] What exactly does *ius* mean here? Boethius's phraseology seems to mean that to be a person, simply to exercise the activity of being there as a real and unrepeatable participant in the convergent, reciprocal pattern of finite life, is something that has the character of *ius* about it, in the sense that it does not derive its worth or solidity from any other finite source. It has a 'right' to be there as the unique embodied substance it is. This certainly did not mean for Boethius – any more than for any other pre-modern thinker – that this 'right' was a private possession, unconnected with anything beyond the individual, or that it was a thing that could be owned by a subject, though not transferred from a subject's ownership. 'Incommunicable' means exactly what it says: the 'right' involved is the proper expectation that this unrepeatable point in the network of relations should be seen as having value as such – not in virtue of its performance or its possession of a defined set of characteristics, but (in a robust theological context) as one unrepeatable way in which God's act in creation becomes local and specific. It is very close to Stein's 'zero point' language – and indeed suggests a way of thinking about human rights in terms of embodiment that brings together several themes we have been discussing. We might recall Stein's point about the body itself in its relation to the 'zero point' being something literally incommunicable – not in the sense of being self-sustaining or self-sufficient or independent of any relation of sharing, but simply as non-'fungible', incapable of being exchanged. To put it in more provocative contemporary terms, this amounts to saying that its value is not a market value; it is non-convertible.

So we can grant that it is still broadly right to say that a 'subjective' view of rights as properties of an individual is not at all what the high medieval language of *ius* has in mind; this language absolutely takes for granted the relational context of *iustitia* as a virtuous state of directedness towards the good of the neighbour. But this is not quite the whole story: realizing the neighbour's good, and the good of the community overall, is also a matter of acknowledging the incommunicable/inconvertible value of any and every specific neighbour within that pattern of relation. In this context, it is not wrong to say that it amounts to a doctrine of the intrinsic value of each subject.[17] And it is this implied view that connects Aquinas's discussion with the more recent terminology of human 'dignity'. The word is not used in its modern sense by Aquinas or by any pre-modern writer; it emerges mostly in twentieth-century statements about human rights, and is frequently found in theological contexts where it is deployed precisely to qualify an over-abstract or forensic, claim-dominated doctrine of rights.[18] The medieval use of the word is, in other words, still focused on something separable from the bare materiality of a person's embodied presence.

Ernest Fortin, one of the sharpest critics of the idea that there is any real continuity between medieval conceptualities and modern rights doctrines, goes so far as to assert that the medieval use of dignity was essentially as a moral term implying worthiness to be treated in a certain way; in this context, 'to be and to be good were two different things'.[19] But this can be argued only so far. Granted that a lawful authority has the job of limiting the claims of any individual in the light of the common good, this does not itself imply that there is no fundamental and indestructible moral status for the human person simply as such. On the contrary; if the state or some such lawful agency limits the freedom of some group or individual, it will presumably be on the grounds that the liberty they are claiming damages the liberty of others and so is at odds with their *ius*, their rightful expectation of both giving and receiving just treatment. My excessive freedom prevents you offering into the common work of the community the gifts that you alone, with your unique perspective can give. And by insisting on that sort of freedom for myself, I abandon the logic of my own 'right', my own position within the interactive or collaborative whole. That fundamental position of 'right', that proper and active inhabiting of the unique place which I have within the interaction of finite agencies, is not something I ever have to earn or achieve; my worth or value is given in my occupying that place and no other. And it is by no means a far-fetched extrapolation from Aquinas's basic position to say that forms of punishment that radically deny or suspend any kind of attention to the incommunicable worth of any human other – extreme punishment, the permanent removal of the privileges of citizenship and so on – can and should be challenged in the name of a more coherent approach to the intrinsic worth of the individual subject. Fortin's point about the non-identity of 'being' and 'being good' holds only in the sense that no one is to be *rewarded* for simply existing; but at another level, that 'simply existing' in this unique position already embodies a 'good', a distinct contribution to the order of the whole. Fortin tartly observes[20] that in the medieval context, it is the 'right' of the criminal to be punished, in the sense that this is the appropriate response to the fact that the criminal agent has abandoned the place in which their giving and receiving of good works as it ought. What is morally due to them, what constitutes *iustitia* in the full sense of action for their benefit, is appropriate punishment. To be *sui iuris* endowed with value is not the same as having an automatic entitlement to be kept happy. But at the same time it is essential to bear in mind that any punishment that denies the inherent possibility of ongoing free and intelligent participation in the realizing of common good, or offends against the body's liberty to exist as body – as an embodied speaker with a position from which to act and give – will undermine the justice it sets out to honour and conserve; humiliating and dehumanizing penal policy, let alone torture, cannot be defended in this framework, whatever ambiguities were entertained on such questions by the medievals.

The debates about the relation or lack of it between medieval ideas of *ius* and the contemporary world of rights discourse can at times give the impression of a weddedness to over-dramatic binaries: either the Middle Ages fully anticipated the key values of liberal modernity, or else the theological wisdom of the high medieval period was catastrophically betrayed by nominalist philosophy, political nationalism and proto-capitalist economics, and the modern discourse of rights is something intrinsically corrupted by the instrumentalism and individualism of modernity.[21] But the narrative does not need to be so polarized. It is possible to see aspects of our familiar rights discourse still tacitly appealing to or negotiating with the sort of concerns that the medievals were interested in; and this is not merely an academic point. It is a crucial reminder that a discourse that we might think of as one of those self-evidently rational products of modernity is in fact the product of a protracted process of learning and debate. It is true that late medieval and early modern discussion of *ius* moved increasingly in the direction of treating right as an individual possession, and that highly problematic theories both of political sovereignty and of economic exchange contributed to this, along with the interest in what Milbank[22] calls '"raw" freedom' in the nominalist thinkers of the late Middle Ages – a notion of the will unconstrained by reason and detached from any idea of a basic level of participation in cosmic, co-operative, 'harmonic' good. At the same time, as Milbank seems rather reluctantly to grant,[23] the ecclesial and political turmoil of later medieval life in Western Europe played some part in bringing into sharper focus those elements of the earlier doctrine that sketched out something like 'subjective' right, even if only as a derivative outworking of a much more comprehensive doctrine. And when we look at the sixteenth-century debates about the humanity and human claims of newly encountered peoples across the Atlantic, to which we have already referred in the first chapter, it is clear that, once again, something like a 'subjective' view of natural right as inhering in human individuals was an important element in the defence of indigenous Americans against the collective self-interest of the colonial Spanish state. What we should now call a doctrine of inalienable human dignity is taking shape.

And it is worth noting that modern approaches to human rights cannot with fairness be reduced to a simple commitment to unconnected entitlements ascribed to solitary individuals. The 1948 Universal Declaration of Human Rights — rather seldom discussed in detail by contemporary critics — retains some of those broader communal perspectives that have been seen as lacking in modern approaches to the subject.[24] In the first article of the text, the ascription of inalienable rights to all is coupled with an exhortation to act in 'a spirit of brotherhood' (sic) with one another — a weak but not completely empty echo of the invocation of solidarity in other contexts. The Declaration also specifies (art. 29.2) that the protection of the rights enumerated is subject to the requirements of a social and political order whose task is to safeguard every citizen in the same way, with every individual again reminded of the respect due to *all*. Again, this can be read as a 'weak but not empty' recognition of interlocking interests in a social unit whose relation with one another needs thought and negotiation. The individual bearer of the rights under discussion is not treated as a purely abstract and unrelated figure: it is made clear that the state is to be regarded as legitimate only when it guarantees not to infringe a set of basic securities and liberties of association – including, significantly, association in families (art.12 and 16), which assumes that our first induction into human society occurs in the context of some kind of pledged relationship between agents who are in greater or lesser measure committed to the labour of teaching a new subject to speak and converse. The Declaration also assumes that communal religious activity and public assembly are aspects of the routine liberties a human subject may expect (art. 18, 20), and that participatory democracy and cultural involvement are likewise matters of routine human activity (art. 21,27).

The problem is, of course, that by casting all this in terms of what an individual may rightfully expect, the UDHR gives the impression that an individual ought to have the *choice* to be part of a nation or family or faith community in a way that does indeed imply that the default human identity is something above and beyond such forms of belonging; as if the basic position were just that 'self-ownership' that raises such problems in the late medieval context. But it helps to remember the historical background of the Declaration, indicated quite plainly in the Preamble. This text is being drawn up in the wake of the devastation brought about through a concentrated and comprehensive programme to deprive human subjects of a range of freedoms through the overriding of assorted 'natural' forms of affiliation – faith, family, co-operative working groups and so on – and the text is clear in warning that a failure to respect these freedoms deprives the state of the right to expect loyalty and compliance. If a state wants stability, it must work for these protections. The UDHR sets out not to list entitlements (though it sails very close to the wind in enumerating rather too many specific and heterogeneous aspirations in its later articles) but to outline what makes a polity legitimate (and by implication what might justify civil disobedience or even more drastic action). Against this background, we should be cautious about assuming that *all* recent consideration of human rights is essentially rooted in an abstract and individualistic set of assumptions. And this should not surprise us, given that the UDHR owed a great deal to the contributions of scholars and thinkers from diverse theological and confessional backgrounds.²⁵ 'The UDHR needs to be read...as crystallising positively the importance of educating a population in the security of being needed and negatively the importance of obliging the state to admit its limitations...The UDHR stakes a claim that the most clearly legitimate society is one that builds in institutions and habits of self-criticism'.²⁶

Drawing together this part of our discussion, it should by now be clear that the language of human rights as currently deployed in national and transnational politics is something of an intellectual hybrid – not simply the unrecognizably degenerate descendant of a more concrete and communal pre-modern understanding, but an often awkward set of extrapolations from that earlier account, in which the idea of an 'appropriate' position to occupy in the network of finite agencies has retreated almost to vanishing point. This attrition of the idea of a given order of proportion and interaction between agents, with its strong religious underpinning,²⁷ is perennially at risk of slipping towards the abstraction that we have seen as a constant concern in recent discussion – and also towards a new positivism, in which human right is a simple 'given', recognizable to any rational individual, self-evident in its imperative force, and thus properly and 'rationally' to be defended or imposed by those who have the power to do so. We are back in the murky waters where modern human rights discourse is stirred into the currents of state absolutism in a way wholly antithetical to the original direction of the language of natural right, as Douzinas and others have argued. Belief in human rights has become the last politically acceptable form of uncritical confessional faith within Western modernity, a grid for universal moral assessment and what Michael Walzer²⁸ calls 'moral maximalism' – but with a distinctly shaky metaphysical basis and (consequently) an embarrassing history of co-option in the interests of geopolitical hegemony and stable market systems. If it is to play any substantive role in a future renewal of political ethics, rather than just being a shibboleth opportunistically applied in the rationalizing of modern conflict, it will need to recover the critical/utopian dimension that Douzinas advocates. And in the light of our considerations so far in this book, this necessitates paying attention to some of the broader questions, however uncomfortably or dangerously 'metaphysical', that link the language of rights with the questions we started with: questions about moral recognition, about the sense of imaginative identification with the standpoint of neighbour and stranger, and (most fundamentally) the awareness of what kind of humanity we are talking about, irrespective of any currently prevailing structures of power and social control. As this chapter has so far suggested, we need to connect an analysis of the empathic awareness that we see as grounding our own account of ourselves with the notion of a *iustitia* that takes as basic the necessary role of the *other*'s well-being in any kind of defensible political ethic. But given the connection traced earlier between the relativizing or problematizing of my individual perspective and the understanding of what is involved in being a body, it makes sense to look a bit more closely in the next section of this chapter at the relation of rights and bodies, with an eye to developing these themes further in the direction of a full explication of human solidarity.

2.

One way of summarizing the knot into which modern rights language habitually ties itself is – as Milbank indicates[29] – to note the way in which so much of it reduces to the affirmation of a contentless freedom of choice, the right to do what I want to do, limited only by pragmatic considerations of social stability. In effect, this translates 'rights' into strategies to minimize violence: how many individuals or groups can you prevent from being constantly at each other's throats? If what the language of rights – or even of 'dignity' at times – is protecting is ultimately the self-assertion of individual interest, it opens out on to a Hobbesian world of primordial conflict and competition, as antithetical as could be to the idea of *iustitia* in the medieval texts. There is a vicious circle at work in this: I hold on to my rights because the aggressive wills of others (persons and institutions) always menace my liberties; I cling on to my firearms because the world is full of people with guns (not an abstract instance, as any citizen of the USA will confirm). Literally or metaphorically, the default setting for my social location is a state of siege.

As with so much of the modern approach, this represents not just a perverse early modern or late medieval capitulation to individualism, but also a rather distorted legacy from the earlier period. Aquinas, in the course of his discussion of slavery and obedience, lays down[30] that the will of the master cannot extend to the enslaved person's freedom of bodily self-preservation or even to their freedom to choose a sexual partner: the will of the master stops at the limits of the body, we might say. So yes, the 'right' of the enslaved person here is indeed a claim to be protected from the will of another; but the mistake is to treat this as the general paradigm for thinking about what 'right' means. What Aquinas is arguing is that no master – and no governing authority in general – can simply prevent a subject from pursuing a natural good like food or faithful sexual partnership; the master's claim cannot override the freedom to do what you need to do in order to lead a human life. But it is not difficult to see how the slippage occurs here. If what you need to do in order to lead a human life is simply to choose what you need to do in order to lead a human life, the stage is set for the zero-sum conflict of will that constantly threatens the peace of a society. For the older tradition, it was possible to answer the question of what I need to do for the fulfilment of my humanity in positive terms: I need the liberty to turn to the true God, I need the liberty to nourish and sustain my body, I need the liberty to exercise my role in the community according to a set of natural and supernatural virtues that will maximize the good of all. No other individual's will can ever lawfully stand in the way of such liberties, and a denial of these liberties is grounds for disobedience.[31] But if such substantive common moral goals disappear, what is left is the bare contest of wills, mine and the other's. 'Right' shrinks to the dimensions of protection from one another. Creating a framework in which it is possible to mediate and interpret individual projects in terms of the good of others, to interrogate individual 'right' in the perspective of what it may do for the good or otherwise of the wider human fellowship, becomes harder. In recent debates over physician-assisted dying, the issue has arisen with some poignancy and complexity: is an absolute liberty to end one's own life (even through the agency of another) something that overrides a set of potential social consequences (such as pressures on the elderly or physically challenged, or the impact on funding for research in palliative care)? These questions do not settle the debate, a particularly difficult and sensitive one, but it is significant that there has lately been a good deal of broadening out of the discussion so as to address this issue more seriously in the light of wider social goods, and to look harder at the naked assertion of an individual 'right to die'.

But to return to the central issue here: the affirmation of the liberty of bodily self-care – significantly including the liberty of creating certain kinds of bodily relationship – is grounded in a picture of the body itself as a site of and a maker of *meanings*: intelligible, consistent 'policies' through which the body participates in communication, giving and receiving significant signs that deepen and reinforce collaborative possibilities. If we could lawfully be commanded to deny our freedom of self-preservation, we should be no more than instruments for inscribing the agenda, the meanings, of another subject. 'The ultimate form of slavery would be a situation in which your body was made to carry the meanings or messages of another subject and never permitted to *say* in word or gesture what was distinctive for itself as a sense-making consciousness.'[32] It is not that the 'right' of the other is always a hostile rival, but that certain kinds of bid for control over others have to be identified and ruled out – within an overall context in which the default situation is not potentially violent competition but mutual intelligibility and shared voluntary labour. The meaning communicated by my embodied action is my unique share in a co-produced meaning, a continuing and intelligible linguistic exchange (taking 'linguistic' here – as noted before – to include a variety of embodied communicative behaviour, so as not to restrict this to verbally high-functioning agents), in which I and the other secure one another's human growth or flourishing within an extended communal pattern of such mutuality. And for this to function, we need something of the perspective we have already been exploring, a literacy about what it is to be a *body* rather than a purely non-reflective organism, let alone a set of programmed operations. We need to be aware of the nature of bodily learning, the empathic knowledge of being seen or read that sustains our own essays in communicating, in seeing and reading others.

So we might begin thinking about rights as something to do with the freedom to act so as to maximize the power of others to act, morally and collaboratively – i.e. in a way that builds up the network of mutuality. A 'just' situation is one in which the particular person receives what is their due – following the classical definition of justice as giving each what is proper to them – but understands that part of what is their due is the capacity to serve the good of the other (the specific and local neighbour and the wider communal network). Thinking of a right independently of this will lead us back to the zero-sum model. Take, for example, the right to free speech – regularly and understandably treated as a test of liberal societies and currently a neuralgic issue for both left and right. That every citizen has the liberty to use their voice in public debate and discernment and to explore imaginative possibilities in poetry or fiction or plastic art is surely implicit in any adequate account of *ius* as the ground of the communicative freedom of an embodied person. But because embodied persons have to work at a shared task of constructing an equitable and sustainable social environment, we cannot simply leave this liberty as the abstract power to say what we like. 'Saying what we like' may silence others or encourage the silencing of others; it may stand in the way of releasing another's capacity to live as a communicating body. The history of racial and gender inequality illustrates what such silencing looks like, and its effect is the denial of *ius* to both oppressed and oppressor, since the oppressor, by silencing another, cuts himself or herself off from the constructive response of the other that should ideally nourish their own liberty.

Most of us recognize this – if not in precisely those terms – when we think about the conventional restraints on 'absolute' freedom of speech; but it is notoriously difficult to determine exactly where the line should be drawn in legal enactments. Framing the problem as I have just done is not meant to offer a quick solution to this, but to move the dial away from the atomized picture of rights as self-contained entitlements (a right to free speech, a right not to be threatened or damaged by what others say) towards a broader consideration of what kind of communicative culture we are committed to shaping – what we are able to say together, as opposed to a culture defined always by what it is not saying or refusing to hear. Legal protections are a part but never the whole of that shaping activity; the heavy lifting is at the level of routine interaction and the possibilities of specific shared work (a point we shall come back to more than once).

In this context, the liberty to 'say what we mean to say' as embodied subjects is not – as John Milbank has argued in a critique of this position[33] – just another version of an Enlightenment appeal to 'the freedom of the adult rational mind' as the basis of rights, recast as an empty 'freedom to be'. Nor does it take us back to an abstract equality for all individual agents that is beyond any kind of mediation.[34] On the contrary: the freedom to communicate in this context is clearly *not* some innate and occult individual capacity, but the liberty that is always already given us in our immersion from the first stirring of consciousness in the circulation and exchange of language; it is the freedom to enact what we are as participants in the construction of an inhabitable and intelligible world. To see this as a universal given is not the same as maintaining a purely abstract equality in entitlement; but it *is* to affirm an equality in virtue of what we might have to call the 'vocation' to participation in linguistic and relational labour, a participation that (as specifically argued in the essay of mine that Milbank critically engages with[35]) does not depend on satisfying prescribed general criteria for 'rational' or even verbal performance: the sheer organic otherness of the other posits a 'being seen' or perhaps 'being sensed' of some kind (which is why the 'imperfectly rational person', the child, the adult with learning disabilities, even the unborn child, can be thought of as belonging in a communicative network).

Milbank considers the focus on the communicative capacity of the body as a focus for discussing rights to be an 'incoherent hybrid'[36] of traditional notions of *ius* and the toxic language of inalienable properties that underpins modern rights discourse. This is to reduce the phenomenological model of bodiliness that we have been considering to a simple variant of basic atomism or 'atomocentrism' to borrow Douzinas's term: there are primitive individual essences called bodies in which inhere a set of entitlements to self-expression, and this, in Milbank's eyes, fails to provide any useful hierarchy or distinction between diverse embodied realities, human, animal or inanimate, that could be called 'expressive'. This takes us back to considerations around recognition such as were discussed in our first chapter, and it should be clear from this discussion that a blanket undifferentiated picture of any material individual substance having the same 'right' as any other generically comparable substance would make little sense, given the variety of intercommunicative models that are at work in different cases. But for Milbank, the worry is also that the 'communicative body based' model, by covertly affirming an individual and proprietorial meaning for *ius*, would legitimize a whole range of decisions to suspend specific liberties 'in the name of "rights as such"'.[37] 'A sovereign power can decide, for example, that, after all, religious liberty is a threat to individual liberty (for example the rights of women, the rights of gay people, or the democratic rights of a congregational body against their own bishop or the norms of their own tradition) and therefore remove altogether any specific mode of freedom to exercise a religious practice.'[38]

This is not a groundless worry, given the way both popular and professional legal attitudes have been moving.[39] But we should beware of simply mirroring the crude binaries that liberal advocates of limiting religious freedom of expressions have clung to. On the one hand: the law of the state can reasonably act against any body, religious or otherwise, that actively and forcibly restrains access to the strictly civic liberties of any of its members as determined by law, or that inflicts what most would see as unlawfully abusive and violent treatment of its members. Conversely, some of those civic liberties or legal freedoms may properly be objected to by a religious community as incompatible with their teaching (the most familiar instance has been the abiding religious prohibition on abortion in the Roman Catholic Church); but they remain formally accessible to believers simply as citizens, and a community's internal sanctions cannot alter this fact or wholly ignore it. The broad rights of association embedded in the prevailing rights paradigm, however, do not encourage the state to try and determine internal questions disputed within religious communities.[40]

On the other hand: any religious theory of rights would have to allow that accepting something like a 'communicative body' rationale would mean (at least) a degree of hesitancy about the assumption that a community would or should invariably resolve the sorts of tensions Milbank mentions[41] in favour of simple collective and traditional protocols. Religious bodies have had to develop some means of dealing with the fact that certain traditional practices – including those connected with precisely the issues Milbank lists as examples – demonstrate a failure to see the internal contradictions that may embed themselves in those practices. In other words, we may and should resist any suggestion that the state (or anyone else) has a prescriptive entitlement to interfere in internal religious matters, while also recognizing that those internal debates can pose their own challenges to the consistency of a community's account of *ius* and *iustitia*. And, as in the case of enslavement or the liberties of women, it may be that non-religious developments and perspectives bring into sharp focus the internal tensions or contradictions of inherited communal practices or assumptions in ways that gradually change the consensus within a traditional religious community. The body-count in many religious institutions is on the high side. You don't have to be a progressive triumphalist to acknowledge this, nor do you have to conclude that you have to deny the priority of associational communities over an impersonal modern state apparatus. But the situation is not as timeless and immutable as some debates seem to assume. One of the results of living in a pluralist society is that the internal consistency and defensibility of communal practices is always going to be exposed to reminders of the universalist horizons that make religious ethics or anthropology what they are in the first place. Defence of the community's own liberty and integrity in determining what it counts as 'right' is not the same as effectively reintroducing what Douzinas calls an 'ancestral' approach to the question, or ascribing to religious communities something like that level of inalienable privilege that is being criticized in the case of individuals.

The purpose of this prolonged discussion of some critiques of human rights discourse is to acknowledge that these critiques rightly highlight some very substantive dangers in versions of rights talk that refuse to ask awkward questions about the abstract individualism that underlies much discussion, about the complicated interweaving of philosophies of rights with theories of state sovereignty, about the implicit and sometimes explicit focus on a content-free liberty of choice. Thus far, the concerns expressed by Milbank and others are reasonable – though it has to be said that much of this critical material engages very little with any actual documentation in recent literature of the full-blown absolutist individualism that is under attack; much of this argumentation is really to do with what are held to be unavoidable *implications* of certain ways of describing rights, and with some of the more journalistic accounts of competing claims that surface in a variety of modern culture-war contexts. But precisely in such contexts, it would be fair to say that a good deal of current debate about rights is subject to deep confusion because of the absence of a coherent basis for moral universalism or respect for persons.

The language of inherent human 'dignity' is often just a way of displacing the problem, every bit as positivist in its implications as the language of rights itself – that is, every bit as dependent on someone claiming the power to stipulate that this is just how things are.

The fundamental uncertainty and confusion here has something to do with our deeply engrained modern assumptions about the connection of rights with contentless freedom; what is to be protected is the maximal exercise of choice. Behind this lies a further and more complicated set of assumptions. We are still held captive – in the Wittgensteinian phrase – by a picture held over from early modernity. Defenders of the normative status of the self-determining subject taken for granted in a superficial rights discourse seem blissfully unaware of Marx, Freud, Nietzsche or Weber, as if the self-determining subject had never had to interrogate its own learning of desire. Identity – in a psychoanalytically-informed narrative – is constructed in the process of our movement through the 'desire of the Other' (best to use the upper-case letter here, in view of its technical significance on psychoanalytic theory): we deal with our primordial sense of lack by turning to an Other that is seen not to be lacking; we want what that Other wants because their wanting is beyond need, an 'excessive' desire that is never dictated by need; we want to *be* wanted by the Other, we want to be accorded the dignity of being recognized as valued and longed-for. And because of the deep contradictions and unrealities involved in this, our desire for the Other is always frustrated and so always renewed and repeated insatiably. The process generates what Douzinas calls the conviction of a 'right to be loved'. It also focuses attention on the meeting of specific and contingent wants as a sign of that global acceptance by the Other, and leaves little resource for thinking about the body's '"natural" integrity' as a whole. Summing all this up, Douzinas characterizes the outcome as a view of the world guaranteed to produce anger, despair and paranoia; 'human rights' has become (in a paradox beloved of Derrida, playing on the dual meaning of the Greek word) a true *pharmakon* – something that is both therapy and poison.

For Douzinas,[42] if there is an antidote to the toxicity of this picture it must come through two processes – a model of 'right' as something that *precedes our own individual subjectivity*, as a complex of mobile, always self-challenging and self-correcting interconnections between agents or subjects; and a consistent recognition, inseparable from this first perspective, that the other is not the same as my knowledge of the other – an illusion that Douzinas considers to be a central mistake in the mindset of rationalist modernity. A 'postmodern' conception of justice, he suggests, is one in which the 'metaphysical residue' in rights language is recovered, the acknowledgement that there is an order or pattern to be imagined in which one's own need or one's own point of view is not finally determinative. This is, for postmodernity, an *imagined* order, not a reversion to pre-modern cosmology; but it is a necessary imaginative exercise if we are to resist the totalizing force of the sovereignty/individuality/market cluster of powers that currently paralyse our world. Its implication is close to what Rua Wall calls for,[43] the grass-roots creation of a different form of social life in which we do not simply ask for increasing concessions from the existing order of law, but look to construct patterns of 'right-ing' that are themselves in excess of law, 'not *determined by* law'.[44] In place of the Sisyphean desire for endless individual affirmation, there is an endless desire for the voice or face of the other to be given what its existence demands, given a place from which to act and give.

Douzinas elaborates this in his essay of 2014[45] by way of a reflection on the postmodern 'will'. The pre-modern will seeks cosmic authorization for a right and true choice to make – the *ius* of high medieval theology; the modern will is the possibility of doing something, a possibility increasingly protected and secured by sovereign order. Late modern rights discourse and practice renders this as the guaranteeing of 'socially accepted demands' and 'lifestyle choices'. What then would a postmodern version of rights look like? Not a reinforcement for the possibility of certain specified and chosen actions on the part of legally qualified citizens, but 'the demand not to be treated as an object', and the freedom to work together to construct a social reality in which such treatment is decisively repudiated – an 'agonistic universality' of unending recalibrations of the location of power, moving from individual non-compliance with injustice to 'collective resistance'.[46] Revolutionary resistance takes as its legitimating principle not law but 'solidarity', understood in solidly Marxist style as the universal liberty to *produce according to one's capabilities, to consume according to one's needs*.[47]

This is a provocative and very intricately constructed set of ideas (redolent of a particular moment in recent cultural history, in which the variants of the 'Occupy' movement across the North Atlantic world seemed to suggest a convergent grass-roots shift of political possibility); the problem is that the rhetoric of its culminating celebration of revolution as a 'collective emancipatory will' threatens to privilege resistance itself as preferable to a durable new culture in which specific injustices can be addressed effectively. Back to the question touched on in the introduction: what will actually change the lot of a woman raped in war, a homeless person, a teenager drawn into illicit drug distribution by the pressures of poverty and the absence of employment options? But Douzinas highlights a number of considerations that would qualify the risks of a perpetual self-referential revolutionary pathos. He is feeling his way towards a definition of 'will' that in fact makes the word itself misleading in this context: the individual resistance he commends is not resistance for the sake of one's own security but for the sake of a different kind of social arrangement, one in which goods are not seen as itemized benefits to be parcelled out equally or unequally between individuals but as interconnected elements in a sustainable and morally reflective community that understands the inescapably mutual nature of human living.

But, picking up Douzinas's own language, this is a social vision that looks to something very like a metaphysical commitment.

In this book so far, we have explored a number of approaches that in one way or another draw out such a metaphysical commitment. We have been brought back repeatedly to similar themes, and to a narrative that goes roughly like this:

(i) We need to let go of the myth of an 'already completed' selfhood with desires and needs laid out prior to any relational or cultural involvement.

(ii) The recognition that my understanding of myself is always already shaped by being object as well as subject, receiving as well as giving meaning, is crucial for any defensible account of human consciousness.

(iii) So we must acknowledge the impossibility of abstract definitions of the human self, and accept the inevitability of seeing the speaking and acting subject as a participant in the ongoing construction of a world.

(iv) Following on from this, we have to reckon with the impossibility of a wholly self-sufficient account of the individual's interest or 'good'; as material agents in a material environment, we are bound up in an essentially shared enterprise. This may be the fundamental 'world-making' business of linguistic communication, making shared sense; but it also takes in the unavoidably shared nature of challenges to our practical interest and well-being in an imperfectly controllable environment.

(v) Our empathic connection with what is not ourselves is not an extra enhancement of our routine (individual) perception or sensibility but a central constituent of consciousness itself: we can't *not* suppose the perspective that is not ours, and so our awareness of threat or crisis cannot indefinitely ignore the interwoven character of the world we inhabit. Our embodied nature – counterintuitively – works against a model of mutually impenetrable and disconnected selves in the world. As bodies we cannot help 'reading and being read'.

(vi) Against this background, the language of 'rights' is problematic but not easy to sideline completely. It is certainly unhelpful and untruthful to think of rights as determinate 'things' that we possess, individual entitlements, cheques to be cashed. The roots of the language of right lie in a strong commitment to cosmological order, so that any affirmation of or defence of a right is *ipso facto* a commitment to a good that is not just ours (remember Aquinas's argument about why *iustitia* is first among the virtues because it is not only about the single agent's moral standing). Centuries of confused reworkings of this have had the effect of cementing in the minds of many a model of rights in which priority is automatically given to the freedom to do what we want, stepping away from any idea of a morally interdependent world. But this is qualified by the Universal Declaration and by a good deal even of modern practice. It does not help to categorize the entire realm of rights discourse as corrupted by abstract individualism. The picture of a mutually creative and nourishing universe in which each unique agent needs to be given room to do what only they can do to maintain the shared world and its shared good means that we can't completely avoid speaking of individual subjects – and individual collectivities – 'having' rights; what we need to beware of is the assumption that these are freestanding, separate entitlements always liable to turn into conflicting absolutes.

(vii) Different kinds of discourses about right, recognition, empathy and so on open out, in more than one thinker's work, on to the horizon of an imagined order, a state of 'communion'. This is *not* – for Joanna Bourke, for instance – a state of timeless and frictionless absorption beyond boundaries, in which total reciprocal transparency is guaranteed, but a condition of energetic exchange in which inequities of power or advantage are constantly being upset and recalibrated.[48] There is – to borrow the theological term – an 'apophatic' dimension to this kind of talk: we know where communion is not (here and now), yet we also know it to be present (here and now) as the possibility we are always on the edge of. We can – so to speak – truthfully imagine a kind of human life together in which the priority in act and in labour was the release of one another into greater liberty to exercise the gift that is unique to each.

This brings us to the central issue of how solidarity emerges as a theme that holds all this more or less together. It is time now to look more carefully at its evolution and at some of the versions of it that have emerged in the last century or so. In the next section of this book, we shall briefly look at its background before 1900, and its increasing use after 1900 as a term of art in Catholic Social Teaching; and this will lead into a treatment of a couple of the major thinkers who have used it in the later twentieth century, and of some of the ways in which its use has prompted and might continue to prompt fresh thinking about both religious and non-religious styles of common life and perspectives on human selfhood.

FOUR

Solidarity: the Making of a Discourse

1.

As we saw in the Introduction, one of the problems with the word 'solidarity' is that it can mean both a state of affairs and an ideal kind of behaviour. The earliest uses of the word seem to be in a legal context:[1] 'solidarity' in the Napoleonic Code is the condition of being jointly (*in solidum*) liable for a debt. But by the middle of the nineteenth century, it had acquired a much more general sense. Charles Fourier's utopian communitarianism had rejected the morality of any individual ownership of goods, arguing for a distributist approach to economic and other resources; and Hippolyte Renaud, in an influential monograph of 1842,[2] developed these ideas further, arguing that the practice of individual ownership was bound in with a set of assumptions about the exclusivity of possession that helped to generate insoluble 'zero-sum' conflicts. But the answer was not simple collectivism; it was a culture – and a legal framework – of 'solidarity', that acknowledged the diverse needs of every agent in society and provided for them on the basis of a radically redistributive policy towards wealth of any kind. This included a recognition of the fact that certain goods were *intrinsically* common or public: the absolute ownership of land, for example, was ruled out as indefensible on this basis. Because human beings lived in an unavoidably co-operative context, distributing among themselves the tasks and responsibilities of maintaining social order or social goods, there was an 'organic solidarity' built in to human existence; and a rational and ethical society should reflect this.

The legacy of this scheme was long-lived – in part because the language of solidarity was heard, especially in connection with

Auguste Comte's social vision, as offering a clear (and superior) alternative to the Christian appeal to charity or even the conventional exaltation of fraternité.[3] In the closing decades of the century, it was reworked by Leon Bourgeois into a programme for government in the 1890s, and he elaborates it in his booklet of 1896, Solidarité. Like Renaud, he resists an all-out collectivist approach in favour of what he called *solidarisme*, a policy based on the principle of differentiated social roles and contributions to the common good, according to which government had the task of assessing the 'debt' of each to all, so as to create a system of taxation that would assure all citizens the same level of access to common goods. Bourgeois was not the first to envisage a redistributive fiscal philosophy for government, but he was certainly among the first to attempt (unsuccessfully) to put it into practice, extending its reach beyond the measures to protect industrial workers that had been established, for example, in Bismarck's Germany not long before. A detailed theoretical discussion had already been provided in Emil Durkheim's work on *The Division of Labour in Society*, published in 1893, but Durkheim's vocabulary is a little more complex than that of Bourgeois. He distinguishes between 'mechanical' and 'organic' solidarity – the former being the state of pre-political communality, based on natural similarity between human agents and the basic business of meeting one another's immediate needs, and the latter being what we create as a reflection of the needs of a *differentiated* society, an expression not of sameness but of difference managed or negotiated into some kind of cultural convergence. This is why solidarity is, for Durkheim, a moral issue, not just a matter of sociological description; and it relates also to his analysis of the deep moral challenge faced by modern society in sustaining a sense of common purpose in a context of cultural and economic diversity quite different from what had prevailed in a pre-modern context. Building a social order of solidarity is thus an imperative. The solidarity of the pre-modern society is not essentially a moral matter, but a given aspect of the fundamental patterns of human collaboration. Durkheim has a good deal to say about the need to construct or reinforce those associational bodies that, even within a society of mass identities and impersonal collectivities, constitute training grounds for the sort of moral creativity he envisages. He is clear that there need to be communities of affinity in which conscious interdependence, mutual responsibility, can be nourished, and the weight of 'purposelessness' (*anomie*) which he so famously analysed could be counterbalanced.[4]

As this makes clear, Durkheim does not subscribe to the idea that the modern problem is simply individualism: 'organic solidarity' is – paradoxically – made possible by the emergence of the *moral* individual, and it is precisely this moral (responsible) individuality that is lacking in 'mechanical' solidarity. The gulf between modern and pre-modern is not that between a sense of collective empathy or whatever and the impersonal processes of industrializing or globalizing societies; it is between a social environment in which individual agents are rather precariously prevented from uncontrolled and violent rivalry by the authority of sacralized power and punitive law and one of clearly and consciously differentiated responsibilities in which the individual grows up into the acknowledgement of the debt of each to all, as Bourgeois would express it. Durkheim fairly clearly works with the deliberately provocative intent of deconstructing a facile association of the 'organic' with the pre-modern and traditionally communitarian; it is something that puts him interestingly at odds with some of the other writers we shall be examining, but also casts light on the way in which a thinker like Jan Patočka handles some of the same themes.

But what Durkheim's analysis of solidarity provides is a first attempt to tease apart the two elements in our discourse about solidarity, the descriptive and the prescriptive senses that the word acquires, particularly in the nineteenth and early twentieth-century political context. We shall be looking shortly at the initial reception of this twofold approach in the realm of Catholic political advocacy in the early twentieth century. But it foreshadows a broader set of issues that have come to the fore more clearly in recent years. As we noted earlier in this book,[5] contemporary discussions of solidarity in the field of political philosophy have identified it in different ways and located it in different places on a spectrum between the primarily descriptive (solidarity is a characteristic of any social system of relations) and the primarily normative (solidarity is a virtue that ought to be realized in social relations). They have engaged with the question of whether solidarity is a goal in itself, whether it is a *distinctive* goal or just a synonym for other perhaps less dramatic-sounding virtues like charity or compassion, whether it is a self-evidently good goal, and whether it is best thought of as *primarily*:

(i) a symmetrical relationship between agents participating together in a social practice or project, in which the word designates the fact that these agents share – in some sense equally – in a common interest defined by things they have/do in common (the paradigm here would be the solidarity of workers in a labour organization);

(ii) an *asymmetrical* relationship between agents directly involved in a situation not of their choosing and other agents who freely elect (though they do not in fact share that situation) to identify with and act in the interest of those directly engaged (the paradigm here being the solidarity of the activist with the oppressed minority, the American student demonstrating for Gaza, the *Je suis Charlie* moment; at the extreme, Simone Weil in exile in England refusing to eat more food than she believed was available to her fellow-Frenchmen and Frenchwomen in the later days of the Second World War, or the Russian nun, Mother Maria Skobtsova, encouraging French Christians in Paris in 1940 to wear the yellow star alongside their Jewish neighbours);

(iii) a symmetrical relationship in which agents who do *not* share in any straightforward way a single set of characteristics, experiences or goals, but are united in a condition they have not chosen and may not initially recognize (the paradigm here would be the struggles to find a coherent centre of gravity for a shared practice of resistance or protest about systemic racial or gender-based oppression without presupposing that there is one and only one *normative* experience of such oppression – a single model based, say, on the history of the Atlantic slave-trade, or on a particular moment in the history of middle-class family life in Western Europe or North America in the mid-twentieth century).[6]

Of these, (i) is the nearest to what might be called the descriptive end of the spectrum. It is unarguably the case, it might be said, that workers share a common interest; the job of an activist devoted to persuading a group of workers to come out in solidarity is really the job of displaying clearly the inseparability of the interests of workers in different industries or even different countries. That common identity is not simply *created* (though it might need to be awakened or galvanized); it is at some important level already a matter of demonstrable fact. If we were to take a perspective closer to Durkheim's original pattern, the point holds: we are obviously in a social situation that works in an interdependent mode, such that, for example, an inadequate pay settlement for NHS doctors or transport workers (not exactly an academic question in the UK of 2025) can in principle be shown to be a matter of interest, direct or indirect, to the hedge fund manager or the corporate lawyer, to the extent that a redistributive tax regime would appear obvious and natural (I do not hold my breath).

Equally, (ii) is at the 'prescriptive' end: it is *not* the case that any actual shared interest exists, unless we move into a more metaphysical register and claim that all human good, or, more specifically, social good is indivisible. And, as we need to be reminded, there are enormous moral elephant traps here when the person intending to show solidarity fails to attend to the way in which the other with whom they want to be in solidarity actually understands or experiences their own condition, and to the priorities those others themselves define. Avery Kolers goes so far as to argue[7] that solidarity in sense (ii) must mean supporting the person or community directly engaged in injustice or suffering without qualification – or, more precisely, not simply supporting this or that aspect of their programmes, desires, or demands, but always speaking and acting under their tutelage and as if from their perspective, so as not to create a new kind of oppression or appropriation, a new reduction of the Other to the Same.

The third variation is in some ways the most interesting for our purposes in this book, in the sense that it pushes back against the reduction of solidarity to a kind of fellow-feeling grounded in similarity – a point that has been significant in some religious treatments of the matter, as we shall see – and invites us to step back and assess the weight of a structural fact that may not be experienced in the same way by all whom it affects. The Latin American woman working unregistered as a company cleaner or housemaid in Los Angeles does not share the experience of the committedly feminist female attorney whose life she is making appreciably easier, but this does not mean that the female attorney is absolved from acknowledging that what she finds limiting and demeaning in her experience has its roots in *the same fundamental imbalances of power* (cultural, economic, physical) that at every turn and in innumerable diverse ways constrain the liberty of women. In other words, there is *work* to be done here, work that entails a particularly complex process of recognition – mutual recognition, to the extent that the cleaner too has an imaginative journey to go on. Not that this means, as a fatuously sentimental response would suggest, that she is likely to see the attorney's situation as a mirror of her own – the pathos of the wealthy, like the 'white victimhood' that many Black authors pinpoint[8] – but that she, like the attorney, comes to see something indivisible about the liberation they both hope for and may acquire the confidence to challenge the attorney to recognize the imperative that affects them both.

The solidarity in view here requires us to grow beyond a simply 'tribal' fellow-feeling based on clearly comparable experience; but it also challenges the idea that the paradigm of any solidarity that can be considered ethically significant is the unqualified adoption of the other's definition of their interest, as in (ii). If a relation of inequality and oppression adversely affects both oppressor and oppressed, the oppressor needs options other than the maintenance of the existing power imbalance in order to flourish as a human alongside fellow-humans. Solidarity with the less powerful is not necessarily a total abandonment of 'self-interest'; rather, it is a way of radically *reimagining* what is in my interest as something that is bound in with the flourishing of others. It is perfectly true that a necessary part of this reimagining is learning to hold back from just reproducing the old patterns of dominance in the way my support is offered, learning how to attend fully to what the other's need actually is and to how they themselves imagine responding effectively to it, without just reframing it in the terms of what I can understand or achieve 'for' the other. Kolers is surely right to the extent that there is, we could say, an unavoidably 'asymmetrical' moment in this; but there is also a deeper level at which my interest as a privileged person is no less at stake than the interest of the less privileged. It is one thing to flag up the perils of the 'white saviour' mentality; another to say that the person freely undertaking to act in solidarity with some person or group whose experience is foreign to them has no *investment* in that affirmation of solidarity, in the sense that they are simply bracketing their own interest for the sake of the other. This treats the other as isolated from a genuinely common future. And the risk of simple 'abjection' in the face of the other is that solidarity becomes first and foremost an obliteration of one of the parties involved, or, as Gillian Rose has pointed out, a 'substitution' by which I seek to stand in for the other without qualification or mediation;[9] we can't speak of mutuality here, only of the cancellation of an identity in favour of another (historically effaced or cancelled) identity. What might emerge from the dialectical recognition of a more nuanced engagement is ignored.

And ignoring this dimension would mean that ultimately the very idea of solidarity must collapse, to the extent that it becomes no more than another way of reducing otherness to sameness, no more than a 'negative print' of the existing model of power. Once again, recent discussion, especially of racial injustice, has articulated the fact that the oppressed do not necessarily want the oppressor to create a drama of radical self-denial (remember, from the Introduction, Reni Eddo-Lodge saying that she does not want 'white guilt' as a response to racial injustice). What is needed is an acknowledgement by the privileged of the reality of where they stand, and a readiness to work, with consciousness and clarity, from that point. What I as a privileged agent bring to solidarity is not a pure act of self-sacrificing 'substitution' but a history of how I have been shaped by, how I have *learned*, this kind of exercise of power (conscious or not). This is indeed a different history from that of the non-privileged or subaltern or oppressed subject. But its difference is precisely what I bring to the relationship. 'Simply to command me to sacrifice myself...makes me intolerant, naïve and miserable...because the insistence on the immediate experience of "the Other" leaves me with no way to understand my mistakes by attempting to recover the interference of meaning or mediation.'[10]

In brief: we need to be cautious about defining solidarity in such a way that it amounts to a straightforward prescription for adopting the viewpoint of another without reservation. Adopting the *cause* of another as one's own does not *ipso facto* mean that one ceases oneself to be a historical subject with an unrepeatable and unreplaceable viewpoint. As has become clear in the discussions of our first two chapters, the otherness of another's point of orientation is irreducible. This is not first and foremost an appeal to the mysterious unfathomability of another consciousness – though there is an essential truth in that – but a statement about how language, consciousness and recognition actually develop and operate. What Rose calls 'substitution', the erasure of selfhood in sacrificial identification, sidesteps the labour of continuing, intelligent recognition, given and received, the movement between two or more subjects/agents. The moral imperative of solidarity is a summons to learn in and from difference, not to seek for a shortcut around the difficulties of language and exchange. But it is also – as our consideration of (iii) above suggests – something to do with a perspective on connections that already exist. The cleaner and the attorney are in fact already implicated in each other's situation, quite apart from what they might think about it, and the 'labour' of solidarity includes working towards a shared recognition of what is the case in respect of their wider social identities. Action in solidarity is an imperative and a virtue because, like other virtues, it is an appropriate response to what is so; it is (to go back to discussions in the last chapter) an exercise in manifesting *ius* – not in the sense of giving someone their rights as an abstract individual claimant, but, to quote Rose again, an attempt to respond 'to this profound and unchanging expectation [that good will be done to each of us]', rather than responding to and adjudicating the comparative demand of person against person.[11] But it is also, importantly, about responding without the kind of absolutist disdain for law and mediation that imagines that a 'just' response can be achieved just by the erasure of the self – the error that (for Gillian Rose) Simone Weil and Emmanuel Levinas both make. This 'profound and unchanging expectation' is what makes sense of the *virtue* of solidarity as a response to the *fact* of solidarity: the presence of the other demands an answer, asks to be 'read', as it also asks to be enabled or emancipated to 'read' fully, to make sense of others. Solidarity as substitution renounces the invitation to read and be read, the aspiration to make sense in shared language, in the multiplicity of voices and perceptions. The solidarity of speakers[12] involves radical upheavals in the language of both parties, demanding interrogations of the formulations and symbolic worlds of both, unceasing scrutiny of how power relations are encoded in what is said and how it is said; but it is something other than the plain abjection of one speaker before the other.

This begins to make the link between our earlier discussions of recognition and empathy and the challenge of defining solidarity with more precision. It should be clear that, for such a definition, we need to be able to presuppose a broad picture of how 'selfhood' itself is formed and articulated in the processes of embodied imitation and imagination. It is against the background of such a picture that we are able to make sense of the conviction that the face of the other or the stranger is not only a site of claim or imperative – as Levinas would have it – but also something that is to be *desired*, something that is offered for and into our own construction of a meaning that we can confidently inhabit. Responding to the call to solidarity is not a matter of some episodic selfless heroism on the part of the privileged, but an acknowledgement of the invitation to work at a shared world of meaning – which (I'd better emphasize) does not mean simply a construction of common ideas but a material and social environment characterized by what Rua Wall calls 'right-ing', the unceasing practice of questioning the balance of liberties in our common life, negotiating with, resisting, adjusting the frameworks of law so as to deal with the endless misrecognitions or denials of one another that drive the historical process: a mutuality always incomplete, always lost, always sought again, always hoped for.

In this light, we can better understand why solidarity can be a term used in contexts that do not seem directly political. The 1964 gathering in Mexico City that called itself *Nueva Solidaridad* was a congress of mostly Latin American artists, especially poets, working towards what they called an 'interior revolution'. One of the leading spirits in this initiative, the Colombian writer Gonzalo Arango, stated in a letter that the ideal of this network was 'not the old and stupid [notion of] human fraternity', but fraternity reconceived as shared 'poetic labour'.[13] Although envisaged clearly as an anti-imperialist movement,[14] its emphasis was consistently on the ideals of inner revolution and the 'transformation of reality'.[15] The *solidaridad* of the participants was a many-layered affair – identification with all who were silenced or stifled by society,[16] identification between different kinds of artists in different Latin America contexts (Mexico, Argentina and Colombia prominent among them), connection with artists and poets in North America, ranging from figures like Allen Ginsberg to the Black Mountain poets and the radical monastic poet and essayist Thomas Merton.[17] The animators of the 1964 meeting were convinced that 'the same poetic and politic-cultural current' flowed in Latin American artists and in the more radical voices heard in the United States. The periodical *El Corno Emplumado* carried extensive correspondence to and from North American artists (rather more to than from, it has to be said), and the Latin Americans followed with deep engagement the movement towards more overt political involvement on the part of their northern contacts, especially in the Civil Rights struggle.[18] Subsequent events fractured this relationship, and some of the prominent figures of the Mexico meeting came to see the hope for solidarity with North Americans as futile or worse, as failing to recognize the deep structural inequalities and hidden imperialism of the relation between the two continents. But the rich and slightly chaotic matrix out of which *Nueva Solidaridad* emerged provides a significant sidelight on the history of the word's associations in the mid-twentieth century: there is a strong perception of a 'natural' human communal identity that is buried under the externals of capitalist and scientific modernity, and a commitment to a 'new humanity' of common work and vision.

As the historians of this movement have observed, its relations with anything resembling effective political action are slender, and its naive utopianism about the Cuban revolution, shared by a good many of its North American friends, generated a fair amount of conflict and disillusion. It serves as an instance of what we could call the imaginative labour of solidarity, a subject we shall be coming back to.

2.
But before examining this further, we need to retrace our steps a little and look briefly at how the nineteenth-century political discourse around solidarity began to make an impact in a context in which it was to prove increasingly important, the world of European Catholic thought. Bourgeois and Durkheim had sketched a model of co-operative decision-making and economic redistribution that for a time helped to shape the policies of the Third Republic in France; but the pressures of labour relations had produced a partially parallel development in Germany, where Bishop Wilhelm von Ketteler of Mainz (1811–77) had, initially in a series of sermons in 1848, attempted to unite a theory of subjective rights rather loosely grounded in Thomist ideas of *ius* with the organic social vision of German theologians like Möhler who had

been influenced by Romanticism.[19] While, like later nineteenth-century Catholic writers, he regarded the right to 'private property' as the cornerstone of a just social ethic, he was also clear that this is not a theological justification for *absolute* ideas of possession (a parallel here with Milbank's analysis of later medieval debates about ownership); Christian theology necessarily qualifies the very idea of 'possession', in the light of its commitment to distributive justice. In this perspective, the individual is not imagined as having fixed, inalienable control over their property in a way that stands over against the community's lawful responsibility to the common good. Ketteler's advocacy of workers' rights and his critique of state absolutism in the name of what was to become the principle of 'subsidiarity' (he was among the first to use this language to designate the principle that decisions should not always be taken at the highest level of social or state authority but be taken at the level where they were most effective and accountable) were immensely influential in the background of Pope Leo XIII's encyclical, *Rerum novarum* in 1891.[20] His views are often seen as the origin of the *Solidarismus* that characterized some Catholic discussion of economic issues in the early twentieth century. Like the French *solidarisme* of the Third Republic, this entailed a strong critique of capitalism and the free market and an insistence on recognizing the basic mutuality of human society, which required both redistribution of wealth and fundamental protections for the vulnerable. In contrast to Durkheim's historical model of pre-modern solidarity as imposed to keep the peace between essentially rivalrous agents, this approach was strongly opposed to any 'naturalizing' of a state of competition and conflict: solidarity as collaboration was in some sense written in to the nature of humanity (rather than being just a necessary condition for the avoidance of unmanageable competition), and the just society would be one that released the possibilities of co-operation and mutual nurture.

The most prolific defender of *Solidarismus* in the early twentieth century was the Jesuit Heinrich Pesch (1854–1926). His five volumes of essays on *Liberalismus, Socializmus und Christliche*

Gesellschaftsordnung[21] explore at great length various ways in which the modern market-based system is inadequate to secure any kind of ethical social order. He looks back to Leibniz's monadology as the source of the idea that maximizing one's own individual 'utility' is the key moral principle in socio-economic matters. When this metaphysical assumption is combined with John Locke's transactional and functional view of social relations and the canonizing of the satisfaction of individual instinct as the fixed point in thinking about human behaviour,[22] we are well on the way to the toxicity of modern capitalist culture. With Herbert Spencer's Social Darwinism in his sights, he denies that human cultural development can be assimilated to biological evolution,[23] so that any picture of primordial or natural conflict between individuals is a mortally dangerous myth: 'Rivalry in its brutal form, the demise of the weak, is not a law.'[24] The notion that self-love or self-protection can of itself be a 'social principle' or a bond of cohesion in any way is obviously nonsense: and the idea that the market can secure any mutuality in sharing goods is simply an abandonment to sheer chance of the 'yardstick of reciprocity'.[25] This attack on the free market is elaborated further in a brief but dense essay on 'Solidarity as an Obligation in Economic Affairs':[26] human identity is always bound up with 'association', and without this co-operative and reciprocal dimension, we lose 'the capability which is altogether necessary in order to lead a life worthy of a human being'.[27] The influence of Durkheim – with whom, as we have noted, Pesch otherwise has major differences – is evident in the link made between solidarity and the differentiation of social roles or tasks: not only can many do what one can't in any given present situation, the principle also holds across generations. Solidarity is what we experience in the plain fact of inheriting *what has already been done* for the well-being of the human community[28] (and the implication is worth noting that solidaristic action here and now must entail a dimension of attending to the needs of future generations). Thus Pesch can speak of a 'law of solidarity' implying that there is no true prosperity that is not everyone's (in the present and the future); the free market cannot deliver this. So the pursuit of an economic practice other than market capitalism is more than just a pragmatic solution to problems of localized inequality, it is a 'sacred obligation', a matter of conformity to natural law.[29] Importantly, Pesch concludes this summary of his understanding of solidarity by distinguishing it from any kind of 'instinct' – that is, from a mere natural empathy (in the common sense of that word); it belongs in the realm of reason and conscience, and so is a proper subject for the imperative of collaborative political labour to realize it.[30]

Interestingly, Pesch is sceptical of some previous Catholic attempts to identify 'solidaristic' practice simply with a benign traditional communitarianism in which the differentiation of social roles is accepted without contestation under the umbrella of patriarchal authority. Nor is he imagining that the workers' organizations he supports should be no more than 'friendly societies' (as they would have been called in Victorian Britain) for emergency practical support. The labour union for him is emphatically a vehicle of solidarity *in its capacity for action and negotiation*; a 'patriarchal reciprocal relationship', in which employers and employees share without conflict, is not enough.[31] In other words, to claim that solidarity is a matter of universal and fundamental human mutuality does not mean that we look back wistfully to organic patterns of common life in which everything can be seen in the light of 'pre-existing harmonies'. Pesch seems to assume that we are irreducibly *historical* agents, whose 'natural' solidarity is repeatedly broken and compromised by the facts of where economic power is actually located at any historical moment. He had studied Marx closely enough to accept the 'agonistic' aspect of the imperative to solidarity, the call to struggle, even if he did not accept the particular vocabulary and programme of class warfare envisaged by Marx himself, let alone by Marxist-Leninism.

Another monumental series of discussions appeared bit by bit (in ten volumes) over nearly two decades under the overall title of *Lehrbuch der Nationalökonomie*.[32] These studies address some rather more granular issues around policy and practice, but point in the same direction, towards a middle way between collectivism and free-market absolutism. Their influence in post-war German policy-making has been noted[33]: the Social Market economy in the West Germany of that era attempted precisely this middle way, directing the operation of the market towards agreed social goals by way of various incentives that worked against naked competition and indifference to social outcomes (it has been noted that Pesch's approach equally justifies the use of deliberate economic incentives to counter the ingrained habit of ignoring 'externalities' such as the environmental impact of economic practice – i.e. it would support major investment in what we now call 'transitional' strategies for decarbonizing or rebalancing in favour of renewable energy sources). For Pesch, 'Economic Order' was the opposite of the free market (the second volume of his first series of essays is entitled *The Free Market Economy or Economic Order?*); but it was an 'Order' that depended not on a simple command economy of the state socialist variety but on a complex and differentiated culture characterized by the co-operative definition of shared goods, grounded in the diversity of intermediate, ground-up social structures. In other words, effective solidarity in national economic affairs was to be seen as inseparable from subsidiarity, the handling of decision-making at appropriate levels, rather than allied to a uniform centralization of authority.

Pesch argues that solidarity should be acknowledged at four levels.[34] Most fundamentally it is something existing among all human agents in virtue of their shared humanity and their shared relation to their creator; while Pesch did his best to avoid simply confessional language or conceptualities, he did not hesitate to appeal to the religious basis for any robust account of human unity.[35] It is also operative at the level of the family, the citizens of a nation and those sharing a 'common vocation' of one or another kind of labour. At each level we can identify different sorts of ethical imperative, but they are all ultimately subsumed under the general rubric of our inability to be human independently of mutual association. At each level, we are working out the implications of the single underlying fact of our connectedness as creatures. Solidarity – a radically reciprocal social practice acknowledging that the well-being of any individual or group is inseparable from that of all others – thus becomes a unifying ethical ideal because it reflects a unifying ontological status, a 'natural' state of affairs. Pesch was not a metaphysician, but he grounds his prescriptions firmly in this assumption of a given connectedness between human subjects – and arguably between all created beings, though this is not a theme he develops. He is not wholly unlike the English 'Distributists' of his era (G. K. Chesterton and his circle) in seeking a way between competing totalitarianisms of Left and Right as well as rejecting the idolatry of the market, but he brings to his work a professional seriousness about the detail of economic realities, not least the realities of industrial society, that is not to be found in his Anglophone contemporaries.

3.
Pesch's influence was mediated to a wider public largely through the involvement of some of his pupils and followers in the drafting of Pope Pius XI's encyclical of 1931, *Quadragesimo anno*, marking the fortieth anniversary of *Rerum novarum*. The term 'solidarity' is not yet employed in this text, but the themes of mutuality and interdependence are strongly underlined: in the words of Anna Rowlands, 'Solidarity continues to emerge as concrete and universal, personal and structural.'[36] Mutuality is again seen, as in Pesch's work, to require a differentiated social pattern, decentralized and affirming of ground-up civil society association and the life of the family: solidarity and subsidiarity belong together precisely because, we might say, our fundamental connectedness is necessarily an 'analogical' affair, something that will look different in different contexts and at different levels of actual human association. But, as Rowlands shows,[37] following Meghan Clark, although Pius XII actually introduces the explicit term 'solidarity' into his magisterial statements (in 1939, with *Summi pontificatus*[38]) it is only with John XXIII's *Mater et magistra* in 1961 that the language expands to include not only the common good of a society of differentiated roles and levels of organization but the common good of a global community; solidarity is coming to be much more

explicitly linked with an international vision of connection and interdependence. By the time of Paul VI's *Populorum progressio* in 1967, it is seen as inseparable from a morally (and theologically) adequate account of *development*: solidarity fills out the meaning of development by insisting on the goal of a 'complete humanism' in which human interdependence is not merely to do with the sharing of material goods but is grounded in a genuine mutual respect and cultural hospitality.[39] It is this spirit of 'humanism' that makes development a vehicle for durable peace. Pope Paul builds on what had already been said a year earlier in the Vatican Council's document, *Gaudium et Spes* (#1) about the solidarity of the Church itself with humanity as a whole.[40] There is a discernible shift in emphasis away from the idea of solidarity as primarily something to do with what we would now call 'social cohesion', and towards a more radical focus on the claims of common humanity. We have moved beyond the world of differentiated and complementary social roles and effective co-operative structures for industrial societies: what is now uppermost in the discussion is something more like a sense of universal *accountability* for human well-being across national and regional boundaries.

It is in the papacy of John Paul II that an ethic and theology of solidarity comes most eloquently and explicitly to the fore – not surprisingly, given the Pope's continuing involvement in the social struggles of his native Poland; and one way of reading his use of the term is to see it as holding together the older emphasis on internal social harmony with the newer interest in the increasingly evident and scandalous gaps between rich and poor in the world of the 1980s. He had, as Anna Rowlands notes, been influenced not only by his own academic research into the notion of the person, but by contact with the eminent priest and philosopher Jozef Tischner, who played a significant role in the Polish *Solidarność* movement;[41] Pope John Paul's encyclicals, from the 1981 *Laborem exercens* onwards, bring together the local ideals of 'solidaristic' practice in national economies with the global perspective of the magisterial and conciliar documents of the 60s, by way of a more systematic theological approach to the subject, in which solidarity is seen as a central element in Christian anthropology. His address in 2000 at the Mass for the Jubilee of Workers[42] skilfully draws together the classical theme of transforming work and labour relations with the perspective of global emancipation and the struggle for human dignity in every area of life, as a condition for the survival of a properly human culture.[43] Interestingly, in *Centesimus annus* (1991), issued to mark the centenary of *Rerum novarum*, he reviews the 'social' encyclicals of the preceding century so as to show how the underlying idea of solidarity appears in different verbal guises such as 'friendship' or 'social charity': in terms that were to become more common in his successor's pontificate, he was tacitly affirming a 'hermeneutic of continuity' in magisterial thinking about solidarity.

Not the least of John Paul II's contributions is an acerbic formulation in his 1987 encyclical, *Sollicitudo rei socialis*, where he defines the 'virtue' of solidarity as the 'correlative response' to the recognition of our basic interdependence. 'This, then [sc. solidarity] is not a feeling of vague compassion or shallow distress at the misfortunes of so many people, both near and far. On the contrary, it is a firm and persevering determination to commit oneself to the common good; that is to say, to the good of all and of each individual, because we are all really responsible for all.'[44] The Pope goes on in the following sections to commend non-violent protest as an expression of solidarity, to exhort the Church to stand with those protesting, and to insist that what holds within societies also holds 'by analogy' between societies: 'Interdependence must be transformed into solidarity, based upon the principle that the goods of creation are meant for all.'[45] This is the clearest statement so far in the magisterial tradition of two central points in the developing understanding of solidarity: it is not to be identified with a sentiment of fellow-feeling; and it is the proper or apt expression of the Church's resistance to 'structures of sin' embodied in the defence of profit and hegemonic power. Rowlands suggests that what is being proposed is solidarity as a '*way of seeing*, seeing persons, peoples and nations as sharers, helpers and neighbours in the banquet of life, to which all are equally called.'[46] But it is more than vision alone. She also rightly notes that the emphasis on 'structural' sin and active (if non-violent) resistance owes something to the impact of Latin American theologies of liberation (despite Pope John Paul's well-known antipathy to the more uncritical receptions of Marxism in that context): solidarity may entail conflict for the sake of doing justice to an interdependence that is denied or attacked by an unjust socio-economic order. This is a model of solidarity that cannot be accused of simply looking back to a harmonious, 'organic' societal order, a sentimental communitarianism. Like Pesch, Pope John Paul assumes that we are historical subjects, dealing with historically conditioned distortions or perversions of our natural human capacity and destiny. Our weddedness to self-protection, individual and collective, has to be challenged without compromise; solidarity entails not only the risk of struggle, but the risk of loss – loss of privileged and security, to rediscover another kind of security in the mutuality of a new humanity established in the truth. And he also, having more or less identified solidarity with love itself, holds up the lives of certain saints – Peter Claver and Maksimilian Kolbe – as exemplifying solidarity of an exceptional kind in the form of suffering or even death willingly accepted for the sake of the other[47] – a theological perspective that will need some more elucidation in a later chapter.

In the context of our discussion so far in this book, one of the very significant elements in the account of solidarity offered by Pope John Paul is that it does not treat solidarity as dependent on 'identification' with some other, as a shared state of mind, or indeed as any kind of primarily mental event. It is a virtue that, like other virtues, is what it is because of the adequacy of its response to how things are – something congruent with the Pope's linkage of 'fairness, truth, justice and solidarity' as conditions for durable and authentic peace.[48] Solidarity is a form of *truthful* living, in that it does not deny what is fundamental in our humanity as such; it is grounded in our createdness, but also in the shared relation of human beings to Christ as Saviour. And one of the issues that has begun to emerge in our reflections thus far is a question we'll be looking at in more detail later on: in what sense does the idea of solidarity require a sense of the 'sacred'? i.e. of some order to which all are related independently of their relation to one another? If it is right to say that solidarity is a form of action that is in some way a 'just' response to the environment of our moral lives, how much can be said about that environment to make sense of this kind of claim? We have seen that the self-evident claim of 'the human face' is vulnerable in certain ways, and we have also noted the risks of assuming that it is possible to absorb or inhabit the feelings of another subject, and that this in itself provides a ground for appropriate moral response. Pope John Paul's richly and extensively developed theological analysis of what solidarity entails does at the very least press us to consider what it is about our humanity that makes a 'solidaristic' practice the most adequate and truthful policy in our moral lives. And the answer to that – as is clear in the Pope's teaching as much as in our earlier discussions here – cannot be a set of defined human *characteristics*, given the way in which all such bids for definition are implicated in precisely the imbalances of power that the language of solidarity is meant to unsettle.

Pope John Paul's successors, Benedict XVI and Francis, seem to have a slightly less powerfully coherent notion of solidarity, though the substance of what they have to say is largely congruous with what we have just summarized. Pope Benedict, in an address in May 2008 to the Pontifical Academy of Social Sciences[49] offered a definition of solidarity as 'the virtue enabling the human family to share fully the treasure of material and spiritual goods'; in the encyclical of 2009, *Caritas in Veritate*, he describes it (#38) as 'first and foremost a sense of responsibility on the part of everyone with regard to everyone' – referencing John Paul's language in *Sollicitudo rei socialis* – and also cites *Populorum progressio* on solidarity as a reality that imposes a duty (#43). It is specifically a virtue of civil society (#39) – i.e. it is part of the grass-roots culture that allows government to legislate with equity. Because it has to do with *gratuitous* relations between human agents, it is not something that can be legislated. It is also a virtue that should exist between industrialized countries and those at different levels of development (#49). There seems to be some tension here to the extent that it is difficult to see how a nation can exhibit solidarity without some kind of corporate and legal enactments; an unsympathetic reader might see Benedict as moving back towards the notion of solidarity as a 'sentiment' that is so sharply ruled out by John Paul, though that would not be at all a fair reading of the entire document. Benedict's own initial exposition of the themes of social and economic critique also reaches for the language of 'fraternity' and 'charity' (e.g. ##19, 34) before any extended reference is made to 'solidarity'. Anna Rowlands notes that Benedict's use of 'fraternity' – a usage that attracted some criticism because of its gender-specificity – may owe something to a desire to evoke some less secular resonances than the word 'solidarity' might carry, with a definite allusion to the common status of the baptized as adoptive children of God, recipients of divine love.[50] I am not sure that the distinction is quite that sharp; and the fifth chapter of the encyclical, on 'The Co-operation of the Human Family,' does not hesitate to speak of the link between more effective local and communal forms of solidaristic support and mutuality with the liberation of resources for manifesting international solidarity (#60). Nevertheless, it would be fair to say that Benedict's general approach to solidarity is less obviously concerned than his predecessor's with the institutional vehicles of solidaristic virtue, and less outspoken on the question of 'structural sin' as a kind of parodic inversion of solidarity, a collective pathology in which we are doomed to oppress and demean one another.

Pope Francis, despite acknowledging in his first Apostolic Exhortation (2013),[51] that the word 'solidarity' was 'a little worn and at times poorly understood', nonetheless uses it to strong effect as defining the motivation that leads us to combat privatized or localized notions of human good; structural reform is necessary, but it must be grounded in a clear sense of personal and communal accountability to and for one another (#189); and in *Laudato si'*, this is extended to include intergenerational solidarity as a principle that should reinforce our will to combat ecological injustice (#159) – a point mostly implicit in earlier documents, though not wholly absent.[52] The third magisterial document in this sequence, *Fratelli tutti* (2020), as its name indicates, once again looks to the language of 'fraternity'[53] – with its strong implications of a familial unity established by the grace of baptism – but its overall focus is unmistakeably in tune with that of Pope John Paul in urging us to look for human affinity across boundaries. The word 'solidarity' is used sparingly – most intensively in a short cluster of paragraphs (##114-16), underlining the priority of care 'for the fragility of others' and the necessary and costly embodiment of this. But other sections of the text reflect some familiar themes in fresh guise. We read of the 'cultural covenant' that allows for cultural diversity (#218), and the interdependence of human communities as a necessary entailment of the fact that no one community can be materially or spiritually self-sufficient (##149-50). Among the questions we are urged to ask ourselves in the presence of God is 'what bonds did I create?' (#197). And there is extensive use of phrases like 'social friendship' and 'social love'. We are summoned to the creation of a systematically reciprocal pattern of personal and communal life, in which our spiritual self-transcendence is inseparable from and expressed in the transcending of social and cultural boundaries in the name of a 'truth' that exacts attention and obedience (#226). The outcome is a society based on 'covenant': '[Solidarity] results in a secure and firm social compact' (n.88).

Tracing the steady growth of solidarity language and its extension into a broad theological/anthropological principle takes us some distance from the world of the sociologists and politicians with whom this chapter began. But it will have served to underline how a limited but flexible set of ideas about social differentiation and the need for models of co-operative working practices and economic arrangements could be grafted, with increasing and considerable success, on to a theological agenda connecting the characteristic forms of the Church's life with the facts of social interaction. The Catholic defenders of 'solidarism' had the advantage of being able to spell out in clear terms exactly what the facts were that made solidaristic behaviour intelligible and desirable – a model of human personhood, and a narrative of divine vocation that bridged the gap between solidarity as fact and solidarity as virtue. In this framework, the enemies of solidarity (as Catholic theology conceived it) are the enemies of humanity as such, as Pesch argued. There can be no coherent account of human good that sidesteps the foundational truth of creaturely dependence on a creator, and the revealed truth of life-giving interdependence in the Christian community, the 'fellowship of the Holy Spirit'.

The Catholic development of the idea moves it away from two of the basic notions that shaped the earlier and more secular discussion, while not by any means ruling them out of the discourse entirely. Solidarity as the complementarity of diverse skills meeting diverse needs in a complex community becomes *solidarity as the basis of subsidiarity* – the organization of society in differentiated and decentralized modes of operation: and the right of the state to dictate the shape of human communal life is challenged by the fact of ground-up social affiliation in a diffused multiplicity of 'solidaristic' associations, from family to workers' co-operative to churches. As we have seen, Pope John Paul does not hesitate to call it an 'analogical' notion in this connection. And the approach to solidarity that begins from the acknowledgement of common interest in specific groups is relocated in a more ambitious account of the common interest of humanity itself. As Rowlands' discussion helpfully brings out, solidarity is no longer a *tool* to be used to obtain certain communal goods: it is a good in itself. The deeper sense of mutual involvement and mutual reinforcement that solidaristic action brings with it is not just a happy bonus to effective lobbying; it is intrinsically a proper human goal. To recover our occluded and diminished humanity, we need to nurture a mutual openness and an imaginative hospitality that militate against those habits of mind and heart that hold us back from full recognition of one another. We have seen how, in the *Nueva Solidaridad* network, the goal was what we could call a solidaristic poetics – a shared imaginative struggle in which new human perspectives could be acknowledged and explored. The magisterial Catholic tradition more than once turns back to the point that cultural enrichment is an inseparable dimension of solidarity – suggesting that we need to keep in focus the recognition that solidarity is not merely something that arises when – as a contingent matter of fact – certain groups discover certain concerns and aims in common. It is a connectedness that precedes our awareness of it, and to acknowledge it is to go beyond the level of contingent similarities. In this connection, such a reading of solidarity echoes the debates about whether we can define humanity itself by a set of defined characteristics. And just as any kind of responsible humanism has to negotiate the risks of creating a list of requirements to be met before some agent is allowed to count as fully human, so this dimension of 'theologized' solidarity works against the term being reduced to the shared interest of one determinate 'gatekeeping' human group arrogating the right to settle the definitions of who or what counts as human.

The question of what primary starting point we assume in discussing solidarity is a crucial one. If we assume – as, effectively, Durkheim does – that solidarity is first of all a kind of instinctive self-adjustment to minimize risk within a competitive and risky social order, and then subsequently the development of a pragmatic system, trading services for mutual benefit, it never quite moves beyond a slightly insecure truce in the processes of meeting material needs, based in a recognition of mutual dependence at the practical level. There remains a kind of 'conceptual shadow' in the discourse, a presupposition somewhere along the line that the solid givenness of the individual's identity is always in tension with the perhaps regrettable fact that every individual has to manage their limitations by way of alliance with others. Put more simply, it assumes that the nature of the *self* is always already fixed. If, on the other hand, such selfhood is always being formed in and through what it receives, in and through the work of finding a way to adjust to agency that is not its own, the picture is different – not by any means necessarily simpler or even more morally clear in particulars, but at least not wedded to a foundational presumption of zero-sum competition. Just as (looking back to Pesch and his followers) the assumptions we make about 'possession' may be challenged by a different ontology, so with the notion of 'interests' as a fixed set of claims. In a definition that might have come from the papal declarations of the 1980s and 90s, but in fact looks back to an Anglican moral theologian writing in the late 1930s,[54] solidarity is not 'a question of creating union out of the materials of discord, but rather of combating those forces which disrupt solidarity through a return to the source of solidarity, that is, to God.' It was suggested in our first chapter that there is something distinctly odd about problematizing the recognition of other human organisms as human; so here, problematizing the interdependence of human agents (as if the very fact of co-operation were an awkward compromise) is to go along with a powerfully seductive mythology about consciousness, knowledge, language and socialization. Even before any strictly religious or metaphysical consideration enters in, the sheer phenomenology of our awareness and our linguistic entanglement tells against this mythical model – as the whole of our discussion so far has illustrated.

The language of solidarity in some of the Catholic discussions we have touched on here *can* slip back towards what Pesch himself – very presciently – warned against: a concentration on economic redistribution and co-operative social bargaining that never quite addresses deeper issues around the distribution of *power*. Pesch identified and challenged the patriarchal and paternalist legacy that still hung over some of the ideals of *Solidarismus* that he had inherited. To quote once again from an Anglican writer of the mid-twentieth century, the aim of socialism 'is not only economic, that is the redistribution of the resources of a community from the rich to the poor, but political, the transfer…of political and social power from "the governing classes" across the community as a whole.'[55] Solidarity has to imagine something beyond redistribution, just as it has to imagine something beyond a formal complementarity of differentiated socio-economic roles. The links made in Catholic Social Teaching between solidarity and subsidiarity begin to open up issues around power; but there remains a need for some more focused critique in this area. If existing patterns of social control are not God-given, absolute, and timelessly authoritative (about which the Catholic approach is increasingly clear), there are two possible routes for thinking about the foundations and justifications of power. One will concentrate on holding to account any patterns of power that systemically frustrate equal access to social goods and silence certain voices. The other will concentrate on the 'brokerage' of rival claims and agendas, grounding its continuing legitimacy on its success in meeting demands (the 'market society' classically analysed by Philip Bobbitt[56]). These are not, needless to say, pure types; but they give us some purchase on some of the implications of where we find our starting point in thinking about the ethics of political struggle. In a nutshell, the 'market state' is bound to envisage social good as ultimately the attempt to maximize individual liberty without licensing unbridled competition and unmanageable conflict; the 'solidarist' state will assume that maximizing articulate and constructive interaction at a variety of levels is a good in itself, not merely a tool to secure a better ensemble of individually satisfying deals.

Choices between diverse models of political anthropology have not been academic questions in the last sixty or so years. The history of Eastern Europe in the later twentieth century witnessed an exceptional series of political upheavals; so much is common knowledge. Less well-known is the work of several Eastern European intellectuals of the period whose teaching and (often very costly) advocacy attempted to provide a fresh vocabulary for social imagining. It is significant that some came from a background of study in phenomenological thought of the kind we have discussed in earlier chapters, and that the language of solidarity played a major role in their writing. For them, it was indeed a positive social good as such, not a vehicle for simple 'cohesion'. Their relation with specifically Christian or theological discussion was far from uniform, but it could fairly be said that they acknowledged solidarity to be in some crucial sense a spiritual ideal, a vocation. So in our next chapters, we shall look at two such figures, one from what used to be Czechoslovakia, one from Poland, whose innovative treatments of solidarity relate quite specifically to a particular moment of struggle against both totalitarianism and marketized individualism. Their thinking offers an illuminating counterpoint to the story outlined in this chapter of how the discourse of solidarity was born and baptized.

FIVE

The Solidarity of the Shaken: Jan Patočka and the Care of the Soul

1.

Jan Patočka (1907–77) studied with Edith Stein's teacher, Edmund Husserl, and his doctoral dissertation engaged with Husserl's account of the natural world – a topic to which he was to return at length in his own mature work. In his native Czechoslovakia, he played a significant role in making the phenomenological movement better known; but his philosophical career, like that of many others, was interrupted by the catastrophes of the twentieth century, first by the German occupation (he spent time doing forced labour during the war), then by the pro-Soviet takeover of 1948. Once again prohibited from teaching philosophy, he continued to write, becoming slowly better known in Western Europe. The false dawn of 1968 in Prague offered an opportunity for him to consolidate this reputation, but from 1972 he was yet again removed from university teaching and forbidden to publish. Active in dissident and underground circles, he played a crucial role in the drafting of 'Charter 77', a manifesto for reform and liberalization, along with the future Czech President Václav Havel. His death in 1977 was generally attributed to his mistreatment during interrogation by the security forces. Since then, his stature as a thinker has been more and more widely acknowledged.[1]

For many of those aware of his legacy, his name is most immediately associated with a phrase he uses in what has become his best-known work outside the Czech and Slovak-speaking worlds, the collection of *Heretical Essays in the Philosophy of History*, circulated in *samizdat* from 1975.[2] In the final essay in this volume,

Patočka speaks of 'the solidarity of the shaken' (*solidarita otřesených*) as the cornerstone of a radical ethical vision for European society.[3] How are we to escape the pendulum-swing between moments of ethical clarity and intensity (the moments in which we own our responsibility as we understand that we can no longer outsource our decision-making to the structures of thought and imagining that we have inherited), and the routine relapse into an acceptance of the given and the everyday that traps us in the anxiety of self-protection? We need to emerge into the new horizon of a truth that we cannot possess, a truth equally strange to all human consciousnesses, equally resistant to possession and thus never something that has to be or can be protected as our property. This emergence into the common light of a truth beyond the competitive struggle for ownership or control is 'the solidarity of the shaken', 'the solidarity of those who are capable of understanding what life and death are all about, and so what history is about.'[4] This kind of understanding is the condition of 'spirit':[5] it is not a question of acquiring extra information about the world (extra 'truths', we might say), but of registering and internalizing a presence to or openness to truth as such, a relation to the real that is liberated from any urge to defend what is provided for the self by the structures that are given to it in culture, language, religion or whatever. Such defensive urges are what condemn us to perpetual conflict.[6]

It is a tantalizing few pages of reflection, tied in with Patočka's overall theories about self and society, about the 'sacred' (not for him the same as the 'religious') and the everyday, and a good deal more. In the lectures he gave in Prague in 1968–9,[7] he devotes a good deal of time to considerations (not dissimilar to those of Edith Stein) related to the evolution of the 'I' in relation to the other. To be aware of myself, whether literally as body or in an extended sense as subject, is complex because neither body nor subjectivity is an object in a 'phenomenal field' for me. To form a 'total' picture of myself, I have to inhabit the perspective of another; I have to imagine a phenomenal field in which I have the freedom to look at myself from different angles – a field that is not in fact mine. Whether or not an actual other is present, my awareness of myself depends on this perspective of the not-self. I take up the stance of another's 'intentionality', another's attention directed towards me. 'The other need not be concretely instantiated. It is a constant structure of our experience; I see myself ever as the other, as the other sees me.'[8] This 'personal situational structure', as Patočka calls it, is the starting point for reflection and it is from the start bound up with the imagining of a shared activity: the other is another 'I', characterized by the same intentional movement as I experience, the urge to engage self-forgetfully, which issues in a return to the self with a capability of conceiving selfhood in a way otherwise impossible. My relation to the other is a 'mutual mirroring'; 'I see and am seen'[9] (readers may notice the parallel with what Cavell says about 'reading and being read'[10]). Self-awareness is therefore always already in some sense linguistic: it presupposes recognition (though Patočka does not use quite this vocabulary) – a shared situation in which what counts as an object (and the perception of its use or relevance for my actions) is common to both myself and the self that is not mine.[11] To relate to some definable, 'speakable' thing is necessarily to relate to others. And so to come to a sense of my own distinctiveness as an 'I' is to return from the imagining of the not-self's perspective precisely in the recognition that it is *not* mine: I come to differentiate where I stand from where I have had to stand in order to see myself. 'Only then do I distinguish the I that I live from the I's that I am not.'[12] In other words, I come to the recognition of being a unique and impenetrable subjective life only through the experience of being an 'I' alongside other selves, even though this unique and impenetrable subject is actually the prior reality.[13] It may be ontologically 'prior', but cannot be first in the realm of knowledge.

This already quite intricate structure is further elaborated[14] in the acknowledgement of another kind of relation that is not defined by the reciprocal movement of I and Thou: I also share in a 'solidarity' that is simply a fact of my situatedness alongside others, in a 'we' that is not instantly and necessarily tied to the formative I-Thou experience of reciprocal personal definition but is nonetheless something other than a mere relation to an 'It'. There is a fluid connection between this general sense of 'we' and an expanded network of real reciprocity, a 'you/-all', as Kohak renders it, that moves from simple co-existence – sharing the same space, as we might say – to co-operation. The level of 'co-existence' as such belongs to what Patočka later characterizes as 'living' rather than 'existing', the level at which we are not yet responding to the possibility of grasping the temporal nature of our situation, the processes of learning how to move in and act upon the world around. This mere 'living' is the state of 'empathic harmony' with the world a state experienced by animals and children, a state without self-relatedness and so without a 'prospect'; its movement is necessarily reactive, and '[B]ecause of its character of present immediacy, this life cannot be a life of symbols, it cannot have a language.'[15] Authenticity, in contrast – and this terminology is of course used with explicit reference to Heidegger and others – is not merely the condition of self-awareness but the acquisition of the perspective of a 'soul', i.e. of a subjectivity involved in valuation and so in *care*. Erin Plunkett observes in her introduction to assorted texts of Patočka's[16] that the idea of care as Patočka uses it is closely connected with images and ideas of vulnerability and incompleteness. Like Heidegger, he sees care as what prevents us being indifferent to our environment, what makes us agents; but his interest in the recognition of need, mortality and incompletion as essential to the life of 'soul' resists any kind of existentialist heroics about the appropriation of a contentless 'absolute' freedom. He sketches a threefold pattern of human spiritual or imaginative evolution in which we advance from an original self-concealment to the representation of our humanity in and through labour (including by implication, I think, the distinctive labour of language) to the final gathering-in of all that has been forgotten or repressed in the earlier stages, in an act of radical acceptance of our finite, constrained and mortal situation as the place from which we must speak and act, the only place from which we can speak and act as properly human.[17] As Plunkett says,[18] there is no mythology of exalting the liberated self to replace an absent or defunct divinity; the liberated self is exposed as never before to a reality over which it has no control. It is not an all-conquering *force* – a point that, as we'll see later, is central to Patočka's account of solidarity.[19] We should in fact be regressing to the level of simply 'living' if we concentrated simply on control; the soul, care, the symbolic order, language, are all born out of loss.

As should be clear, Patočka's language about the soul is not specifically religious – any more than Edith Stein's use of the term in both her early and later writings is bound to a conventional doctrinal model. The formation of soul is what is happening when our subjectivity is released from two different sorts of constraint: the pre-reflective and pre-linguistic 'empathic harmony' of the child or animal; and the defensive struggle for a mastery of the environment that will secure our future from struggle and tension. Patočka's self moves out of unthought harmony into a reflective stage in which it becomes aware of its uniqueness and so of its capacity to make a distinctive difference; and that distinctive difference is inseparable from a *shared* project of human self-representation and self-augmentation through speech and labour. But it has yet to become fully soul because it has yet to be freed from its bondage to a dream of material security, the state of not having to hope for anything. As we shall see, this is, for Patočka, the seed of violence. But we find it mortally hard to let go of the dream and expose ourselves to the unwelcome solidity and resistance of the real. And it is this difficulty, this mental and spiritual brick wall, that is the underlying theme of the *Heretical Essays* he was working on in his last years, where he weaves together the intricate anthropology of his earlier lectures with a recklessly ambitious sketch of European cultural and intellectual history, so as to offer an answer to the question of how we may be delivered from our slavery to the everyday – not in a spirit of arrogant dismissal of 'ordinary' human life in the name of the 'authenticity' beloved of existentialist writers, but with the powerfully therapeutic aim of showing just how the everyday has become ever more successful in recent centuries at normalizing atrocity and destruction in the name of peace.

SOLIDARITY

2.

Patočka's *Heretical Essays* is a sketch for a philosophy of history in the grand style, a sweeping (European) cultural narrative in which the essentially human gradually comes to light in the process of social and intellectual change over centuries (or millennia). Patočka acknowledges the Eurocentric nature of the narratives — Hegelian and Heideggerian — with which he engages,[20] and places a question mark against its nakedly teleological structure and its aspiration to translate history into metaphysics; but the essays remain firmly in the tradition of understanding 'Europe' as a unique cultural production nurturing and nurtured by a more penetrating and comprehensive account of human interiority than can be found elsewhere: 'The care for the soul is thus what gave rise to Europe — this we can hold without exaggeration.'[21] We should not misunderstand this: Patočka is not allying himself with any project of European political hegemony, or even cultural hegemony in the obvious sense. He notes wryly that the 'post-European' phase of geopolitics, the 'planetary era' as he calls it, represents both the decisive rejection of central aspects of the European imagination and the adoption and deployment of the technological fruits of European rationalism.[22] Theocratic terrorists use the Internet; totalitarian regimes adopt the techniques of surveillance and mass organization made possible by scientific and bureaucratic modernity. If — as our earlier discussion noted — history is what happens when we step beyond the state of simply 'living', the habitual human mixture of acceptance and defensiveness, then there is a threat of some sort of 'end of history' in the blend of totalizing power and technical control that has characterized the last century or so in Europe.

The ironies are manifold: 'Europe' is formed by and in turn forms an historical consciousness, a possibility for soul to emerge and be educated, yet this very process accelerates a distancing of the self from the material world that encourages an exploitative technocratic mythology;[23] Europe presents itself to the rest of the world as the champion of humanistic and critical sensibility, while itself deploying technocratic modernity in the service of its material interest, and the non-European world responds by using the same techniques to consolidate its resistance to the critical, historical ideal that Europe has simultaneously promoted and betrayed.[24] The result is a 'decadent' civilization in which meaning recedes because we have no orientation in terms of value — that is, of what is in itself desirable, deserving of pursuit and imitation not because of its utility but because of its intrinsic quality. 'A life can be said to be decadent when it loses its grasp on the innermost nerve of its functioning, when it is disrupted at its inmost core so that while thinking itself full it is actually draining and laming itself with every step and act.'[25] What is in danger of being lost is the crucial moment of *becoming a stranger to oneself* — which is the condition of becoming an agent rather than a series of reactive organic responses.[26]

Here Patočka notes that human consciousness and culture bifurcate not only into the 'authentic' and the 'inauthentic' (Heideggerian terms, but used here with some very non-Heideggerian resonances), the historical and the pre-historical, but also into the everyday and the exceptional, the 'holiday'. The pre-historical self escapes from the routine collective maintenance of life by stepping into the realm of the 'sacred' — the enrapturing, self-obliterating force of the real, divorced from ordinary self-awareness, responsibility, agency. In this connection, the sacred is a compound of all sorts of daimonic experiences, erotic and orgiastic, visionary, ecstatic; it represents precisely the realm of the uncontrollable real, beyond the self's capacity and power, that delivers us from the routines of labour and defence. But it does so at the expense of the critical self-estrangement that alone can gather together our fragmented and partly concealed selfhood.[27] *Religion* as a cultural phenomenon is distinguished from the direct encounter, ritual or otherwise, with the sacred because it reconnects this confrontation with an unmasterable and impenetrable world to the care of the soul — the formation of a critical (and thus *constructively* self-estranged) sensibility: religion 'is where the sacred qua demonic is being explicitly overcome'.

In other words, encounter with the sacred in the sense that Patočka gives to this risks being a shortcut out of 'inauthenticity' (or perhaps better, 'pre-authenticity'), and as such poses substantial problems. Encounters of the kind referred to – erotic, orgiastic and the like – highlight the truth that the routine of coping with the maintenance of life will generate an illusion, the fiction that we can have secure power over our environment – physical, social, relational – in such a way that meaning never has to be *made*, never has to be tested, interrogated, risked, lost, misrecognized, reborn; it simply invades or overpowers. And so long as that illusion persists, we have not yet arrived at the heart of what it means to say 'I' in the sense of taking a unique responsibility. Immersion in the ecstatic is another way of refusing to say 'I': we do indeed have to encounter and respond to the transcendent, the uncontainable and overwhelming, but without the total surrender of the historical self – 'without collapsing in self-forgetting into the region of darkness'.[28] The transcendence offered by the Dionysiac self-loss of the sacred is an ersatz solidarity, we might say, a dissolution not only of relation with others but of the crucial relation to oneself as other that is basic to Patočka's understanding of human capacity, and that alone is capable of saving us from perpetual violence (we shall have more on this point shortly). 'Dionysiac' transcendence (not Patočka's own vocabulary) is another form of decadence, in that it does not allow value to be the object of both desire and intellectual or imaginative labour; meaning is simply what *is*, what is given in the surface of things and the immediate fabric of work. Religion, on the other hand, belongs with '[t]he Greek *polis*, *epos*, tragedy, and philosophy'[29] as part of our resistance to self-concealment. And in the light of this, we can conclude that whatever a genuinely ethical solidarity is for Patočka, it must be a matter of *conscious* appropriation of our state of implication with one another.

He turns at this point to a more detailed discussion of the trajectory leading from Greece to orthodox Christianity, picking up and elaborating points he has made about the Christian legacy in an earlier lecture.[30] It is worth spending a little time on this. He is clear that Christian thought is in some ways an essential moment in the European imagination and in the emergence of a mature understanding of the self-estranged, self-interrogating subject. But he also sees Christian language as having contributed to the regressive alienation of self from world that shapes Western modernity. The earlier discussion, in the third of the *Heretical Essays*, contends that Christianity in effect pulls us back from the Greek valuation of *polis* and philosophy towards the seductive promise of a wholly 'given' meaning, a security that philosophy cannot provide, grounded in a 'true world' beyond what had become in the Hellenistic and early Roman world a contested and uncertain life in the *polis*. As the increasing predominance of kingly rule came to obscure the participatory and dialectical life of the city, it also obscured the promise that had inspired Plato, the promise of a political life opening out on to the horizon of metaphysically conceived truth, truth beyond contest and struggle. Into this environment of frustration with the *polis*'s failure as a locus for the creation of definitive shared meaning comes a radically new discourse claiming that human beings are intrinsically incapable of creating meaning, and must submit to a 'world from beyond'. The 'true world' once promised by a politics formed through the reconstruction of human knowing and desiring – the world of Plato's political vision – is now conceived as a transcendent source of communal identity wider and more deeply rooted than any historical *polis*. 'It is not only a community of humans with each other, a mutual recognition in which they guarantee each other a spiritual perpetuation in the memory of glory. It is, rather a community of humans with God who is their eternal memory and the perception of their eternal spiritual being.'[31] Meaning is not sought and found but given. What is more, it is given from beyond the world, so that the significance of wrestling with and interrogating our relation as humans with the rest of the material world more or less fades away. Reason loses its status as a guide to meaning (i.e. a guide to the ordered process of self-questioning that can release us from bondage to mere living); but it acquires a new significance as a tool for the configuring and exploiting of the stuff of the world, now separated off from ethical or spiritual (soul-related) truth. The historical facts of redemption replace the invitation to discover meaning in the cosmos, so that the cosmos becomes both alien and subordinate. Absent the narrative of revealed incarnate truth (which has been effectively discredited or abandoned by modernity), and there is no space left for epiphany anywhere; and the Christian universe collapses into nihilism.[32]

This theme of a 'Christian' alienation between soul and world is explored further (and rather more positively) in the fifth essay.[33] But the theme is taken in a slightly different direction. Christianity warns against a merely negative conception of freedom; its understanding of wisdom includes a positive relation to the act of selfless love that provides revealed meaning in the first place, a love that comes from a mysterious divine interiority, not exhausted even by identifying it with the Idea of the Good. The soul is formed by relation to a divine *person*. 'What a Person is, that really is not adequately thematized in the Christian perspective';[34] all we know is what the narrative of divine incarnation, God's self-identification with humanity, might suggest imaginatively; and also what is implied in the idea of transgression as an offence against personal love, requiring therefore a personal reconciliation. Patočka does not use the language of 'solidarity in sin', a familiar theological trope,[35] but he implies something very like it: we are individual only in the uniqueness of our particular history of transgression, but otherwise all equally and collectively guilty (whatever the detail of our transgression) before God. The soul thus becomes something in search not of 'the truth of intuition' but of 'the truth of its own destiny' in relation to the 'abyss' of the mystery of the divine – and of the human neighbour. It is in an important sense *nothing but* the reality of responsibility, moment by moment, a subjectivity entirely foreign to the realm of the eternal (in contrast to what a Platonist would have argued).[36] If the soul is no longer encouraged to seek meaning in and through its eidetic relation with eternal forms manifest in the order of the cosmos, and if the *polis* no longer stages the co-operative search for meaning in social converse and collaboration, the soul is indeed bound to history in the most acute and uncompromising way.

It is against this background that Patočka can say that Christianity has provided an 'unsurpassed' resource in the battle with decadence, focusing upon the radical absence of any home for the soul – whether in the fixed contemplation of the eternal or in the security and stability of the shared imaginative and intellectual work of the *polis*. The homeless soul becomes actual solely in moments of responsibility that arise out of a profound inner mysteriousness, out of the pregnant void of freedom; and this gives to the human subject, whoever and whatever they may be, a dignity that cannot be eradicated: labour is no longer something belonging to the order of 'things', the following out of a mechanical script. Even the enslaved person engaged in labour ceases to be a thing but becomes a subject with variegated relations and responsibilities. At the same time, what we work *on* or *with* is, so to speak, confirmed in its status as mere object: it gains its meaning not from the transcendent, with which the human agent has a uniquely direct relation, but from its utility. The human subject 'contemplates' the ambient world in the security of mathematical analysis and technical effectiveness – a set of ideas whose remote ancestry is a strictly spiritual discipline designed to protect us from 'orgiastic' forgetfulness, a set of ideas circling around the rigorous attention to structures that we have not invented for ourselves. And this ultimately becomes the basis for the spiritual vacuity of disenchanted modernity.

Patočka's discussion of all this is exceptionally compressed and often unclear; like most of the *Essays*, these passages convey a sense of intense urgency, a passionate concern to get down a series of very intricately related insights, without the delaying brake of granular reference and evidence. Most specifically, his account of the impact of Christian discourse is powerfully shaped by a particular kind of twentieth-century Protestant sensibility: his use of Karl Löwith as a spokesperson for 'essential' Christian perspectives on nature and history ties his discussion in to the history of the reception of Karl Barth's theology, with its absolute insistence on the causeless liberty of God in revelation – a concern grounded in Barth's uncompromising rejection of the sacralizing of given forms of nature and society (including race) by German Christian supporters of the Third Reich.[37] The thesis that Christianity posits a drastic separation between soul and world is a perspective that can be found also in Hannah Arendt's work (which Patočka clearly admires),[38] and a fuller discussion would need to look at how her understanding of what she sees as the Christian marginalization of genuinely *temporal* experience, the ongoing uncertainty and fluidity of human conversation, parallels and reinforces Patočka's focus on the necessary openness of the soul's life to a strictly unknowable future. But as a rendering of any classical Christian worldview, it is eccentric:[39] the assumption that relation to God as person is essentially an exposure to a formless *mysterium* unrelated to the order of the actual cosmos sidesteps the enormously diverse tradition in Christianity (and its parent tradition of Judaism, which Patočka handles rather awkwardly and patchily) of seeing human wisdom or holiness as alignment with a divine 'Wisdom' that is the ground of all finite order and which is the vehicle of some sort of participation in the love that is offered in revelation or incarnation. Both the Greek and Latin theologians of the early centuries – Origen, Gregory of Nyssa, Marius Victorinus, Augustine, Maximus the Confessor – in their different idioms argued for a continuity between the truthful contemplation of the world's order and the liberation of the spirit from destructive self-obsession and slavery to reactive instinct (passion). The continuity, in medieval thinking, between ethics and the natural order (the idea, much misunderstood and sometimes trivialized, of *lex naturae*) plays no part in Patočka's version of Christian cosmology, so that the sacramental role of the natural order and of material life is obscured. Like Arendt, Patočka seems to begin from the assumption typical of certain strands of twentieth-century Protestantism – the Lutheran Anders Nygren as well as the Reformed Karl Barth – that the definitively and uniquely Christian perspective is one in which meaning is not to be sought in either natural or social order (not quite the position of classical Reformed theology, it has to be said), and in which divine love is always and only the bestowal from outside upon humanity of a divine love that can no more be shared or internalized than it can be earned. It is a scheme which leaves relatively little place for the idea of a spiritually grounded solidarity in which there is an active mediation of grace in and through the relation of distinct material persons and the shaping of a 'culture' of reciprocity.[40]

But the salient positive point for our wider discussion is that Christianity is here seen as not simply distancing soul from world but affirming the world as a *task* – an 'agenda' for understanding. Even if it is also responsible for misconstruing (misrecognizing) this task in terms of objectification and reduction to pure functionality, the original sin of technological ambition. Christian discourse about the givenness and inexhaustibility of the world leaves the path open to Patočka's project of care for the soul, the emergence of a radically new kind of subjectivity on the far side of the dissolving of all inherited certainties and meanings that have never needed to be laboured at. Christianity represents a major step towards that 'solidarity of the shaken' that is the position of the transformed spirit: the position of 'soul'.

We could describe the whole argument roughly in these terms:

(i) The self discovers itself as unique, indefinable, free, in the reflexive or recursive moment when it recognizes that it must occupy a space of difference in relation to the imagined perspective of the other which allows it to 'see' itself in the first place.

(ii) At the same time, it is constantly drawn back into a primordial 'empathic' relation with its environment that minimizes its agency, its capacity to *change the terms* of its relatedness with what is around it.

(iii) The linguistic risk and innovation represented by political argument and imaginative creation ('*polis, epos, tragedy*', and the rituals of public religion) resist this pull towards collective security, the world of 'living'. They preserve the idea of meaning as something constructed in an active exposure to a truth that is beyond usage and routine.

(iv) The decadence of politics, art and religion that we see in the sacralized monarchy of the Hellenistic era denies the possibility of such meaning.

(v) But into this void comes a new religious mythology that embraces the meaninglessness emerging from the decay of classical politics and posits a wholly different kind of community, a solidarity of betrayal or guilt on the one hand and of gratuitous divine invitation on the other.

(vi) The drastic disenchantment and 'functionalizing' of the ambient world that this finally produces in Western modernity leaves in its wake another kind of void, once the narrative of divine love, incarnation and atonement has faded; Christian solidarity cannot survive the death of God because it has never fully realized what it needs in order to become a solidarity of true reciprocal recognition.

(vii) And so, while Christian discourse has maintained the notion that the meaning we create in struggling towards fuller exposure to the real is never something to be read off from the givenness either of nature or of culture, it fails ultimately because it still thinks in terms of a meaning that is comprehensively given by an agency beyond the world rather than a meaning that is created. And this – on the one hand – leaves Christianity exposed, like other comprehensive metaphysical and mythical systems, to the corruption of absolutist power, and – on the other – leaves human society abandoned in the face of meaninglessness, *anomie*, boredom and violence.[41]

What is needed, as a specific against the dual threats of religious fascism and soulless techno-consumerism, is a solidarity that does not deny the imperative of making meaning within history – not by constructing a grand narrative showing that the past leads with inexorable rationality to the totally 'justified' and unimprovable present (the cheapened Hegelianism of various philosophies of progress), but by allowing the crushing effects of loss and senseless disruption in the narrative to liberate us from the addiction to security and defence that condemns us to constant violence.

3.

And so we come finally, in the last of the *Essays*, to the theme of the solidarity of the shaken. In the second of these essays,[42] Patočka had quoted a well-known and much-debated fragment of the pre-Socratic Heraclitus, which is rendered: 'We need to know that *polemos* [conflict] is what is common, and that conflict is the right (*dike* = *eris* [discord]), and that everything takes place through *eris* and its impetus.'[43] For Patočka, this identifies the central paradox of thought itself: seeing comprehensively or coherently seeing the universality of incoherence, or rather of irreducible tension. To understand anything is to see it emerging against the dark background of undifferentiated process; and this moment of dramatic emergence, of differentiation, is 'the flash of being out of the night of the world', allowing the *particular* to come into focus.[44] As such, *polemos* is the foundation of the *polis* and of history, and so, ultimately, of the soul as Patočka understands it. He returns to this fragment at the very end of the final essay, insisting as he has done earlier that the foundational 'conflict' he and/or Heraclitus is speaking of unites rather than dividing. What *polemos* brings to light is the universal truth that 'existence' comes to light in the shattering or refusal of unexamined living. Conflict dramatically shows the divergent possibilities of slavery and liberty that stand before every human subject; and so it makes sense to see it as the fundamental law of authentic human identity.

This is not, Patočka insists, to imagine some kind of primordial clash of forces at the ultimate root of being. 'A metaphysics of force is fictitious and inauthentic.'[45] What is in view in his language of conflict or 'warfare' is something more elusive: we live as humans in the midst of a complex of potentially colliding energies of transformation; and if we come to understand our own human agency as primarily one among – even if the strongest of – such transformative forces, we identify 'Being' itself as force. What most fundamentally *is*, is on this basis going to be configured as violent and mindless change – pure process, we might say, in which what 'works' is identical simply with the greatest accumulation of realized potential. We lose sight of our own human identity as an authentic relation to Being, a relation of attunement and understanding. All that matters is our capacity for successful manipulation of the mindless processes of the material world; all that counts is function – not quality. We can only (to borrow St Augustine's language) use and never enjoy, and we are trapped in an identification of being with function that deprives both us and the world we inhabit of any internal substantive uniqueness.

Yet this release of force in modern technocracy, this apparent abandonment of the project of authentic history in the name of a universal problem-solving management of the environment, is not simply a matter of 'decadence'. It exposes the deep risk facing humanity, it offers a series of solutions to any passive acceptance of human fragility and the struggle for survival, and as such it ought to challenge the pervasive anxiety that repeatedly draws us back into the desperate fight for security. If we are able to salvage the questioning spirit in the midst of all this, if we are able to throw an unprecedentedly clear light on the nature of the soul, and to rethink political power and moral purpose in this light, the future of the soul may yet be more promising rather than less. But – and this is the burden of Patočka's final 'heretical essay' – this involves a degree of fundamental disruption to our self-attached and self-protecting habits; and this is how we must think about twentieth-century warfare, as a generative disruption. From the First World War onwards, modern armed conflict has revealed itself as the pure conflict of force, wholly detached from any contest over truth: violence sets out to create meaning by the sheer annihilation of the other and the overcoming of the status quo.[46] To this end, the maximal resources of technology are harnessed, releasing the maximal capacity of mindless force (Patočka touches a little later on the phenomena of Hiroshima and Nagasaki as the final stage of this logic[47]). And so to have experienced and understood the nature of modern warfare is to have been exposed to the most basic threat imaginable to the project of historical meaning, exposed to the effective abolition of meaning in the name of power.

Patočka points to two commentators on the experience of the First World War to clarify what he means – the German novelist and essayist Ernst Jünger and the French Jesuit and scientist Pierre Teilhard de Chardin. Both share the *Fronterlebnis*, the direct experience of the trenches, with all its terror, humiliation and dehumanizing potential; both see this experience as also having brought about a decisive epiphany. For Jünger this seems to be the realization of what total mobilization means for a society; for Teilhard, the discovery of a profound sharing of life at the very edge of annihilation which is also the very edge, the 'crest of a wave', of the advent of some total transfiguration.[48] For Jünger, the mobilization of an entire society for the purpose of destructive conflict, and of a monumentally resourceful and brilliant repertoire of technological means for securing victory, demonstrate the effective dissolution of all we have previously thought of as 'value'; nothing (and no one) is of value in itself, but only in virtue of its function in conflict. And the deepest and most troubling paradox of all is that this waging of total war is done in the name of peace: defeat is unthinkable because it will bring the destruction of all we take for granted, all that makes us secure, and we cannot live in insecurity. So we actively plan for radical and unconditional destructiveness in the name of life, peace and light. 'How do the day, life, peace, govern all individuals, their bodies, their souls? By means of death, by threatening life. From the perspective of the day life is, for all individuals, everything, the highest value that exists for them.'[49] In stark contrast, the perspective, the 'illumination' of the *night*, the understanding of what this terrible passion for peace brings with it, is the realization of a situation shared with the opponent. We are returned in the most vivid and extreme way to the theme touched on earlier of the grounding of solidarity in a shared plight. The enemy is utterly at one with us in that the enemy is, like us, trapped in the lethal and inexorable mechanism of self-protection at all costs; and so, in the final and deepest paradox, 'absolute' conflict creates reconciliation with the enemy. The total devastation of the inherited landscape – physical devastation and loss of landmarks being a metaphor for the deeper devastation of value[50] – leaves no boundaries standing between people.

SOLIDARITY

This is the 'solidarity of the shaken'. The *Fronterlebnis* is a 'summit' experience from which there is no going back into unexamined everydayness – back into the 'peace' that (we now see) can justify any imaginable level of violent atrocity. 'History is the conflict of *mere life*, barren and chained by fear, with *life at its peak*, life that does not plan for the ordinary days of a future but sees clearly that the everyday, its life and its "peace" have an end.'[51] Understand this, and you have a grasp at last on what is essential to the spiritual, to the care of the soul, on what a humanistic and tragic politics would entail. Intrinsic value would return to the world simply because the things and persons of the world would no longer be identified with what can be mobilized. Conflict in its most brutally unrelenting form, has exposed the complicity of security with violence, and so exposed the connection between non-violence and the embrace of mortality – but in this process it also exposes the nature of real liberty. Freedom is the very opposite of collectivism, the slipping back into the ecstatic and orgiastic; and it defines the nature of the soul as something over against the 'world', without settling for the 'worldlessness' that Arendt, for example, identifies in Christian discourse.[52] Heraclitus's aphorism is vindicated in the moment when the opposing sides in modern conflict become – as Jünger says – a single body.[53] *Polemos* reveals once and for all what is involved in refusing the soulless everyday and its slaveries; to do so is to discover the fundamental belonging together of mortal subjects who *cannot* ultimately protect themselves and so have no need to struggle to protect themselves against each other. What is fatal to them is not their otherness to one another but the humanity they *share*; accepting this solidarity, this relativizing of all the ways in which death is denied and anxiety is enthroned, is the only way beyond an endemic spiral of violence that is made more and more catastrophic by the triumph of technology.

This climactic point of Patočka's ethical philosophy – virtually a theology, in many respects – is a striking fusion of very diverse themes, and they are not easy to disentangle. Teilhard's apocalyptic rhetoric about the profundity of shared experience in the trenches and Jünger's exaltation of the common sensibility of

THE SOLIDARITY OF THE SHAKEN

opponents in war are both of them deeply ambivalent tropes, with their glorification of extremity and their erasure of the reality of the terror and actual intolerable, dehumanizing suffering of trench warfare. Patočka seems to accept too readily the Romantic sensibility indulged in these texts, in a way that does less than justice to his own intuitions.[54] And there is an uncomfortable shadow of elitism in Patočka's characterization of the solidarity of the shaken in the wake of the absoluteness of modern conflict as something that 'shows some to be slaves and others to be free'.[55] 'Some' and 'others'? Not, you might think, the most promising structure for imagining a genuinely radical human togetherness. The trouble with utilizing Jünger and Teilhard is the obvious risk of identifying the solidarity of the shaken too closely with a very specific kind of individual experience, confined to a very specific kind of apocalyptic imagination. It sits jarringly with the impersonality of mass annihilation in modern war, whether in the trenches or in the bombing of Dresden or Hiroshima (or in the drone warfare of the twenty-first century). The schoolchild in Hiroshima or Baghdad is vanishingly unlikely to experience that heightened sense of exalted convergence with an enemy that Jünger describes, but only agony. What has Patočka's solidarity to say to them? Yet his overall insistence on care for the soul – along with the specific way in which he spells out the implications of recognizing the complicity between security and atrocity – seem to call out for something a good deal more than just a comparability of individual 'peak' experience, or indeed a 'movement of inner detachment' (as Andrew Shanks characterizes it in a gently interrogatory summary[56]) from the mechanism of total mobilization.

The solidarity of the shaken is imagined by Patočka as a deep and empathic resonance among those who have discovered the absurdity of the ways in which peace is weaponized in order to make war, and who have also grasped in that discovery the absurdity of using philosophies, theologies, ideologies and so on as markers of impenetrable alienation from others. That this form of solidarity is a morally significant matter is obvious enough; and, in the political context of Patočka's mature writing, it is not difficult to see the importance of the notion of some sort of critical, sceptical, marginal 'clerisy' (to use Coleridge's term), an intellectual or imaginative avant-garde, their perceptions sharpened by persecution, as a necessary element in the technocratic state. Patočka imagines a culture in which the comfortable administrators of routine scientific rationality are consistently exposed to the challenge of the 'shaken' to the extent that they become 'uncomfortable about their comfortable position', and are reminded that they need to stand at the 'front' of unsettlement and dispossession, for the sake of the vulnerable and dispossessed, and to avoid accepting the tyranny of force.[57] It may well be the case that our societies are 'demobilized' at an external level, that cold war has replaced naked violence, simply because of the alarm generated by the scale of destructiveness promised in the nuclear age. But this is not a real rejection of universal mobilization; it is simply a militarizing of economic competition, a mobilizing in terms of growth and productivity, that is no less a capitulation to 'force' and no less generative of bitter and absolute conflict — conflict now between the successful manipulators of economic growth and the vast populations of the deprived. The mechanics of growth can delude us into thinking that war has been transcended and history is over: the presence of the 'shaken' is there to disabuse us of this fiction.[58]

To this end, acknowledging, even celebrating, the solidarity created in extremity is a crucial moment; the recognition, above all, that war is the enemy of meaning insofar as it absolutizes the defence at all costs of whatever particular system of security we have inherited, as if that system were not itself contingent, the deposit of historical labour and learning — this is an essential element in escaping the vicious circle of peace that needs protection by means of indiscriminate violence. But all this needs a further 'turn' to save it from the problematic elite Romanticism we have noted, and to reconnect it with Patočka's central theses about the nature of the *polis* and the necessary implication in and with the other's perspective that stands at the root of every identity. To put it a little differently, the *polis* has to find room for more than the heroically 'shaken', the clerisy of sceptical martyrs; for those whose suffering or exclusion or dehumanization does not readily find expression, whose fate is unmarked and uncelebrated. And the ground of this has to be thought of as, ultimately, the always already given involvement with one another of self and stranger in the shaping of the human subject, and so of human meaning. Patočka's compelling diagnosis of the universal functionalizing of knowledge in late modernity, and the erosion of the idea of humanity as 'relation with Being', can be read as developing his basic analysis of the universal relatedness between subjects, an analysis that concentrates on acknowledged dependence, reciprocal gift and shared meaning-making (rather than self-obliterating ecstatic collectivity). A truthful and durable political expression of the 'solidarity of the shaken' has to involve the solidarity of the human as such. The sensibility uncovered or restored in the trauma of modern war, as understood by Teilhard or Junger, cannot be something overriding or working against the basic rhythms of human identity as it evolves in time and embodiedness. It is better seen as a drastic clarifying of what happens when – as the *Heretical Essays* attempt to trace in detail – an instrumental reason capable of radical detachment from value and contemplation reaches an unprecedented peak of sophistication – more specifically a sophistication directed at the defence at all costs of existing (rival) securities. The acknowledgement of 'shakenness' is a key to understanding what it means to refuse understanding, to ignore what is involved in prematurely closing down the possibilities of reciprocity – including the possibilities of reciprocity with those who do not share our articulacy and privilege, a point that easily gets lost if the focus is too insistently on the exalted insight of those who have fully experienced and internalized the 'shaking of the foundations' (in Paul Tillich's famous phrase).

In short, Patočka's solidarity of the shaken invites a certain demythologizing. The picture of a fellowship of exceptional individuals, exceptional in their courageous embrace of the lack of firm foundation and their equally courageous commitment to the creation of shared meaning, itself needs to undergo a degree of 'shaking', in the name of a solidarity between the heroic and the unheroic. We have to imagine and explore a unity between the conscious pioneers who recognize one another across the battle lines and the 'infantry' for whom deliberate heroism is not an option, and whose vulnerability and suffering is so readily forgotten in more or less every philosophy of history. This is in fact something that Patočka's own anthropology ought to draw us back to: the involvement of each subject in the reality of the stranger, the perspective that is not theirs, already lays the foundations for something rather different from the effect of apocalyptic moments that reveal who is a slave and who is a free person. To define the authentically human in terms of a historical consciousness torn open to the groundless 'night' of an uncertainty that has to be illuminated by the insight of the 'shaken' – this has an uncomfortable echo of precisely the urge to decide who counts as 'really' human that we have already seen as a breeding-ground for moral confusion.

Patočka is not guilty of any kind of doublethink here. He makes it entirely clear that the task of the 'shaken' is to challenge every divisive structure of ideology and of social or ethnic privilege that reinforces the sense of threat from the other, so that all may find a way towards a stability that is not dependent upon material status or achievement, and so is not menaced by the plurality of the human world. But in the spirit of Patočka's own concerns and warnings, it is important to unsettle any rhetoric that might collude with the privilege of the 'choice spirit' who is aligned with the 'true' trajectory of history. Patočka's power and originality lie partly in his insistent refusal to yield to any version of Nietzschean ambition, because of his fundamental recognition that loss and exposure to groundlessness are the conditions of truthful insight. The idea of any superhuman 'force' that commands our allegiance, including the force of historical 'logic', 'being on the side of history', is always and necessarily for him a regression to the world of pre-history and pre-humanity, the world where 'life' is what matters rather than 'existence', and where sacrifice – a significant category in the *Heretical Essays* and elsewhere[59] – is made and demanded for the sake of external and therefore contingent goods. The solidarity of the shaken entails a deep fellow-feeling between those who have embraced the imperative of sacrifice, not for a 'cause' external to them but for the non-contingent truth of self-gift and selfless risk in itself, for the 'openness' that ultimately renders us human. But it is worth recalling the insistence of Pope John Paul that fellow-feeling is an inadequate account of solidarity; and worth also remembering the question of how the drama of sacrifice connects with the unchosen suffering, loss and impotence of the majority of human subjects. Without some way of addressing this, Patočka's solidarity risks slipping towards a realm of private understanding between heroes; it may have the external or public effect of challenging the prevailing myths of power, but it falls short of offering any account of mutual *interdependence* as an aspect of solidarity, and has little to say about the nature of the common good for a social unit. In terms of the wider typology of understandings of solidarity that have been sketched in this book so far, Patočka's notion stands closer to solidarity as condition rather than solidarity as virtue; and even as such, it is a condition that results from certain limited historical circumstances in the experience of certain particular human subjects.

This is by no means to suggest that identity in fragility or loss is irrelevant to the ethics of solidarity. On the contrary. Patočka wants us to see that a solidarity emerging from the *Fronterlebnis* does indeed tell us something about a common hinterland and a common destiny for human subjects: we must all stand before the 'night' of our groundlessness without despair, passivity or messianic utopianism. And the affirmation of this as a universal vocation – the only universal vocation that can make us see the futility and falsity of universal mobilization – is indeed, as Patočka argues, a dimension of what the 'shaken' bring to politics, relativizing the absolutes of collective self-protection. But this universal fragility is – and Patočka is clear about this too – inseparable from the foundational 'lack' that we find in our human subjectivity: we are not self-sufficient units who may or may not enter into accommodations with others, but are constituted by difference and distance. We see ourselves only from the perspective of what we are not.

The social question then becomes one of whether we can understand this aspect of shared fragility or non-solidarity as connected with an active obligation to the other. Patočka makes some significant adjustments to the fundamental structures he inherits from Husserl in this respect by insisting upon the convergence of authentic consciousness with the 'historical' sensibility, but – perhaps too much influenced here by Hannah Arendt – he sees human labour as finally a pre-historical and so in some way pre-human (certainly pre-humanistic) reality. The idea that labour itself can be the setting and vehicle for conscious solidarity and that the category of work need not be so closely tied to subsistence-level labour does not come clearly into focus, except in the problematic disjunction of work from 'production' that Patočka assumes.[60]

This is worth noting at this juncture because our next chapter will be looking at the writings of a thinker who has a good many points of intellectual contact with Patočka – not least a shared ancestry in the phenomenological tradition stemming from Husserl – but who takes a conspicuously different approach to work, to mutuality and, ultimately, to value, and whose philosophy is less inflected by the 'world-historical' register of discourse. More of that shortly. But Patočka's importance in mapping the meanings of solidarity remains. Like Edith Stein, he outlines a basic understanding of knowing and being that begins in the inhabiting of the other's perspective – begins, we could say, in a kind of imagining, not in a primordial self-transparency. Like several others we have discussed so far, he sees the irresoluble tension between the recognition of foundational human solidarity and the world of technocratic management of our material environment: he understands the radical opposition between universal ethical reciprocity or responsibility and global 'mobilization'. Some of his most penetrating cultural analysis can be found in the pages where he explains how the all-pervasive mechanisms of the global technological market have become a (not wholly successful) displacement of the universal mobilization or conscription of populations in modern warfare.[61] And Patočka's exposition of how the *Fronterlebnis* can bring into focus as never before the reality of a common exposure to terror, pain, meaninglessness and death, and so can relativize every contingent justification for violence against the stranger, is in its way a classic of ethical imagination, even if the working through of its detail uncovers a range of difficulties. Patočka's work is formidable and formidably serious; the issue that remains is whether this seriousness can be sustained and even enhanced by an understanding of solidarity that, while it has its own vision of the demands of heroism, is more consistently liberated from a 'heroic and tragic' mode inherited from the Romantic imagination.

SIX

Solidarity Without Enemies: Józef Tischner and the Conversation of Human Labour

1.

On 19 October 1980, a large congregation of Polish trade unionists gathered in the chapel of the Wawel Castle in Krakow to hear a sermon from Fr Jozef Tischner – one of Poland's most prominent thinkers, a philosopher who had trained in Western Europe and also had a reputation as a charismatic pastor. The sermon, on 'The spirit of solidarity', was to become something of a canonical text for the moral and political thinking of the activist and reformists who made up the *Solidarność* movement that had been founded in the same year, and Tischner's intellectual and moral legacy has continued to play a significant role in Poland and elsewhere. As we noted in the Introduction, the Polish workers' movement of the 1980s did a great deal to give fresh currency and fresh immediacy to the language of solidarity in the Western consciousness.

After its foundation in 1980, *Solidarność* continued an underground existence during many years of repression and persecution, eventually becoming a political party after the collapse of Communism in Poland.[1] In its earliest days, it proclaimed in unmistakeable terms its debt to Catholic Social Teaching; the influence of a number of Polish clergy and theologians was of lasting significance in its initial self-understanding as what could be called a 'para-political' movement, a form of organized social co-operation that did not immediately seek a role in the management of a state. Foremost among these influences, of course, was Pope John Paul II, the former Karol Wojtyla,

Archbishop of Krakow, who, as a teacher of philosophy and theology, had been deeply marked by the phenomenological thinking of Edith Stein and Roman Ingarden (1893–1970), the latter being the leading advocate of this philosophical school in twentieth-century Poland. But Tischner (1931–2000) was without doubt the most prominent and original supporter of the workers' movement. Already, by the time of *Solidarność*'s foundation, he had established a national reputation and held several senior academic posts. His first research degree had been supervised by Ingarden.[2] In the difficult decade that followed the foundation of the movement and his Wawel sermon, he was widely regarded as a 'chaplain' to the *Solidarność* network as a whole. His writings and addresses from the first years of the movement were published in Paris in 1982.[3]

These brief essays, non-academic in style and aimed at a general audience, have proved a fertile source of inspiration and provocation; Tischner himself revisited some of their themes in an essay that was posthumously published in a new edition of his *Etyka Solidarnośći* in 2002,[4] to which we shall be referring a bit later. The chequered history both of the movement and the term 'solidarity' itself has continued to prompt discussion in Poland, along with Tischner's own political evolution after the end of the Communist regime. But in 1980 the sermon spoke with exceptional force into a particular cultural moment: along with the other short addresses and articles with which it was published, it outlined a quite comprehensive social philosophy, clearly grounded in elements of Catholic social thought but seldom making explicit reference to this, and drawing on a notably wide range of sources, strongly influenced by phenomenological thinkers and connected in various ways with Tischner's own earlier academic work. Very broadly speaking: Tischner's account of solidarity in the Wawel sermon connects the idea with three significant themes – conscience, faithfulness and work. We shall begin looking at his understanding of solidarity with these three points in mind.

First, *conscience*: the Wawel sermon concludes with thanksgiving for 'our solidarity of consciences',[5] which seems to coincide in some loosely defined way with the awakening of 'consciousness' he has mentioned earlier in the text as accompanying the birth of solidarity.[6] The words in Polish are distinct – *sumenie* for 'conscience' and *swiadornosc* for 'consciousness'. But the consciousness in which he is interested is above all our awareness of the pressure or burden that is carried by another human being: we awaken to the recognition that we are connected with the suffering of the other, and it is in that recognition, Tischner argues, that speech itself is born. This awakening is what St Paul means by exhorting Christians to 'carry one another's burdens' (Galatians 6.2). In the next address in the collection, Tischner reinforces the point by asserting that '[t]he ethic of solidarity intends to be an ethic of conscience'.[7] His definitions of conscience are mostly vague and fairly conventional to start with – grounded in generalities about the ethical sense that is natural to human beings – but they then narrow down to the specifics of recognizing suffering, with an appeal this time to the parable of the Good Samaritan. But this reference to the parable slightly shifts the emphasis of his exposition. Conscience, Tischner says, is activated when we see that someone else's pain is not caused primarily by contingent or 'natural' factors but is actually designed by one human agent for another; and the recognition of such a 'gratuitous wound' stirs something deeper than mere sympathy. It is here that the difference between solidarity and support or sympathy comes most clearly into focus for Tischner: conscience is what awakens in the moment in which we perceive the deliberate, willed, non-necessary suffering of another and understand our accountability in relation to it. As he puts it in a later address, it is the presence of a deliberate intention to injure that gives someone's suffering 'a moral character'[8] – presumably because it is then identifiable as a willed *breach in relation* rather than a neutral (if distressing) set of unchosen occurrences. And this moment of being struck by the moral – not just physical – gravity of the offence to another's humanity is what generates not only an individual response to the other's suffering but also a solidarity with all others who combine to meet that need – because the moral character of the pain is so deeply connected with the recognition that someone has been betrayed, abandoned. What they need, therefore, is not simply the alleviation of bodily pain or distress, but the faithful attention of a community. In this level of solidarity, we are united not by our looking at each other but by our common looking towards the person in need. '"For him" is first and "we" comes later.'[9] This is, says Tischner, what makes the kind of solidarity he is describing a unique kind of communion, in its primordial directedness towards the suffering other; we shall find our communion in active shared response to need and pain, not in exploring or nourishing an inner sense of common interest (it is hard to be sure, but this sounds as though Tischner is in part rebutting the argument of those nineteenth-century social thinkers in the lineage of Comte who found Christian 'charity' to be unduly limited by a potentially selfish focus on mutual benefit[10]). Solidarity of conscience ultimately means the creation of a community in which what prevails is *fidelity* to one another and specially to those who know what it is to be victims of unfaithfulness, betrayal.

So to the second focal point, *faithfulness*. The further dimension of solidarity and conscience that has to do with faithfulness is spelt out in subsequent pieces in Tischner's collection, and is presented as the polar opposite of exploitation or abuse – an exploitation that is not simply about poor or unjust conditions of work or remuneration but is most evident when people are not allowed to be what they are but are instrumentalized in a way that traps them in untruthfulness.[11] Solidarity cannot coexist with illusion, with the pretence that work is something it is not; and when labour is exploited – as, by implication, it is in the systemic distortions and propagandist fictions of a corrupt Communist regime that has no concern for work that is meaningful for the worker – illusion reigns. One of the insights that the awakening of conscience brings is 'feeling the pain of a lie';[12] falsity is seen as something that actively diminishes the dignity of the person,[13] and so becomes an even more urgent issue than the injustice of a wage system, for example. If the worker is understood only as an individual with physical needs, there is a fundamental failure to see what both work and humanity really entail; and only if we grasp the absolute necessity of faithfulness to one another do we begin to address the wound inflicted by the corruptions of a social and economic system. 'Solidarity of consciences is an ethical movement, the basis of which is *fidelity*; but '[f]idelity arises and grows where clear light reigns.'[14] There is a tight interrelation for Tischner between honest work, honest language, conscience, faithfulness, trust and communion.

And, thirdly, key to this is the understanding of *work* itself understood – in one of Tischner's tantalizingly original axioms – as 'a particular form of interpersonal conversation that serves to sustain and develop human life. Even briefer: Work is a conversation in the service of life.'[15] This is explained in terms of how work, like language itself, builds up from raw material a synthetic object with a commonly recognizable purpose; material acquires meaning through the processes of labour. In other words (and does he have Hannah Arendt at all in mind here?), the distinction between work and production is artificial. Tischner would not recognize Patočka's relegation of labour to the pre-historic realm; in sharp contrast, work, all kinds of work, is here *essentially* cultural, linguistic. The conventional picture of some primitive human sallying out alone to find an animal to kill and eat and gradually discovering that it is easier to accomplish with help from others is, in Tischner's eyes, not very convincing or important. We can't readily identify a stage of human development in which co-operative labour is absent. The labour we are familiar with as fully historical and conscious beings in social relation always presupposes agreement, common purpose, collaboration: 'By working I am joining the conversation that was already in progress before I was born. I am a link between the past and the future. I am an heir of the work.'[16] Solidarity is both the collaborative business of refining and enriching the conversation of work and a 'conversation' between past and present: in both respects a view of labour conspicuously different from any idea of it as somehow 'timelessly' repetitive.

Taken together, these elements make up a quite complex picture of solidarity, one that has obvious roots in earlier thought, not least in the theological and philosophical traditions out of which Tischner comes, but remains highly distinctive.[17] Solidarity is certainly the recognition of a pre-existing relation, to the extent that there is always already something that can be injured or 'paralysed' (as Tischner puts it) by those acts of betrayal, exploitation and oppression that create suffering. Encountering the victim of such betrayal, we recognize what has been lost. But at this point we are also challenged to recognize solidarity as a vocation or duty: there is a form of human behaviour that restores dignity and integrity for others, and this is embodied above all in practices of faithfulness, trustworthiness. The marginalized, paralysed victim is promised an unconditional accompaniment and advocacy. And those who share this response to suffering, those who – in Tischner's terms – actively 'desire to have a conscience', to live in obedience to conscience,[18] are bound more deeply to one another as they address themselves to the need of the betrayed. The embodiment of this binding together is a new kind of work in common, a form of labour that acknowledges the dignity and distinctiveness of each and also the dignity and distinctiveness of various kinds of labour. It is a 'truthful' form of work, in contrast to the superficial and illusory patterns of working that are imposed in a society that no longer has a real 'axiological' basis, a proper grasp of how values are judged (we shall return later to Tischner's use of the word 'axiological').

'When we read the gospel, we read it as a great textbook of fidelity.'[19] And our reading of history too becomes a complementary process of learning who we are as humans: Tischner's vision of humanity itself is of a species capable of faithfulness, and capable of faithfulness because it is open to truth – which is why[20] fidelity is also the primary principle of education. In the formation of the young, 'betrayal is not permitted', because it destroys hope, which is the only motive power of true human formation and maturation. This (hopeful) openness to truth involves a faithfulness to oneself as well as the other: responsibility begins with a fidelity to truth expressed in the resolve not to lie to oneself and not to collude with being lied to.[21] What is perhaps most striking about all this is the relatively muted role of fellow-feeling in the understanding of solidarity. We respond to the unjust suffering of the neighbour with outrage and active compassion, partly because this suffering adds to our own already serious suffering;[22] there is a very clear sense of the distance between the felt suffering of the other and my own, at the same time as a recognition that the resolution of the other's suffering is inseparable from the resolution of my own. When Tischner writes about 'dialogue',[23] he does indeed begin with the proposition that dialogue occurs only when we 'feel' the other's point of view; but this is 'not simply a question of compassion'. It is unpacked in terms of the willingness to imagine what is 'right' in the other's standpoint – right and therefore in some sense necessary to me – and the resolution to work towards a truth that both can acknowledge as including what matters to them.

The resolution of the suffering of the other is thus more than the ending of unjust conditions, it is the reconfiguring of how we understand shared labour and the process of continually discovering the solidarity of common *meaning* in that common action. We come to see work as, paradoxically, not just the meeting of a need but the *deferral* of the meeting of a need as we work out how to meet it *collaboratively*, as we talk it through and clarify its purpose (work as conversation) and attend to the granular distinctiveness of what makes the other 'other', both in terms of capacity or gift and in terms of the difficulty of adjusting to the reality of another who shares the same work in such a way that something new can emerge. The worthwhileness, the meaningfulness of such work is bound up with the mutual reliance that develops. We know it is worth suspending our immediate wants, making certain sacrifices, minor or major, because we are confident of a shared good will and a clear common goal; once again, 'conscience' and 'consciousness' are aroused as we see more fully what is lost in the act of betrayal.[24] And when Tischner speaks of 'heroism', as he does from time to time, it is in this context, of a sacrifice that is validated by the trustworthiness of those around us whose share in the common task makes sense of it, even if it is also a matter of risk and isolated decision.[25] In the process of dialogue (and here Tischner builds on some of his earlier and more theoretical work), there is an irreducible element of moving into the unknown. But this is not quite the same as Patočka's 'shakenness', in that it is connected here with the pre-existing and continuing process of trust between human agents. As in Patočka's world, solidarity entails a 'common openness to the world';[26] but here it is grounded not in the shared experience of the dissolution of received values and systems but in the shared commitment to build – or rebuild – the mutual credibility of human agents divided by narrow accounts of class interest, by ideological polarization, and by the endemic corruptions of a true ethic of work in a totalitarian society.

2.

In the background of all this is Tischner's philosophical formation – specifically his attempt in his doctoral and habilitation theses to reconstruct aspects of the phenomenological method so as to connect it more systematically with hermeneutical questions – issues of meaning and shared interpretation. His teacher Roman Ingarden's challenges to Husserl were crucially important, but so was Tischner's own reading of Levinas and Rosenzweig.[27] In brief, his concern is to move away from prioritizing questions around the relation of subject and object and the realism/idealism debates of Husserl's disciples towards what he described as an 'axiological' framework, a scheme in which *values* played the central role. Rather loosely summarized, what this means is this: the question is not how to establish what is entailed by the relation of subject to object in terms of knowledge, self-awareness and the like, but how to understand the orientation of self to other in terms of attitude, engagement and desire. The I-Thou relation is radically different from that of subject and object: it represents the way in which an other of some kind both makes a claim upon the self and, in so doing, reveals the self to itself as 'for' another (whether it wants to be or not).[28] What should be our primary question is not how or whether we truly know states of affairs in the external world, human or otherwise, but how we make sense of the fact that from the very first we are invited to *take up a stance* towards the world: some things *matter* in ways that other things don't. And in their mattering they become something other than 'just' things, enumerable objects. On any other basis, philosophical anthropology becomes no more than a description of determined behaviours, third-person accounts of processes. Tischner insists, especially in his *Philosophy of Drama*, that any purportedly 'ontological' account of the I needs to be corrected and supplemented by his phenomenology of the I as engaged, *questioned* by what it is not. The first-person perspective obstinately remains and cannot properly be ignored, coming into focus as a point within a reciprocal relation, as being for the other: I as 'addressed subject' do not stand among the list of objects contained in the world, and I as subject literally cannot speak about myself on such a basis. I cannot meaningfully say that 'I' as the receiver of an address or the making of a claim am a determinate object within my own field of perception. I cannot avoid taking up a stance *towards*, in responding to questioning. I allot significance to this rather than that, I learn to work with differentiated and 'hierarchized' meanings, according more and less significance to elements of my environment. Crucially, I can grow into this kind of practice only in continuing company. Which is why in turn it will not do to fall into the diametrically opposed error of supposing that the fact that I occupy a distinctive first-person position is the sole *source* of worth or meaning, that my ego's relation to 'being' is the primordial truth. Tischner's 'axiological' perspective is as critical of Heideggerian or Sartrean rhetoric as it is of materialistic reduction.[29]

Central to this perspective is the encounter with the human other – the linguistic other. The other's presence is what realizes the self's freedom, because this presence directly requires me to make choices. I can respond or I can withdraw; I can help or I can hurt. This confrontation with the choice that the other presents means that encounters with an other who is recognized as a subject are unlike any other kind of encounter in the world; indeed, they are in some sense *not* 'of the world' in that they require a passing beyond the realm of simple instinct or feeling and a drawing on some inner creativity. Tischner's preoccupation with *drama* is important here: he sees 'dramatic' engagement as the essence of the distinctively human. The persons of the drama are — in the old literal sense of the word 'person' — masks through which we both reveal and discover what or who we are. The uncontrolled and unpredicted initiative of the other towards us or in response to us is what sets defining boundaries for us in certain ways: we could not know ourselves without this engagement.[30] But this is not the last word: axiology is a relatively clear summons to take up a stance of one sort or another, but it has to be supplemented by the much less clear but more foundational invitation that Tischner calls 'agathology', the recognition of and response to the Good. I encounter not only a sort of 'bare' otherness but an otherness that *attracts or repels*. I can't 'register' what I encounter in a reaction of simple and static neutrality; I am drawn closer or pushed further away. So in affirming 'value' in this way through my response, I am also acknowledging *what should and should not be*, in the sense that I am conscious of wanting or not wanting some state of affairs; and the oddity of not wanting, not 'consenting to', some existing state of affairs, should alert us to the fact that we are invited to define ourselves not just in terms of 'values' in general (this happens to matter to me more than that) but in relation to good and evil (this is without qualification *to-be-desired* rather than that). The immediate facts of our environment open out on to a more challenging horizon in a way that has been called 'a biblically dramatized Platonism'.[31]

This is the point at which the metaphysical implications of Tischner's scheme become clearest: there is an order of relations (not quite the same as an order of 'things') that is what it is independent of our conditioned state of mind or heart, an order that has what could be called a *just* claim on our desires. In sum, axiology alone simply tells us that we cannot avoid taking a stance; agathology tells us that this action of self-definition cannot be an arbitrary affair. Why not exactly? I think because this would leave us with an 'I' that was simply the sum of its natural impulses and needs, never actually provoked or interrupted by the reality of a real other, whose demands were not defined by my preferences, skills or concepts. The face of the other, in Levinas's language, is never one thing among others, a phenomenon towards which I can take up whatever attitude I like; its claim on me is presented (as we have noted) as something beyond the realm of 'ontology'; Tischner here agrees with Levinas. The other's claim is not something that I can either describe in a third-person narrative or absorb into the ego as an occasion for my self-realization. The 'I' is always implicated in the other's reality and vice versa, and this means that I cannot consistently see myself as legitimately having the kind of liberty that can act without constraint – without the constraint of a reality that is always defined by mutuality and responsibility before my own standpoint as subject is even determined. So the sense of what should and shouldn't be is always on the edge of my axiological thinking, and I shan't make final sense of this inescapable world of values unless I open it out on to the agathological horizon.

All this is significant for our topic, and for the understanding of Tischner's specific discussions of solidarity, because it helps us grasp why solidarity and conscience, solidarity and fidelity, solidarity and the labour of language are inseparable in the addresses of the 1980s. I am always constituted by the linguistic other – and Tischner would, I think, want to insist, as many others have done, that to talk about a 'linguistic other' is not to confine linguistic presence and identity to articulate users of words; communicative gesture of any kind, allied to the recognizability of the face, is the point here, the point that would allow us to include the non-articulate, the non-'standard' forms of bodily communication, even, at the extreme, the communicative reality of the newborn, the unborn, the 'locked-in' and so forth. This 'being-constituted-by-the-other' in the axiological relation of having to take a stance towards them means that without the sustained engagement of self and other, the engagement embodied in 'drama' in the broadest sense, we could make no sense of the reality of *desire* in our lives – desire not as the hungry craving for something to silence the begging of the ego but as the hope for a future. In simple terms, to be involved with the other in the axiological context is to be faced with having to decide what we *want* in respect of the suffering of others: are we content that the suffering of another should persist? How can this be a desirable future for me any more than for the suffering other? Are we able successfully to detach that suffering from our own well-being? If so, there is in fact something about our own humanity that we are actively suppressing, something untrue to what we actually are as constituted by 'dramatic' interaction. And if we do acknowledge that this is the kind of choice that faces us, if we grasp that this choice is something to do with not lying to ourselves, we shall see that 'conscience' carries with it an element of hope. This situation should not be, but it does not have to be: I have the capacity for a choice that will resist and perhaps destroy what should not be. I am able to choose fidelity and to embody it. Something new can come into the situation of suffering, something not determined in the way that the cause-and-effect systems of the material world are determined.

As Tischner says in his *Etyka* pieces, the capacity for solidarity thus becomes a distinguishing feature of our humanity (though not a *condition for recognizing it*; we also, sadly, exhibit the distinctiveness of our humanity by exercising our liberty to refuse and betray). The good is always vulnerable to destruction in any particular circumstance, but it is not absolutely destroyed because the reality of interpersonal involvement is always present and always capable of being restored by our response. This is why sacrifice for the good is intelligible; the persistence of the good is a trustworthy belief, inseparable from our belief in human dignity itself; and so we continue to try to find words and practices to share that will affirm such a belief and make it more trustworthy for more people. To a question about whether solidarity is primarily a state or an imperative, Tischner might reply that it is a state that makes the imperative intelligible and credible, and an imperative that makes the state imaginable. Solidarity – as the realization of mutual fidelity and communicative freedom – is what we most deeply want because it is what is most deeply real in us, what we always in fact inhabit. The repulsion of conscience in the face of the unjust suffering of others is inescapable because it reminds us of what is lost of our (shared) humanity in this situation of injustice. And, to connect this with another part of our discussion, it is the point at which the notions of human right and human rights come into focus: we become aware of the gravity of those responses to the humanity of others that are fundamentally 'untrue', unfitting to the reality of humanity as such.

This anchorage in an already-given connection, by way of the 'axiological' and 'agathological' focus of our discovery of the self's reality, is important in Tischner's thought because it gives him the freedom to identify precisely where the ideal collapses and is distorted. He famously insists in his Wawel sermon that he is speaking about a solidarity that does not need enemies to make it real.[32] But, looking back in his reflections on 'The Ethics of Solidarity Years Later', he pinpoints the way in which solidarity can become weaponized if there has not been a real change in the *subject*.[33] He discusses what he calls the spirit of 'clienthood' – the moral or spiritual dependency that arises from looking to be *rewarded*, whether by the system, the hand of history ('being on the right side of history'), or simply by a social order that provides me with basic gratification and security (Bobbitt's 'market society' perhaps). Such attitudes speak of the lack of any transformation of fundamental self-understanding. And the other side of this coin is that, if motivation is reduced to reward, moral sanction takes on the form of shame or ostracism, which produces and nourishes a pattern of simple moral binaries, petty absolutisms. As he goes on to argue,[34] this ends up enshrining 'solidarity' as merely group loyalty. It becomes the rationale for a polarizing negativity about the past: if, as Tischner puts it, all we can say about the legacy of Marxist hegemony is that it was tyrannical fantasy, we absolve ourselves from any understanding of the past that will assist our learning in the present. The past is not allowed to be *our* past, and so there can be no continuity of critique and learning. Power becomes an all-or-nothing contest, a realm of absolute demands accompanied by the radical delegitimation of any system that fails to meet those demands. The world of labour regresses to factionalism and pragmatic self-interest. 'Heroism' has been refused, as has the 'courage to think'. And the Church, which has the potential, according to Tischner, for clearly embodying every level of the ideal and the reality of solidarity, has retreated to a position of 'fear of the world', replacing the Christian personalism that provides the seedbed for shared dignity and mutual trust with a Christian 'integralism' in which confessional loyalty obscures the universal call to solidaristic action and witness.

Tischner believed that dialogue was possible only when the other partner was regarded as 'a necessary source of knowledge'[35] in respect of whatever was being talked about. The stark polarization he attacks in his later reflection is incompatible with this understanding, and ultimately with the more abstract convictions around drama that shape Tischner's basic anthropology. To see the dialogue partner (past or present) as necessary for my process of learning is not to adopt a passive and uncritical approach to that partner, but to acknowledge that without the partner's presence and intervention *there will be things I shall fail to learn.* The encounter itself, in the context of all kinds of other encounters too, will lead into a fuller apprehension of the truth to which all are finally held accountable. The assumption that I can know my situation adequately without this openness to the partner, even the partner with whom I am in bitter and apparently irreconcilable disagreement, condemns me both to a partial knowledge and to the violence that results from this separation from the other. Tischner interestingly implies, as we have seen, that this kind of dialogical perspective must apply in our reflection about the past as much as the present: the past – including, in Poland, the recent past of totalitarian repression and pervasive public corruption – has to be listened to as having something necessary to say. Letting the past speak in its own terms, and letting it speak as *our* past, is not a thoughtless rehearsing of a history immune to challenge, but an acceptance of the universal incapacity of any person or society to see itself truthfully outside the context of relations, welcome and unwelcome, convergent or divergent. And this is a further dimension of solidarity, the refusal simply to silence or forget the radically other, even the repellently other, including the repellently other in our own memories of our collective selves. Including them in dialogue is not collusion but the attempt to explore what the world feels like to the stranger. Unless I know this, I know less about the world than I need to (we might recall again Gillian Rose on what it is to recognize in dialogic encounter the other's 'investment' in their belief or argument). That the world *can* appear differently to the way in which I experience or configure it is a truth about the world – and it is in fact – according to Edith Stein, Patočka and Tischner alike – the truth that literally makes it possible for me to know myself. Further, connecting this to Tischner's meditations on labour, we could say that intelligent (truthful) labour is possible only when we have found ways of negotiating the different perceptions of reality that come into play, even at the simplest physical level: we see different aspects, and we also identify different features as significant, depending on the skills and/or needs we bring to the task. In other words, solidarity and a certain kind of pluralism belong together. The solidarity we recognize in the bare facts of shared language and action impels us to work towards a more conscious, reflective solidarity, a deeper level of shared labour; and the triggering factor in reawakening the basic facts of shared speech and action seems to be the awareness of the deliberate breaches in this primordial co-operation created by the laziness, greed and hunger for power that drives us to try and silence the other and deprive them of their freedom to take a part in defining the nature and goal of any exchange.

Tischner's vision is a powerful and rhetorically coherent model of human interconnection; but its coherence at a more theoretical level has been questioned by some generally sympathetic commentators, and we shall look briefly at two such responses. Charles Taylor, in a generally positive discussion of Tischner[36] helpfully spells out how the basic analogy between socio-economic interaction and conversation (an analogy that, he says, brings Tischner close to Jurgen Habermas in some respects) grounds the idea that social equality and real economic freedom imply that no one party has the power or right to dictate the conditions of the relationship. But he also notes a complication in Tischner's account. Solidarity is grounded in existing relations; but if we are using, as Tischner does, the parable of the Good Samaritan as an instance of solidaristic action, there is also something that goes beyond this, in that there is no prior relation between the Samaritan and the victim of the thieves. 'The good-will of the Samaritan is able to cover up the gap in social relations...Not a thing in the world as it exists calls him to act.'[37] Taylor suggests that the more basic aspect of solidarity as a function of existing relations is what Tischner is more focused on in his *Etyka* pieces, rather than this latter — should we say 'super-natural'? — expression of solidarity.

Only up to a point, I think. The truth is that throughout these essays, Tischner shows little interest in drawing boundaries between natural and supernatural. There is indeed a sense in which the Samaritan's act is prompted by no localized natural affinity; but that kind of affinity is not the whole story about any kind of solidaristic action, especially those acts arising from the outrage generated by the arbitrary denial of another's humanity. That other may be a fellow-worker or trades unionist, as is often the case in Tischner's examples (and as is very understandably the case in his specific political setting). But even here, while in one sense 'the world as it exists' may be thought to prompt compassionate action out of an identification with the other that is fairly obviously connected with what I have called localized affinity, there is even here no simple cause and effect relationship: as Tischner insists, there is a choice of response or flight. Fidelity has to be chosen. The fact that it is chosen over against an option that is neither natural nor life-giving, that it is chosen as what is most fundamentally defining of human existence, does not mean that it is any less a moment of self-determination that moves beyond the surface level of affinity or group loyalty. The Samaritan's action is neither something arising out of group loyalty nor a context-free, *ex nihilo* upsurge of sacrificial detached selflessness. It is an acknowledgement of what is owed to the truth of a tangibly immediate human otherness that is just one instance of a human commonalty beyond tribal boundaries, always constituted by mutual involvement, reciprocal definition and actualization; and so it is an act of obedience to what we collectively are.

But Taylor's question is not misplaced. What is not always very clear in Tischner's analysis is how exactly the decision for truth over illusion, fidelity rather than withdrawal, is made and sustained. In theological terms, he has apparently little to say about *grace*. To use his own rather awkward vocabulary, the turn from axiology to agathology is obscure. We take for granted – or we should take for granted – that our actions are shaped by judgements of value, and we discover that such judgements are concentrated in a very distinctive way around the presence of the face of the other; in some way, we come to see that this discovery entails a further judgement about what is and is not to be sought or desired, for self and other, a judgement about the Good. It is the nature of this last transition that is left surprisingly vague by Tischner. It is not that reciprocity or mutual transparency somehow work in themselves as definitions of the Good; the reciprocity between agents has as its goal the communication of a kind of life that manifests the Good. To turn to another sympathetic critic, there is an appreciative but probing assessment of Tischner's work, heavily influenced by the political history of *Solidarność* and of Poland generally in the post-Communist era,[38] by Dobrosław Kot, who argues that Tischner's account of solidarity in his *Etyka* is less a theory of solidarity, more a reflection on how the vocabulary of solidarity illuminates a range of significant topics, as part of a general project of allowing a certain kind of ontology to emerge by way of the discussion of ethics.[39] Dialogical mutuality alone cannot provide a dependable ground for a critical and substantive ethic, and must turn in the direction of what the shared good in view actually is; the focus of solidaristic action is not just the relation between sufferer and observer, but looks towards a more comprehensive horizon.[40] Tischner is so preoccupied with the damage done to social reality by the pervasiveness of unfaithfulness and untruth that the appeal for a solidarity that will overcome or cure this dominates his discussion to the detriment of a fuller analysis of how and why untruth has come to be so pervasive, and exactly what sort of inner transformation is needed to take us beyond its reach.

It is true that Tischner is inclined in the *Etyka* pieces to stress what he elsewhere calls the 'obviousness' of the Good,[41] and that the precise contours of an argument from ethics to ontology are not mapped out. Nevertheless, there *are* elements in these essays that would answer some of Kot's challenges. As we have seen, the emphasis on fidelity and the importance of working practices and conditions that do not alienate or dehumanize the worker clearly assume that what Kot calls 'dependability' is very plainly in Tischner's view as the way in which solidarity is embodied. But Kot is right to say that solidarity is as much a tool for clarifying a variety of issues as a topic in itself in *Etyka*; which is why it is necessary to look a little more deeply at the hinterland of Tischner's anthropology, and at what he means by 'agathology'. And, putting it all together, it is possible to extract a slightly more systematic picture that offers a response to the suspicion that dialogic mutuality has simply overtaken any more substantive ethical structure.

The agathological perspective is one that recognizes something to-be-desired for human subjects that is not simply dictated by their contingent wants or preferences; and this something-to-be-desired is the full liberation of reciprocal generosity, the process by which persons are brought to life. Mutuality is not an exchange of peripheral acknowledgements but an exchange of life-giving energy and knowledge (remember Tischner's account of the conditions of dialogue, including the recognition that the other has what I need to negotiate my own life in the world).

But the implication of this is that my fidelity to the other, my painful awareness of their suffering, my resolve to alleviate both their pain and mine, is all predicated on the assumption that I relate to the other ultimately as a subject who needs to be liberated to give what they are able to give for the life of their own neighbours and the life of the entire human and global community. Put more directly: I do not serve the selfishness of my neighbour, their (probably) imperfect and patchy realization of the Good. I acknowledge and share their suffering precisely as the suffering of those who have been robbed of their birthright of freedom to serve or share or love. I serve their imagined future as responsible and generous agents. There is a good for them that they may not fully acknowledge and is not necessarily what they currently happen to think it is – any more (crucially!) than it is necessarily what *I* think it is. I can rightly perceive what it is about their situation that frustrates or stifles their dignity – dignity in the sense of their freedom to play their proper part in the interdependent life of the human community, making life possible for their neighbours, enhancing the humanity of their neighbours. I love them as I love myself, in the sense that what I am called to love in myself is not the bundle of anxieties, cravings, obsessions and mythologies that I create for myself but the self as person, as a unique centre of perceiving, receiving and bestowing, object as well as subject of exchange; myself as free to 'displace' myself for the life of the world. Insofar as the 'agathological' turn in Tischner's anthropology, a movement away from a more narrowly phenomenological approach, imagines all agents to be commonly answerable to a Good that none of them in isolation can control or fully define, we do have here precisely that 'reconstituted Platonism' that some have identified in his work. Solidarity opens out on to some sort of transcendental horizon.

3.
Tischner in his later writing – as well as several of those who have commented on and developed his thinking – shows a clear concern about the way in which solidarity language can be

conscripted into a new pattern of binaries and exclusions. The affirmation of an ethical world that is able simply and comprehensively to negate a rival ethical world – even in the name of solidarity itself – is a profoundly troubling development for Tischner. It is something that reduces solidarity to that confident definition of the authentically human in terms of what one group agrees to be 'essential' that we have consistently seen in this book to be a driver of denial and violence. Shared interest is not enough; nor is solidarity in the most robust sense to be identified with any kind of impersonal redistributive scheme.[42] Shared interest comes to a halt when we cannot find any interest that we recognize in another; redistributive equalization comes to a halt when the natural self-evidence of redistributive calculation is turned into an absolute such that no argument is possible about how it works – rather as a forensic and abstract doctrine of human rights may paradoxically lead to violence because there can be no debate about its correctness.[43] Tischner insists that it is – so to speak – 'dialogue all the way down'. But this commitment to dialogue, to that often counter-intuitive belief that the other knows something I need to know, must not be read as a kind of 'Rortyan' solidarity in which consensus substitutes for truth and objectivity. It is the agathological moment that obliges us to step aside from this tempting shortcut.

In dialogue, we seek what we need, not fully knowing what we need, except that there is something we shall not know without listening to the stranger. If this is so, we are acting on the assumption that the stranger also needs what I know, but does not know that is what they need. What I and the stranger have in common in the dialogical process is that we are both aware at some level that our knowledge is incomplete; so when I say that the stranger needs what I know, the irony is that I may not *know* what I know – i.e. that I may need the other to enable me to see what the limits are of what I think my world is. But this nudges me further towards the recognition that discovering the truth I need to know is a backwards and forwards movement of 'reading and being read', to revert to the language of earlier chapters, in which what comes into focus is what neither of us has previously seen or possessed. Yet what makes it compelling to our acceptance is not simply the fact of some kind of convergence but a genuine recognition of something that has a *claim* on both of us, something that embodies what we both desire for a truthful life, not merely a peaceful one. It will be a shared good towards which we can both work as a legitimate ground for sacrifice or struggle.

As becomes evident, Tischner's subtle interweaving of solidarity with fidelity, truthfulness and shared labour is designed to create a model of solidarity that cannot be reduced either to an instant and uncritical sense of affinity, a sort of tribal loyalty, or to a merely pragmatic co-existence. It is about the cost of truthfulness; it is not only the aspiration to lift the neighbour's burden, it also requires us to create forms of collaborative labour that, as we pursue them, teach us more of what we do and can share, in a co-operative engagement with a world we did not make, a world with whose givenness we must negotiate in imagination and humility, in truthfulness. Tischner's proclamation of the imperative for a solidarity 'without enemies' is intelligible against this background: not a passive tolerance of diversity but the daunting project of discovering a form of human togetherness that does not at some level depend on identifying who is an outsider or a threat. It does not preclude sharp and prolonged contest; Tischner fully recognizes that there will be a struggle against those who deny or stifle conscience in themselves and others, while never actually urging violent regime change. But the two crucial points he holds on to are, first, the danger of identifying this struggle with some absolute binary of good and evil, in which the victory of one side is the victory of humanity itself over its enemies; and, second, that an effective revolution changes not simply the governors but the governed.[44] Habits of servility and fear are overcome, because the mode of effecting change is no longer a top-down process but is grounded in the necessarily co-operative activities required for deploying new technical resources. His somewhat naïve picture of technology providing not only solutions to traditional problems but a new way of working together for human agents weakens the argument in important respects. But the notion worth salvaging here is that a solidarity without enemies is a social bond that looks beyond the seductive drama of absolute conflict, final and mutually exclusive binaries, to something more demanding. Precisely because it appeals to a shared and interactive identity that does not depend on our grasp or achievement, it warns against imagining that the other's moral world is completely inaccessible and alien. Even more importantly, it warns against supposing that the triumph of my/our view is the vindication of it absolute rightness; the truth we seek is what it is independently of what I/we achieve. If we believe otherwise, we are in danger of reducing truth to what is endorsed by successful power. Once again, the Platonist hinterland of the argument comes into view: if truth or justice is *not* the interest of the stronger – the question with which Plato's *Republic* begins – then it is discovered by something other than calculations of power; we need to reflect on how we come to know what is real, and we need to turn our backs on what Tischner calls the spirit of 'clienthood' – acting on the assumption that fidelity to truth is imperative because it brings immediate and obvious reward. And for Tischner it is clear that central to the learning of what is real is the revelatory importance of the moment in which I acknowledge the other's suffering or lack as *my* lack also – not an identical form of privation but a privation that entails privation for me as well as for the primary sufferer. Not to *imagine* what the other lacks is to fail to think what the other needs; not to think what the other needs is in effect, in Tischner's scheme, to fail to acknowledge my own need or incompleteness. And that way lies the absolutism of conflict that in his later years he saw as increasingly displacing the solidarity he defended and believed he had glimpsed in the early days of the reform movement in Poland.

As this summary suggests, his treatment of the issues is unsystematic. We are moved very briskly from consideration of the immediacy of the suffering other within an existing community – paradigmatically, the disadvantaged or oppressed fellow-worker – to the recognition of the position of the hostile or indifferent other, the other, indeed, who may be responsible for the fellow-worker's pain and frustration. We have to shuttle backwards and forwards between the obvious form of solidarity that is embodied in the relief of another's pain and the far less obvious kind that seeks to sustain intelligible, reciprocal exchange with those *responsible* for pain. To repeat a point made earlier: what we love in them, pity in them, that in which we affirm solidarity with them, is not the power and advantage they wield, the power that causes the diminishment of others: rather we love what they are damaging or destroying in themselves, the capacity for life-giving. And Tischner's thoughts about the dangers of ignoring or demonizing the recent political past are of real relevance if this tendency results in supposing that there is no legacy from that past that needs to be worked with. Tischner clearly has no time for the 'Day One of the Revolutionary Era' mentality. It will be a mixed legacy, obviously; but it is ours. It will have formed what is possible for us in the present, for good and ill, and as such it needs to be worked at as much as any relation with a current interlocutor or opponent.

So we are committed, it seems, to a model of dialogue that always requires us to imagine why a belief or programme matters as it does – or fails to matter – to the hostile or indifferent other. It is a search not for general convergence but for the (perhaps vanishingly minimal) ground on which it might be possible to identify a recognizable shared good. This entails not a shrug of the shoulders and a bland acceptance of difference, but a determination to imagine what counts as a substantive good for the other, what they want and why, in a way that does not resort to caricature or contempt; a determination, therefore, always to examine my/our rhetoric for these labour-saving tactics and to try and avoid them. And there is no guarantee that we shall find lasting solid ground here. What is clear is the perspective that is demanded by what Tischner calls axiology and agathology: the 'grammar' of dialogue as the basic human condition, finding out what matters and what sense of the goal of human desire is at work. We may and must oppose the oppressor; we must not at once imagine that the oppressor's desires are not recognizably human. To put it in the context of a range of contemporary issues: it is imperative to oppose racism, so most of us assume; but if we care about more than just 'defeating racism' but changing how power is understood and exercised, how the pathologies of power generate racism, we have to work at disentangling both the contradictions of racist discourse, *and* the nest of fears and myths that it is trying to manage – rather than ascribing everything immediately to a single incomprehensibly evil desire to hurt members of other ethnic groups. In the toxic environment of current debate about gender identification, the race to absolutism has been particularly evident. It is all the more important for some to remember that a person seeking gender reassignment or surgery is typically a person whose experience of their environment is largely one of a comprehensive lack of safety, and whose experience of their own physicality is largely one of a comprehensive alienation and desperation. Important too for others to remember that the woman whose experience includes being the target of abusive violence is likely to be living with similar levels of unsafeness and self-alienation of a different kind. If the language of the debate ascribes to the former a cavalier and arbitrary disdain for the constraints of material existence or an arrogant revolt against the creator's purposes or a systemic contempt for one gendered identity or another, or a predatory desire for access to the protected spaces of another gendered identity; and if it imagines the latter as wedded to inflexible discrimination, the deliberate perpetuation of unchallengeable gender stereotypes, the belittling of lifelong social and physical suffering – then the prospect of an absolutist clash of pseudo-solidarities is clear enough.

What is involved in taking both kinds of unsafety seriously? That is a question calling for a different and more first-principles-based account of solidarity,[45] one in which the idea of dependability, faithfulness, becomes central. The injunction to 'check your privilege' has become for many people a tiresome cliché; but it represents an essential moment in any conflictual encounter. What is it in my word or stance that will diminish the security of the other and intensify their sense of mistrust, their belief that their interests are radically at risk? Solidarity of Tischner's kind invites something more like a search for the vulnerability I share with another – not so as to create a rhetoric of suffering that can compete with that of the other (the rightly challenged language of 'white distress' or 'white victimhood' in the face of accusations of racism, for example[46]), but to begin to see better how I/we have been acted upon as well as how we have acted, how we have reacted to perceived threats, how we have colluded with bad, violent, uncritical or unbalanced solutions to our fear, and so on. If we begin from solidarity as the state of irreducible interdependence in which we all stand, then the imperative to realize this solidarity in the detail of finite biography, finite choices, must ultimately be an imperative to be consistently suspicious of any position that allows us to declare any other group and their perspective simply deserving of obliteration. To repeat the point – we may and we should struggle for certain views and policies to disappear. It's not much use saying or thinking that 'there are fine people on both sides'. But we cannot pretend that others have no history and no 'investment' – that there is nothing to understand. And if understanding is what we seek, there has to be some sense in which any final position at which we and our interlocutors and opponents arrive is going to be shaped by the narratives of both parties. If we work towards a world in which racism is a thing of the past, we need to see what the process of learning has been that allowed us to grow beyond racism; what the definitive arguments and experiences or encounters were that sharpened the case for leaving this abuse behind. To make a point frequently made in this context: it matters to acknowledge what we have learned, what the outrageous errors or betrayals of our own past and the past of others may include, if only to ward off the idea that Tischner himself clearly finds seductive, the timeless self-evidence of truth. To be able to tell a story of error and struggle as a story of learning is part of the intellectual (and spiritual) discipline that keeps us from the tyranny exemplified in the perspectiveless and abstract rationalism whose disastrous costs we touched upon in the first chapter.

A solidarity without enemies does not mean, then, a universalism beyond conflict. Each community, like each person, brings a history to the encounter with the stranger and does not simply abandon that specific narrative. Each community, like each person, acknowledges that they are still in the process of learning and that part of such learning is learning how to survive the wounds inflicted on the self by the hunger for control and possession. But the horizon within which we all work is not the hope of a straightforward consensus any more than it is the hope for the unqualified victory of one party, licensing it to forget its own history of learning, risk, misrecognition, self-challenge. It is rather, as we have repeatedly seen, the horizon of shared labour, the creation of meaning by the discovery of how we work together to sustain the world. Tischner's very remarkable aphorism,[47] 'Work is a particular form of interpersonal conversation that serves to sustain and develop human life' (or, more briefly, 'Work is a conversation in the service of life') opens up the idea of labour as a constant adjustment of meaning under the pressure of making practical sense of communal life, each material element in the technical/constructive process making and demanding an adjustment of the imagined whole and being itself qualified and changed by that imagined whole. Thus we can say of the process of dialogue that it is in some ways most clearly itself in the linguistic but non-verbal mode of joint work.[48] Solidarity as a virtue is the commitment to culture-building, we could say: it is (with due respect to Dobrosław Kot) more than a method to resolve problems or balance out deficiencies. It is indeed in one sense instrumental, not an end in itself, in that its goal is a radical redistribution not of resources but of power, in a social order of free and equal participation that embodies the abiding, underlying structures of human mutuality and releases individual agents to play their constructive or life-giving roles. This is why a *merely* redistributive programme is inadequate; the socialism that matters has to entail an interior conversion, overthrowing not a system but a myth of the self. The attempt to create mutuality by legal enforcement is a mistake and potentially lethal one.

And talking about conversion brings us finally back to the question touched on earlier. How does our reorientation to the imperative of solidaristic culture-building actually happen and how is it sustained? We have noted the importance for Tischner of the idea of the Good as something owned or comprehended by no finite subject; do we need a fuller account of the way in which that Good comes to be seen as active, as 'taking an initiative' in our regard? Time, then, to turn briefly to the theological perspective that Tischner so tantalizingly suggests and never quite spells out in full.

SEVEN

Solidarity, Responsibility, Guilt: Dietrich Bonhoeffer's Helplessness

1.
'Love for real human beings leads into the solidarity of human guilt.'[1] Dietrich Bonhoeffer died at the hands of the Third Reich in 1945 before he completed the work on ethics that had been his major theological project in his final years of freedom; and although the word 'solidarity' does not occur often in the drafts that he left, it is clear that much of his reflection bears on the themes we have been discussing here. The unfinished *Ethics* drafts are both an intricate ensemble of theoretical perspectives on human life together and a thinly veiled self-interrogation. Bonhoeffer was already engaged (exactly how closely remains a matter of dispute) in a conspiracy that involved the planned assassination of Adolf Hitler – an engagement that ran against both the historical Lutheran commendation of non-resistance to the powers of the state and against Bonhoeffer's own earlier commitment to Gandhian non-violence. The *Ethics* fragments are in part his attempt to make sense of where he had found himself as a political activist, working in secret with the group plotting Hitler's death while maintaining a public role as an agent of the government's intelligence network. In these late writings, a recurring theme is the temptation to think of virtuous or even holy action as entailing a withdrawal from the compromised public world; Bonhoeffer insists that the contrary is true. 'The solidarity of human guilt' is a strong phrase and a difficult one, but it reflects his conviction that ethical action must embrace the fact that we are always already implicated in

the same destructive or disorderly circumstances that we seek to resist and transform.²

In the background of course is the longstanding Jewish and Christian framework in which the individual is eternally caught up in 'mysterious solidarities'³ that condition and limit possibilities in the present. In the complex and resonant metaphor deployed by St Paul, we are elements in an integral organic system, a 'Body'. Injuries experienced by one part are injuries to the whole; the well-being of the whole is the well-being of each element. The fact of relatedness at this level guarantees that there is no sphere of existence in which we live clinically protected lives for which the injury of others is immaterial. The myth that we can preserve or construct such a sphere is the foundational error of humanity, the sin of Adam. We harbour the longing for a self-contained identity in which knowledge and pleasure can be divorced from the passage of time, from dependence on others, and from the reality of cost and struggle. This 'Adamic' role is what we are all offered, what we are all inducted into, as soon as we are born into human social interaction. The rather unhelpful language of 'original sin' in traditional theology is an attempt to capture this sense of an inescapable 'being implicated'.

And Bonhoeffer's phrase at first sight presents the sharpest version of this intuition by using the terminology of 'guilt', *Schuld*. His thinking here shows unmistakeable signs of the influence of Dostoevsky's language in *The Brothers Karamazov*, where more than once spiritual awakening of one sort or another is represented as a recognition that one is 'guilty for all'.⁴ In a sense this points us back to the earliest uses of solidarity language in the legal setting where it designates a shared 'liability' in law:⁵ we are to be held accountable collectively and inseparably for a certain situation, whatever the degree of strictly individual culpability we might recognize. 'Guilt' is a matter not so much of the psychological awareness of responsibility, but of the bare fact of being implicated: this situation here and now would not be what it is without our involvement and/or complicity.

SOLIDARITY, RESPONSIBILITY, GUILT

This tradition of characterizing our human condition owes a very great deal to St Augustine as well as to St Paul; and for Augustine it is in significant part a corrective to the notion that the agent is in principle able to choose a course of action without any constraint deriving from inherited and ingrained patterns of human behaviour – or, ultimately, from anything beyond the individual will. It is, we might say, the shadow side of what we have repeatedly been discussing here, the irreducible role of the other in the constitution of the self. Granted this starting-point, what if the other's presence and agency is constituting in me a selfhood that is damaged or distorted? What if from the beginning we are each of us at the mercy of a pattern of information or a structure of desire that reproduces a dangerously diminished, misdirected form of selfhood? But the point that Bonhoeffer is making takes this a stage further: if we cannot escape the shaping influence of these patterns and structures (any more than we can escape the grammar of the language we first learn as infants), the hope to act justly or truthfully can't be grounded simply in a confidence that we are able to shed or ignore what we have inherited. The paradox is that truthful action – 'just' or appropriate action – begins in the acknowledgement of our *lack* of freedom, clarity and truthfulness, and in our willingness to accept that the judgement we make of the failure or corruption of others is also a judgement on ourselves. If we are to engage in the kind of creative, empathic and work-directed solidarity that we have seen advocated by various thinkers discussed in earlier chapters, we must confront the unwelcome fact of a solidarity that already exists – a morally clouded solidarity, in virtue of which we are all constantly both subverting of and subverted by the actions of others. This is not to indulge the 'we are all guilty' cliché so popular and so much mocked in some modern discourses. It is not an invitation to *feel* the kind of self-repugnance that would belong with a recognition of specific and deliberate wrongdoing on our part. It is a question of understanding our interdependence in a particular and not very welcome way, understanding that the fidelity identified as central to the project of any life-giving solidarity is always made harder by the delusive images of selfhood into which we have been educated or conditioned. Because of this, any ethical project depending on the idea that I as an individual am able to identify and realize an unshadowed, unqualified good is a dangerous myth. For Bonhoeffer, 'love', the opening up of some kind of life-giving connection with the other, must be separated from the ideal of unconstrained self-perfecting activity; and if it is so separated, it will have to reckon with the uncontrollable 'ecology' surrounding any specific action, in which both motive and outcome are not going to be readily controllable, and ambiguity and complicity are unavoidable.

In short, unambiguous decisions for clear right and wrong outcomes are going to be rare. And this, so far from relativizing or weakening our sense of conscientious loyalty to unchanging values, should reinforce our sense of the imperative of fidelity. If I cannot act without my action being implicated with the actions of others, as well as being already shaped and compromised by what I have inherited, I am bound to recognize that my own fate is not separable from that of others. If we are all implicated in destructive patterns, the turning around or redemption of our agency can't be a matter of individual change alone; the new life of any particular agent will still be affected by and have impact upon others. My obligation to work with and for a healing version of mutuality is underlined, and the mythology of individualistic notions of human possibility is further exposed. The decision to stand with a human community that is compromised and vulnerable to judgement – rather than withdrawing into a self-fashioned image of perfection – is a form of *self-dispossession*. I accept solidarity in 'guilt' (the inescapable blurring and blending in with a shared human responsibility for our shared situation of dysfunctional, destructive habit) so that I may become able to act more truthfully, to act for the sake of the gifts that solidarity is meant to bring. And not the least of those gifts is the trust between people that is generated by a truthful admission of involvement/complicity.

For Bonhoeffer, this is grounded in a distinctive – though not unique – reading of the religious narrative within which he thought and lived. It is a narrative of gratuitous involvement on the part of the divine saviour in the compromised condition of humanity, and it is worked out by way of an analysis of two interconnected concepts, 'responsibility' (*Verantwortung*) and 'representation' or 'vicarious action' (*Stellvertretung*). 'A human being,' writes Bonhoeffer,[6] 'necessarily lives in encounter with other human beings and [...] this encounter entails being charged, in ever so many ways, with responsibility for the other human being.' If we seek to act for ourselves alone, we deny what actually makes us the selves we are – our entanglement with the lives of others. Denying this doesn't free us from these entanglements, it simply means we handle them badly rather than well.[7] The foundation of ethical life is thus the question of how we rightly identify our responsibilities, how we rightly discern the claim of reality upon us within the net of relations in which we stand. But so far from this meaning that we must do our duty in the station in life to which God has called us (to echo the terminology of an older Protestant social morality), it entails something difficult and transformative. Because the world we encounter is the world that God has always already decided to embrace and affirm, even in its chaos, ambivalence and violence, two things become possible. First, we are able to see it as having a solid claim upon us because, since God has embraced it, it is where God's claim on us becomes immediate; and second, we are also released from the fantasy that we have the responsibility either to sustain or to change *everything*. Grasping that we are responsible in this context means precisely grasping that this is not about our lonely *individual* responsibility but about a shared challenge and summons. Ultimately, God's sovereignty is the premise of all we think and do.[8] Our calling is therefore not to perform a series of perfectly just or justifiable acts in the world (an impossibility), but to discover what it is that *we* are specifically summoned to do and are able to do in every encounter. It is not in the least a relativistic or 'situationalist' model (in which circumstances dictate what's right or wrong): the absolute measure of all that is done in the world is the sacrificial identification of Jesus with the sinful and suffering so that they may be released into their proper humanity.

Thus the goal of our action is not individual ethical achievement, let alone perfection; it is a 'just' and appropriate engagement with others that arises out of a self-forgetting attention to their needs within an overall vision of what human flourishing, life in the divine image, looks like. We may recall the sense of 'justice' and 'right' explored in an earlier chapter: the point is to identify a response that is true, 'just', to what is actually before us – both the human situation and the reality of God's act and nature.

This then opens out on to the notion of *Stellvertretung* – a notoriously difficult word to translate. 'Representation' is not the most satisfactory term. In ordinary German usage, it designates 'standing in for', 'deputizing': taking the place of another so as to act on their behalf or in their name. For Bonhoeffer, this is what Christ does: he has no 'agenda', no interest of his own to be served or advanced, but takes on the position of human beings in their neediness and loss, doing what they need to do but cannot do to secure their own well-being. Christ 'is the responsible human being par excellence. All responsible action is rooted in the real vicarious representative action of Jesus Christ on behalf of all human beings.'[9] In the light of this reading of the work of Christ, we can say that 'responsibility' is nothing other than this kind of willingness to have no agenda exclusively of one's own, but to act 'in the place of' or 'from the position of' the other, with an eye to their release or flourishing. This does not mean that the position and need and capacity of any particular self are simply *cancelled* in favour of the neighbour (we have noted the moral awkwardness of this position, and its critique by Gillian Rose, in an earlier chapter[10]). It is rather that my initial, flawed self-perception, involving the idea of a purely private agenda, a purely individual account of my need and so on, has to give way to the idea that whatever resource I have is ultimately at the disposal of the human community instead of being a vehicle for self-advancement or self-protection. I discover *another sort of selfhood* in the process of standing for and with the other. Part of this resignation of the idea of a solitary self with privately defined needs and goals is the recognition of *already existing complicity* in the continuing turmoil and dysfunction of the world. We have to leave behind the aspiration for a moral purity that has no connection with the reality of the needy, guilty, compromised, helpless other – and no connection with the implicated, collusive self that I am.

So Bonhoeffer attempts to position his vision of ethics between an ideologically dictated activism – for which the essential thing is to secure a set of maximally correct answers to various problems and to present a record of indisputable moral achievement – and a pietistic indifference. And he also differentiates his conception of responsibility from 'the dark glow of tragic heroism',[11] in which the moral/Christian agent is crushed by the claim of conflicting principles; we might well want to speak of a tragic element in Bonhoeffer's picture, but it is not the tragedy of a lonely individual compelled to choose between incompatible absolutes, and so doomed to one or another kind of unforgivable betrayal.

To be 'responsible' is to acknowledge that I do not answer for myself alone. I already exist in solidarity, a solidarity I have not chosen; so that with or without my conscious will I am 'guilty' – that is to say, I am part of the densely textured fabric of action that causes whatever present pain or evil is confronting me. It is never the case that I as a purely benign or innocent agent confront a situation of pain or disorder in which I have absolutely no part. And in the light of this, I see that the action required of me must flow from a truthful attention to a point of view that is not my own – not from a morally over-ambitious desire to be innocent or virtuous. I must learn to inhabit in my imagination a self other than myself, a subject over against me that is aware of itself as suffering or sinful or simply in need of nurture and help. This awareness about my context opens up for me as I gain a truthful perspective on the fact that 'I' as an individual live with a pre-existing 'moral deficit', a solidarity in sin – the 'lack of the glory of God' that Barth speaks of.[12] As soon as I acknowledge candidly where I stand and own my illusion-driven attempts to position myself as an independent centre of unchallengeable and unrelated claims, I begin to see obliquely how my inextricable involvement with the other might be a vehicle of life rather than death – how the subject over against me is in fact inseparably bound up with me for both life and death. And this comes most clearly into focus in the narrative of Christ's gratuitous embrace of humanity in an act of divine solidarity, and in the reality of a solidarity in 'communion' within the believing community – the governing theme of so much of Bonhoeffer's earlier theological work.[13]

In this context, I am able to experience solidarity as life-giving instead of life-draining. I know that I am inseparably bound in to the patterns of life-draining relation, self-oriented and protective, that I encounter around me; but I also know that both I and whatever other I encounter are together already affirmed and embraced by God through Jesus Christ. In Christ's incarnation, God has denied that there is any gap between God's own divine will and the peace, absolution and transfiguration of human beings. God is identified with what humans most deeply want and hope for. So for the Christian believer, the starting point of ethical action is a handing over to Christ of all my individual aspirations, my moral ambition, my self-images of abstractly 'good' behaviour; I simply identify with Christ's commitment to the healing of the other. In practice, this may involve me in complex and compromising decisions (like Bonhoeffer's own affiliation with the group planning Hitler's assassination). I shall not be able to appeal to some abstract verdict on the unqualified goodness of my actions. To defer action until I am certain of such a verdict is to abandon responsibility. And it is worth saying here that Bonhoeffer is emphatically not arguing that some general sentiment of love is what makes actions ethically good; that would be another way of guaranteeing a positive verdict, being able to know comfortably what is good in a specific situation. It would reintroduce the greedy self-dramatizing ego that wants to know how good it is. Bonhoeffer is saying that a serious and self-forgetful attention to the urgency of what we encounter is the vehicle for allowing into the situation something of God's unqualified and unflinchingly faithful presence. Human solidarity, taking responsibility for the other and acting 'representatively', acting as if from the heart of the other's own need and deepest desire, is within the finite world the imperfect but necessary vehicle of God's solidarity with creation.

This makes sense of a difficult and tantalizing passage in the *Ethics*[14] where Bonhoeffer is addressing the question of the distinction between 'ultimate' and 'penultimate' expressions of faith. The 'ultimate' is, we might say, the essence of faith, or the fulfilled culmination of a process of growing in faith. Must every expression of faith have this character? Or does faith have a real history, in which its expression is conditioned by what it is actually confronting in this specific moment? In other words, says Bonhoeffer, we are asking 'whether...the gospel can be extended in time, whether it can be expressed in the same way every time, or whether here, too, the ultimate differs from the penultimate.'[15] Bonhoeffer attempts to clarify the kind of question he is asking by describing the experience of accompanying someone in a 'serious' situation like bereavement, where we may respond in 'helpless solidarity' rather than by a confident declaration of the triumph of the resurrection or whatever. 'Why is my mouth often closed when it should give voice to the ultimate, and why do I opt for a thoroughly penultimate human solidarity?'[16] Perhaps, he suggests, this silent and inexplicit standing alongside may be a more faithful witness to the 'ultimate' in that it leaves God to 'speak in God's own time', rather than insisting on my own capacity here and now to transmit the Word of God directly and unambiguously. There is a tyranny of the 'ultimate' that wants to make the gospel the immediate and visible enemy of all worldly compromise, all the claims of the 'penultimate' (that is, the routine order of human relation and obligation); just as there is a tyranny in embracing compromise as a principle, on the grounds that the life of complete openness to grace has not yet arrived and we must not therefore expect too much of ourselves.[17] 'Neither radicalism nor compromise': the solidarity called for is born of an attention to the truth of the particular moment and its needs, and we can neither insist on a completely explicit proclamation in season or out of season, nor on a tired pragmatism. If we are silent, and so accept the 'penultimate', it is because we are trusting that God's solidarity precedes and undergirds our efforts to stand in solidarity. Pushing to articulate the ultimate in all circumstances might imply a confidence that we are so perfectly aligned with God's sovereign will that our words or acts will automatically be vehicles of that will. Accepting life in what seems to be the 'penultimate' frame of reference – in which the manifest presence of God is not insisted upon moment by moment – but accepting it in genuine faith that we are making a path for the divine solidarity to be more effective in the world, is an appropriate embodiment of responsibility and vicarious representation and humility before God's sovereign presence. We embrace and become answerable for the condition of the other – whether they have faith or not; we try to enter into where they stand in order to speak both with and for them, for their longing or their need.

2.

This language is a long way from most of what we have so far been discussing in this book. But it highlights an aspect of the understanding of solidarity that deserves serious exploration. Bonhoeffer is developing a theological theme whose origins lie in the earliest Christian literature. For Paul of Tarsus, writing in his letters to the churches of Rome and Corinth in the third quarter of the first Christian century, what was distinctively new in the life of Christian communities was the formation of a community in which any gift, skill, insight or whatever enjoyed by any one individual was given so as to enrich the lives of all in the community – and conversely, any loss, diminution or wound experienced by any member was a privation for all. Paul's imagery of the 'Body' for the Christian community echoes a commonplace in republican Roman political rhetoric,[18] but develops it a good deal further. It is not simply (as in the classical use of the metaphor) that subgroups within the social organism have diverse and equally necessary functions, but that each individual person within this organism both gives and receives life and capacity in a comprehensive process of exchange (I Cor.12.27 ff.). The process of building up the Body, understood as the Body of Christ, is a process in which 'Christ is formed' in each and in all (e.g. Gal.4.19, and cf. Eph.4.4–13). Each particular member, with their distinctive gift, becomes a channel for the divine creative and healing action to flow towards others; no individual therefore is dispensable within such an organism. Each particular member, created in the image of God, comes to realize this image in a unique manner, mediating to others some aspect of divine life/gift. Each therefore deserves unconditional honour as a vehicle for such a gift. In its context, Paul's elaboration of the organic metaphor is a fusion of the classical language of the body politic with a more distinctively Jewish interest in the active vocation of all members of God's people, touched by and empowered by the divine Spirit (e.g. Num.11.29) so as to be a community collectively exercising royal liberty and priestly mediation (Ex.19.6, picked up in Christian usage in I Peter 2.9).

This is the root of Bonhoeffer's schema. If this is the nature of the connection between persons in the Body of Christ, we are answerable for how every act and word and thought expresses the conviction that we are acting, speaking and thinking on behalf of the neighbour in the community; the issue of their healing and well-being is the centre of our understanding of who we are and what we are to do. We 'represent' the other not by replacing their agency with our own, not by assuming the right to act *instead of* them, but by committing ourselves to acting *from where they stand*, along with them, sharing their point of orientation in the world, being 'at' this point, in Edith Stein's language – seeing the world from their position, and grasping that, while this is an alien place for us to stand, we must inhabit this strange place in order for us to be at home with our *own* calling. We are ourselves in and only in this deep imaginative displacement in which we refuse to see the world only as it relates to our individual or partial construction of it and our own individual or partial agenda for it. As we shall see, this is particularly material for how we understand the business of shared labour, in which (recalling Jozef Tischner's idea of labour as 'conversation'[19]) our solidarity is actualized in the process of sustaining meaningful and purposive action together. Labour is impossible if we are not capable of imagining the perspective of a physical other. But more immediately, it opens on to a significant further insight – that in the 'imagined community' of the Body of Christ, in the theological projection of a form of human life together that is maximally at the disposal of divine agency, I am perpetually seeking to stand in the place of another *who is at some level equally committed to standing with the other* (potentially *including* myself, but not at all necessarily *beginning* with myself; this is not simply a neat exchange of individual benefits). Each, we might say, becomes the 'guardian' or 'trustee' of the individual security and affirmation that every other is in the process of leaving behind or bracketing out in the labour of serving the healing of their own neighbour. More simply, each of us takes responsibility for the safety that the other is called to sacrifice. But – and here is the most significant implication – whether or not the other is *in fact* committed to this displacing of the self, my obligation remains – to stand where they stand, to shelter and serve their vulnerability so as to release them to act for others; to seek to act 'from' that point of the neighbour's reality as if my own interest were at stake. I do not act on their behalf as a way of rewarding them for their moral reliability or their participation with me in an agreed common task or common vision, but because their sheer presence puts me under obligation. Yet when I do act from that point of identification with the neighbour, it is still emphatically *I* who act, with the specific gifts given to me and no one else. I exhibit care for the other by putting my gift at their disposal; I thus come to exercise what is most distinctively mine in the act of care for the other's life and flourishing. And of course in the entire economy of such action, it is finally God through Christ and the Spirit who is acting – actualizing in successive circumstances the focal act by which redemption is won, the act of gratuitous identification with the need and hope of the other.

This is, incidentally, a pattern that suggest some strong complementarities with Tischner's bold language in *The Philosophy of Drama*[20] about the experience of 'being a burden for someone' and 'to have someone as a burden'. When a question is asked by one subject of another, says Tischner, the one questioned assumes a 'burden', a responsibility to speak in a way that is not conditioned simply by their own stance. And the question is intelligible only if the *questioner* has also already in some sense assumed a burden in finding words that I can understand in order to ask the question in the first place. Questioner and questioned come to share a world, a history; and they also share a kind of 'liberation'. 'I am myself when you are a burden to me, and when you are my liberation, because you truly are that too. When I met you, I felt liberated in some degree. From what? From whom? Perhaps from my own thoughts, maybe from another I that followed me like a shadow? The experience of burden-lightness is very important.' [21]

Bonhoeffer in his last months in prison was becoming increasingly conscious that the courageous resistance to the legal enactments of the Third Reich that he had encouraged in his earlier ministry was still, in spite of every good intention, an exercise in collective *self*-protection.[22] Above all – though he does not say this quite explicitly – the Church's resistance maintained on the whole an unpardonable embarrassed silence in respect of atrocities against the Jews. The most challenging implication of the model with which Bonhoeffer is working is that if we are genuinely 'displacing' ourselves for the sake of the other within the Body of Christ, we cannot make our displaced identification, our solidarity, dependent on being able to recognize in the other exactly the same commitment that (we hope) is in us. The failure to defend, to 'represent', the genuinely other – in this case, the Jew – is a failure in manifesting the solidarity that exists not only in our humanity as such but more deeply in the identity between all human creatures as those *with whom God has chosen to be*. Clinging on to a set of criteria for recognizing the 'deserving' other, so to speak, is to slip back into reducing the other to one who can comfortably be reduced to sameness. And as such it is a refusal of real displacement, and ultimately, for Bonhoeffer, a refusal of God's choice of unconditional embrace of this other: *my* criteria, *my* conditions, are still at work, so that the truly alien other is excluded – so that the radical identification of Christ with any and every other is not being allowed to work through my action.

And this in turn means that I shall not be acting in fully responsible or representative mode, and so not aligning with the defining movement or rhythm of the work of God in Christ; I shall be at odds with the saving work of God.

In brief, identification in faith with the action of God in Christ always has the possibility of being an identification with the stranger, not a solidarity based on obvious common interests or common culture – even religious culture. Hence Bonhoeffer's final moves (in his letters from prison) in the direction of a discourse about Christianity freed from 'religion', in the sense of a system among rival systems – an aspect of his thought still much discussed and much contested.[23] It is as if solidarity is given both in nature and in grace 'at an angle' to all human efforts at self-definition: just as God creates the human world in a condition of irreducible interdependence, so God renews and heals the world by 'activating' that interdependence in ways and in places that are thoroughly opaque to human explanation or expectation. And God does so, in a focally embodied way, through the incarnation of Christ, in virtue of which God affirms, takes hold of and commits to an ensemble of human histories, more or less deeply flawed, characterized at different times and in different contexts by both faith and faithlessness.

For our present purpose, the most salient point here is the emergence of something like the 'solidarity without enemies' that Tischner speaks of. A solidarity that is given by God, through the gratuitous act of identification with flawed humanity, cannot by definition be vulnerable to the contingencies of whether or not this or that other or group of others satisfies the conditions for recognition that we want to lay down. We always come too late for this; we are implicated before we have any choice. If God identifies with all of us, then we are identified with God; if God is identified with those who are radically different from us – culturally, morally, religiously, whatever – so are we. If in the light of this we consciously embrace solidarity as a 'policy' in our moral (and thus social and political) world, we are set free from the compulsion to imagine solidarity as a loyalty to those we judge to be adequately like us. We are opening ourselves to be vehicles of the divine 'loyalty' to creation as a whole, a solidarity that begins from the total *unlikeness* between finite and infinite life and between unchanging divine holiness and the historically evolving and spiritually uneven lives of finite moral agents, the unlikeness that is overridden by the divine act of assuming representative identification in the incarnation.

So when Bonhoeffer writes of the 'helpless solidarity' that accompanies the one with whom I have no Christian vocabulary in common, and when he castigates the anti-Nazi Confessing Church for ultimately defending only its own, both themes have their origin in the basic conviction that the territory of solidarity has been mapped for us by God's action in advance as a territory in which boundaries are always suspect. As we have noted, Bonhoeffer's argument for our universal responsibility is not an impossible demand for an absolutely homogeneous universal compassion, nor for the unqualified 'abjection' of the self against which Gillian Rose warns so pungently. Of course our experience of realizing and acting upon solidarity will be *first* a summons to the immediate neighbour in the context of work or family or social bonding – themes central to much of the *Ethics* texts. But beginning from the particular is not the same as a principled refusal to cross frontiers; our 'unlimited' call to solidarity, representation, responsible standing in for and standing with the other, is a matter of understanding that what will call us to solidaristic action cannot be restricted in advance to circumstances we shall be able to understand, circumstances where we can grasp what it is that might *justify* solidarity. We must let go of any confidence that we shall be called alongside people like us. Not only do we already belong with them within the ecology of the whole creation – so that we are not ourselves without them – we must be ready to activate that belonging whenever and wherever we encounter the denial of the other's humanity. I do not have to strain my imagination to feel an unlimited guilt or an unlimited liability for the good of every subject in the world; rather, I need to have, in every contingency that I encounter, a simple readiness to stand with the vulnerable other in an identification that is above all an outworking of the limitless readiness of God in Christ to embrace human life.

3.

And non-human life? There is admittedly not a great deal here about solidarity with the entirety of our environment.[24] This, we may say, is up to a point fair enough: the focus of the argument is very much bound up with the conscious attention that is required in human interaction, and the very specific problems of recognizing the human other in a context where cultural pressures are pushing so strongly against such recognition. In the early 1940s, it is understandably a more immediate priority for a writer like Bonhoeffer to acknowledge and honour the human other, the Jewish other above all, but also the Roma and disabled and homosexual other, dehumanized by the state's policies, than to turn too rapidly to the honouring of the claims of the non-human environment. Bonhoeffer stands close to Tischner in this. Both of them speak out of the very particular historical urgency around the claims of solidarity over against totalitarianism. But the logic of the argument can hardly be arrested at the frontiers of the human race. If the actual tangible form of solidarity has something to do – as St Paul so clearly indicates[25] – with the fact that the exchange of life is fundamental to the *entire* created order, then the embrace or affirmation of humanity is also an embrace of what makes humanity human, and so of the material and animal world as much as the social or cultural. I am summoned to responsibility for this whole network of life within which I exist as an inseparable element, recognizing that my service in and to this wider network is an aspect of my service to the human world and vice versa. I am serving what gives me life so that life may be given in turn to what is other to this particular other with whom I am now engaged. And so, recursively, cyclically or spirally, world without end. I give so that another may give – but not necessarily directly to me, even if the giving I enable is indeed *ultimately* another element in what makes me alive.

What holds together the call of the human other and the non-human other is – following Bonhoeffer's own logic – the fact that both alike have been already 'embraced' or 'affirmed' by God. This language is, of course, not what most would call precise. And although complete precision is not easily to be found in this area, it could perhaps be spelled out further. Briefly: the other (human or not) that I encounter, this specific cluster or intelligible field of presence, is already related, independently of its relation to me, to an infinite agency that is at work in both the sheer thereness of this specific substance, and in its particular concrete or active form. In the simplest possible terms, what it *is* does not depend on me – even if, mindful of the perspectives of quantum theory, we can rightly say that it would not have its specific present mode of intelligible action without my participation. The recognition of it *as other* is the recognition that it is related to more than myself. I do not exhaust its possibilities. It resists the totalizing ambitions of my will. If I approach it on the assumption either that I *am* capable of exhausting its possibilities, or that whatever possibilities it has that are not relevant to me may safely be ignored, overridden or destroyed, then I fail to see it truthfully – and at the same time fail to see myself truthfully.[26] I give permission for both human and non-human others to be reduced to their role in regard to myself, and so come to imagine myself as essentially the site of a particular bundle of determinate needs for which I seek determinate satisfactions from a set of determinate, atomized providers in the 'outside' world.

But if the world is a system within which every identifiably distinct cluster or pattern of agency is a 'carrier' of divine agency, there is no possibility of either subject or object being comprehensively reduced to a set of localized needs and functions. What makes them alive and active is an inexhaustible source, underlying and giving cohesion to the entire network of exchanging life and exchanging information that is the intelligible universe. For the religious believer, especially in the Jewish, Christian or Muslim worlds of reference, the fact of this inexhaustible, sustaining and pervading action is identified with divine love, the diffusion of life and enjoyment throughout the finite world as a reflection of the unchanging and unconditioned bliss that is intrinsic to divine life. Or, once again to put it as simply as possible: what we encounter is always already loved – brought gratuitously into being, sustained in life, intuitively and comprehensively known or seen; and loved. Different religious vocabularies concentrate on different elements in this overall picture. As we have seen, a committedly Protestant theologian like Bonhoeffer reads outwards, so to speak, from the fact of God's identification with humanity in the human life of Jesus, and so is able to give his account of solidarity a very distinctive slant towards our call to identification with a history of guilt and woundedness. Christians of a different tradition lay more emphasis on the primordial fact of God's act as creator, in which God imparts to the finite order the possibility of manifesting something of the divine and eternal intelligibility. This is the idea of the *Logos* that is definitively embodied in Jesus, but is also present in every finite structure. The idea of the universe as a system of manifested *logoi*, interlocking intelligible and animating structures held together in the eternal *Logos* is characteristic of some significant strands in Byzantine theology, especially the thought of the seventh-century Maximus the Confessor.[27] Jewish thought approaches the theme through meditation on the diffusion of 'Wisdom', 'Glory' or 'Presence', the *Shekinah* of God, within the world, most dramatically in the Kabbalistic tradition of the primordial 'shattering of the vessels' through which the eternal glory is fractured and scattered within creation, waiting for the righteous to restore it to where it belongs – 'reconciling the glory that is above with the glory that is below', in one formulation – by their actions of love and justice towards God and creation.[28] Islamic philosophy has in recent decades appealed to the Qur'anic language of *mizan*, 'balance', as the foundation for a Muslim ethic of environmental interdependence, as well as the traditional insistence on sole divine sovereignty (so that humanity has no authority finally to determine the functions of other life forms in creation).[29]

In all of these discourses, the world of finite substances is imagined as a world of interconnected and interacting 'nodes' of divine agency, points of convergence or intersection within a cosmic network of interrelation. Each identifiable subject is a vehicle for divine purpose and so arises from the single and unchanging act of the self-sharing of God's life. The world is not a system of uncomfortably adjusted atoms or monads, but of particular 'points of orientation' – to borrow again from Edith Stein's language[30] – whose ultimate identity lies in the (always partial, always re-workable) actualizing of a field of possible structure and meaning in a way that generates further possibilities. Each of these is the object of love in the sense that they are understood both as recipients of creative gift and vehicles to others of creative gift.

In such a light, the final ground of 'solidarity' is simply the reality of a manifold, always pre-existing, interaction between the lives of finite beings; and since such interaction between *human* finite subjects naturally includes what is distinctive about them – the activities of language and intelligent labour – we can see that our human life is unavoidably a 'culture', a matter of collaboratively created meaning. This is true whether or not we acknowledge it or consciously work with the grain of it. But if we do focus more directly and consciously on the idea that what we encounter is always already not only seen but loved, then solidarity shifts from being simply a foundational fact in our constitution as finite substances to being a *vocation*; the appropriate, the 'just', response to encounter with the other is a faithful commitment to the life and fulfilment of what is encountered. 'Justice' in such a context *is* love. The truthful perception of what we encounter is the loving perception.[31] Whether this is theologically spelled out in terms of the incarnational embrace of a wounded and compromised world that Bonhoeffer stresses, or the 'cosmic architecture' of Maximus the Confessor, the ultimate direction of imaginative travel is the same: we are summoned to stand in the place of the neighbour – human or not, familiar or not, deserving or not – as the natural expression of the underlying pattern of the world itself, whereby each lives in, from, and for the life of the other. The deepest structure of the finite world is just this consistent exchange; the ethical life is the deliberate representation of such consistency in the form of moral faithfulness (to echo Tischner's emphasis), the displacement of a central and autonomous ego, a commitment to the life of the other, an imaginative engagement with that otherness so as to avoid the anxious imperialism by which we seek to reduce it to what we want or what we can cope with.

All of this locates the language of solidarity within a context that is very definitely not limited by the idea of 'common interest'; it works with an assumption, not only of human recognizability – the issue from which we began – but of the moral recognizability of an entire field of encountered objects and embodied lives. No element in this field is divorced from moral claim, from the presupposition that there is at every point a node or focal point of agency that has a proper ('just') claim to attention, respect, care. This does not mean that we are surrounded by a chaotic plurality of conflicting individual rights (the sort of issue that has led to agonizedly complex – and sometimes faintly absurd – legal discussion about what sort of rights ascribed to non-human agents might be enforceable in court). It simply affirms two things about what we encounter – that each element contributes significantly to the whole (an empirically straightforward matter, more and more so as ecological science advances), and that each element is both object and channel of love – i.e. of some energy that responds with affirmation and joy to what is there, and that also itself bestows life, and the steadily fuller fruition of life ('well-being' is sadly and paradoxically a rather tired term these days). We may very well still be faced with difficult and conflicted choices about how all this is to be honoured, but what matters is the imperative not to satisfy a series of atomized demands but to reflect and act upon the need to sustain a life-giving and self-renewing balance of exchange in any environment. The balance of the system within which we live is constantly readjusting itself (not always rapidly or easily); the question for the consciously deliberating agent is not how to avoid disturbance of an existing balance but how to avoid long-term distortion of or depletion of whatever resources within a particular ecology best allow it to rebalance and regenerate.[32] Not a simple task and not guaranteed success in the social environments we are most familiar with.

But to configure solidarity itself in this perspective may be helpful. Throughout our investigation of its many contexts and senses, we have noted from time to time the concerns expressed by some that the notion may be regressive or static, simply a matter of registering and conserving a shared identity. But what if solidarity is the labour of repeatedly 'readjusting' to others, responding to growth and change, more than an affirmation of what already is? We've seen how the theological perspectives outlined in this chapter lead us into more reflection on active solidarity as an act of boundary-crossing, the discovery of some sort of continuity and mutuality in relation to what is strange. Bonhoeffer's incarnation-centred model rests upon the story of divine agency 'embracing' the places where it is apparently/functionally absent, embracing 'godlessness'. Acting in solidarity then becomes in an important sense an act of faith: trust that the environment we inhabit is comprehensively held in and pervaded by grace – however we understand such a word – and trust that faithful engagement and attention will reveal the possibility of convergent lines of fulfilment and mutual gift, despite the immediacy of conflict. The labour that goes into this discovery is certainly not without tension, even confrontation: we are not thinking about a frictionless and rapid assimilation of radically different interests. But – to pick up the term that has been around in some of our earlier discussion – the prospect of a 'labour' that will change all our existing accounts of identity, interest, agenda and so on continues to provoke us to hope. The theological perspective proposes a view from both beginning and end – both 'protological' and 'eschatological' in the jargon of theology. There is something at the roots of our finite existence that is inescapably communal and mutual; and there is something at the end of all our history that secures reconciliation without dominance, without cancellation of one by another, without the triumphant silencing or occluding of some elements/agents in the finite world by others. Like other imaginings of beginnings and endings, this is not something that philosophy itself can generate or vindicate; but the philosopher can at least trace some of what it is in an imagined larger framework that might make sense of acts or policies of solidarity – some of what would count as grounding the hope and the presupposition of the ways in which we try to locate ourselves 'at the point of' another's world of experience (or even 'at the point of' the life forms of the non-human world). In other words, the philosopher is not in a position to conclude to, or to justify claims about such a framework; but they can explore how exactly the framework supplies the context in which this or that course of action would seem desirable, natural, imperative and so on.

With regard to another theme that has recurred in our discussions, there is more to say about the question of 'common labour', and we shall be coming back later to this; but at the present point we might signal the issue of what it is that *prompts* or *generates* this common labour. The simplest immediate answer is, obviously, common need: we know, as soon as we engage with our world with any degree of reflectiveness that if we act purely as individuals we have no chance of securing what we need, even at the most basic level, since as humans we live through a long latency period when we are radically dependent on the care of others. Our emergence as reflective subjects and linguistic subjects is under way well before we can claim any adequate capacity to provide for ourselves physically. We are inducted into cultures as soon as we are spoken to or even gestured to; and in this process we are invited, even before we can effectively contribute any major modification to the cultural world to which we are being acclimatized, into the joint work of cultural construction in our own handling of meaning and symbol together, as we become familiar with increasingly sophisticated and resourceful language systems. Shared labour is built in to the process of maturation and individuation. We cannot build an intelligible world without depending on the labour of others – material, imaginative, intellectual, emotional – and our labour is required to sustain and extend that world. It is impossible to conceive a wholly passive relation to 'culture': any intelligible action, including speech itself, changes what is possible or thinkable to some extent. Intelligently receiving what comes to us from outside is always an act of 'editing', of screening and adapting. To recognize the omnipresence of culture-building is to recognize the invitation to a variety of forms of common labour. In the context of the theological discussions touched on in this chapter, it becomes clear that, if the life of 'redeemed solidarity' envisaged by Bonhoeffer and others – the fully released and life-giving mutuality in which human and non-human interaction is maximally life-giving – is to be actual, it cannot be imagined as something that makes no claim on our capacity to work with others – as simply some kind of pure divine bestowal. This is not in the least to deny the priority of the gratuitous divine act of release as the sole source of the renewed culture in which we are to live; it simply acknowledges that, *as* a culture, it will still involve continuous, conscious, attentive, co-operative agency; what some early monastic writers call digging over the soil of the heart.[33]

Before we return to the issue of 'work' and solidarity in our concluding reflections, the next chapter will be examining some other strands in theology that echo or enlarge some of what this chapter has highlighted. How far, for example, can we take the idea of 'standing in for' the other? It is a common trope in more than one story of modern martyrdom; in what sense is it also a psychological and spiritual element in the activity of prayer for another? And when the language of 'communion' is used in theology, how far does it coincide with 'solidarity'? Does it add anything? We noted earlier[34] Joanna Bourke's fleeting allusion to 'communion' as a deeply ingrained human desire, always existing in a precarious balance with the necessary recognition of real otherness. Bourke's argument (about which there will be more to say in the next chapter) seems to be that anything that could claim to be a 'just' response to the diversity of the world will acknowledge but will not absolutize difference; and her use of 'communion' in this context may give a clue as to how the theological senses of the word might be of some illumination here.

This chapter has attempted to bring Bonhoeffer – and with him a variety of voices and traditions within Judaeo–Christian discourse – into some sort of conversation with the broader philosophical currents discussed earlier in this book. It will, I hope, have shown the continuities as well as the differences, continuities that should not be surprising, given that so many of those we have discussed – notably Stein and Tischner – were entirely familiar with the theological world, and even those who were less so, or less sympathetically so, like Patočka, were nonetheless marked by particular narratives of intellectual and imaginative history that had been shaped by theology. Focusing on Bonhoeffer allows us to bring into focus a quite complex – often far from wholly clear – approach to the encounter between religious and non-religious understandings of solidarity, marked by the acute personal and political pressures of Bonhoeffer's own circumstances, yet rooted in his own most distinctive theological preoccupations. Undoubtedly his most starkly 'confessional' and unphilosophical affirmation is that the world – including the entire world of human suffering and failure and betrayal – is embraced by divine love in advance of and independently of any particular human interaction with it. It is what it is in relation to something completely and without qualification beyond human subjectivity. This fundamental insistence allows Bonhoeffer to sketch a notably challenging version of solidarity, grounded in the idea that the divine life itself is characterized by the embrace of otherness. The greatest ontological distinction that could be conceived (between absolute and relative existence) is thought through not in terms of uncrossable distance, but in terms of the irrelevance of any and all specific distance and distinction. Transcendence is not the *absence* or *distance* of the holy or the ultimate from the immediate and conditioned, but the *freedom* of the holy or the ultimate to live and act within any and every aspect of the contingent world – a freedom defined in and by the identification of Christ with sinful humanity. God is more different from the world than any concept or model could capture; and just because this difference is different from any other difference, it is always 'overcome' by the divine will for *koinonia*, sharing and identification. But in making sense of this in relation to what is demanded of us in 'solidaristic' action, we are starkly reminded of the cost to any surviving myths about our own freedom from involvement and interdependence; we are summoned to let go of our attachment to our own clearly demarcated moral or ideological territory. And this, for Bonhoeffer, meant inhabiting the difficult space of being willing to hold back from what could be prematurely explicit use of Christian language for the sake of a fully transforming identification, an appropriate solidarity, with the stranger.

This is a theology of solidarity that – with a degree of conscious irony – mandates a marked reticence about its own theological foundations, and it remains one of Bonhoeffer's most challenging and tantalizing contributions to an ongoing reflection on solidarity in general. As the next chapter will suggest, it is not the whole story of how the discourse of solidarity affects and is affected by theological themes; but it suggests that any theologically informed approach to solidarity from a Christian background needs to weigh the importance of what we have been calling 'displacement' – not a simple self-cancelling, not even a habit of ascetically preferring another's good to one's own, but a profound reimagining of what and where 'selfhood' is. As we shall see, it offers some crucially clarifying insights in reading other religiously inspired accounts.

EIGHT

Solidarity, Co-inherence, Communion

1.

Around the same time that Bonhoeffer was formulating his ideas in Germany, a very idiosyncratic English thinker was advancing a thesis about solidarity with both striking parallels to and striking divergences from his continental contemporary. Charles Williams (1886–1945) was a poet, novelist and critic, a man with virtually no formal higher education, author of numerous essays and books on Christian history and thought, including studies of Dante; a close friend of C. S. Lewis and his Oxford circle, a correspondent of T. S. Eliot, W. H. Auden, Dorothy Sayers and many other literary figures with theological interests. His complex and tormented emotional life has been much discussed;[1] and his ideas have tantalized and inspired generations of Christian readers. In some respects a theological genius, he left a legacy of immensely complex theoretical and mythical patterns in his writing, both literary and religious, and considerable debate persists about the multiple ambiguities, oral and intellectual, of these patterns.

Basic to his imaginative engagement with the issue of solidarity is a set of narratives to do with the early Church. In a work published just before the Second World War, *The Descent of the Dove; A Short History of the Holy Spirit in the Church*,[2] Williams points to a narrative from second-century North Africa in which Felicitas, the enslaved companion of an aristocratic young woman named Perpetua, condemned to death as a Christian along with her mistress, is mocked by some of her fellow-prisoners as she endures a painful childbirth in prison before execution. How will she face the even worse tortures of the arena? Her reply is that in her martyrdom, 'another will be in me who will suffer for me, as I shall suffer for him'.[3] Williams broadens out the focus of this poignant narrative to unite it with texts from Clement of Alexandria[4] and the fourth-century Desert Fathers[5] about giving our lives for one another and 'putting one's soul in the place of the neighbour's' so as to suffer for the neighbour as the neighbour would – 'to become, if it were possible, a double man'.[6] More simply, there is the well-known saying of St Antony the Great that 'your life and your death are with your neighbour'.[7]

For Williams, this lays the foundations for a wide-ranging reading of the evolution of Christian imagination as a series of variations on the theme of 'exchange', the various ways in which, according to his reading, Christianity returns to the central affirmation that it is possible not only to recognize the pain of another but in some sense to make it one's own within the shared experience of the 'Mystical Body', the Church, in a relation that he calls 'co-inherence'.[8] This theme – repeatedly seen, embodied, corrupted, lost, parodied, throughout Christian history – is, he says, what is alluded to by Dante in his conversation with Folco of Marseilles in the ninth Canto of the *Paradiso*. It is a complex idea: Dante recognizes that in heaven the happiness and vision of each breeds and kindles happiness in others, because that happiness is participating directly in God's own bliss and so enables each to see in some measure as God sees. Dante, speaking to Folco as a fellow-poet, wonders why, when he can see or sense Folco's bliss, he still cannot fully share it. As he has already recognized, for those still on pilgrimage through their earthly lives, there is still a 'shadow' between selves; they have not yet come to inhabit each other fully as they inhabit and are inhabited by God:

'God sees,' I said, 'all things, and your own sight,
you happy souls, in-hims itself in him
so no desire can steal away from you.

> Why, then, does not your voice (which so delights
> these spheres with that same song from holy fires
> who make themselves a hood of six great wings)
>
> bring my desires the satisfaction due?
> If I in-you-ed myself in you as you in-me
> I would not still await what you might ask.'[9]

Dante does creative violence to the Italian language in those awkward verbs (*inluia, intuassi, inmii*)[10] so as to evoke the action by which self comes to be in the other – in God, but also in the human other, in the ideal relation that characterizes the heavenly vision of God and, simultaneously, the fulfilled life of the Christian community, the Body of Christ. Williams connects it with the whole theory of 'romantic love' that he ascribes to Dante: 'the recurrent image of this in-meing and in-theeing is the eyes of the Florentine girl [Beatrice].'[11] Without going into the intricacies of Williams' reading of Dante and his entire theology of romantic love – a singularly complex area – it is clear enough that *The Descent of the Dove* makes a strong case for the idea of exchange and even 'substitution' as one of the focal and distinctive novelties in the Christian worldview. In his earlier work in poetry and fiction, he had regularly explored these ideas, insisting that the exchange of life was fundamental to 'the City', to any durable and intelligible social order. In one of the poems in his sequence *Taliessin Through Logres*,[12] Williams picks up and adapts the phrase from Heraclitus that also helped to shape some of the imagery of T. S. Eliot's *Four Quartets* about 'dying each other's life, living each other's death' as the principle of the universe's harmony, and thus of social or interpersonal communion also. And several of the novels, most notably and unambiguously *Descent Into Hell* in 1937, dramatize the possibility of very directly assuming the suffering or terror of another person. *Descent Into Hell* includes a lengthy chapter entitled 'The Doctrine of Substituted Love,' in which the playwright Peter Stanhope – a rather transparent avatar of the author – explains to a troubled young woman, Pauline, that the scriptural injunction to 'bear one another's burdens' is not a metaphor for 'listening sympathetically, and thinking unselfishly, and being anxious about, and so on'.[13] It is actually a matter of carrying something for someone else as one might carry a parcel: 'If you give a weight to me, you can't be carrying it yourself.' 'The law of the universe,' he claims is that you must give up your burden and carry someone else's.[14] As the book's plot unfolds, it becomes clear that this process can act backwards in time, not only between contemporaries; Pauline finds herself able to 'carry' the terror of an ancestor condemned to be burned at the stake, and a lonely young man who has committed suicide some decades earlier is liberated from the state of frozen bafflement and disorientation that has followed death by the substitutionary love of Pauline's dying grandmother. As we shall see later on, this idea of a retrospective solidarity has some implications for thinking about how we imagine our relation with past agents – with our history, individual and collective.

The theme is developed further in Williams' last novel, *All Hallows' Eve*,[15] with an even more extravagantly complex plot, involving magical ceremonies and a retrospective saving substitution exercised this time by a dead person on behalf of a living one. The connection with romantic love is a good deal less dominant here (though by no means wholly absent) – less dominant, certainly, than in his brilliant and startling little book, on the Incarnation, *He Came Down From Heaven*;[16] or rather, it is easier to see how for Williams' romantic love has become not so much a supreme embodiment of the process of 'exchange', the 'substitution' of one subject for another, as a focal and illuminating crystallization of this process of mystical substitution; a key to unlocking a broader theme, rather than the heart of the argument itself. Paul Fiddes, in his excellent discussion of the unfolding of these ideas, looks at how the language of co-inherence develops in Williams' work, and argues that the use of the actual term 'co-inherence' comes only quite late in his writing. The word is borrowed from his reading of a book on early Christian theology, where it is used to describe the life of the divine Trinity.

Each divine person or agent (Father, Son, Holy Spirit) exists only in and through the lives of the others; each is who/what it is in virtue of the others having – so to speak – renounced any independence, any assertion or defence of an autonomous 'self' so as to let the others be. So for Williams, this divine archetype of mutual gift and mutual surrender of defences now comes into focus as the ultimate theological rationale for his idea of 'substitution': the work of grace within the community of believers is something that steadily erodes our unwillingness to be affected by the need of others and intensifies our capacity to offer life-giving love to others – and, most specifically, to offer them a release from whatever most oppresses them by volunteering to bear their burdens. By the time of the last novels, certainly, Williams is pointing his readers more explicitly to classical theological themes, drawing rather more directly than before on a doctrinal vocabulary, and his brief 1941 essay on 'The Way of Exchange' is unusually explicit about this doctrinal anchorage: the substitutionary pattern and the movement of mutual indwelling is the 'overspill' in creation of God's eternal relational life in which believers together participate.[17]

Alongside all this, it must be mentioned that Williams' personal practice incorporated these ideas in some very problematic forms. He involved himself in a succession of intense if unconsummated affairs with younger women, with whom he enacted various rituals of a vaguely sado-masochistic character.[18] One of the regular features of the spiritual apprenticeship to which these women were introduced was 'substitution'; they were invited to take on the suffering, anxiety or doubt of specific others. At least some others outside these exceptionally intimate relationships were laid under similar obligation: Williams, from around 1938/9, spoke and wrote a fair amount about the creation of a 'Company of the Co-inherence', dedicated to realizing the notions he had been developing in his theology, criticism and literary work. The principles governing this 'Company' or 'Order' were initially circulated to some close friends in 1939, and the overlap with what he was discussing in *The Descent of the Dove* is very clear, down to the citations that feature in the outline of the 'Order's principles included in the circulated document.[19] Several of these – *figlia del tuo Figlio*, 'another will be in me', becoming a 'double man', the insistence on the eternity of exchange and relation in the divine life of which created life is an image – are prominently flagged in *The Descent* as keys to understanding the novelty of the Christian vision. In his more ambitious or extravagant moments, Williams seems to have conceived of his Company as contributing to the spiritual warfare that he saw as underlying the international military conflicts of the years in which it was formed – an intangible force pushing back against the powers of disintegration, rivalry and hatred.

The ideal remained (remains) both elusive and ambiguous, and, as this last detail might suggest, there was a real risk of a rather melodramatic appeal to spiritual heroism. Williams is not unaware of the risks, but he was a compulsive mythologizer. To do him justice, he is careful to distinguish the 'substitution' he describes from anything like an intensified state of empathy, a strong feeling for another's pain. The 'carrying' of another's suffering was not envisaged as a transfer of *feelings*: for Williams, someone offering to exchange with a person facing acute agony (like Pauline's substitution, in *Descent Into Hell*, for her ancestor's terror at the prospect of being burned alive) might not actually *feel* anything much at all. The point is to relieve the sufferer by 'displacing' the pain, not literally experiencing it for them. This makes some attempt to avoid an obvious moral pitfall in the schema: someone's suffering is what it is in significant measure because they are the person they are and have been; and there might be something both arrogant and invasive about simply instructing them to 'hand it over' to another. But this is less of an issue if what is in view is primarily the *removal* of a burden rather than the *transfer* of a set of experiences from one subject to another. What this might look like in practice is not all that easy to tease out, but it would need, surely, to be at least something like promising to be alongside in facing the effects or consequences of another's extreme jeopardy, an action that informs the sufferer

SOLIDARITY, CO-INHERENCE, COMMUNION

that they are supported in a way that might/should release them from paralysing fear or anguish. In a very literal way, someone else is making themselves answerable for this. And – in a way that has some discernible echoes of Bonhoeffer – the person so relieved or liberated is in turn obliged to take up the burden of another, and so on, ad infinitum. Williams' structure can be read as restoring agency to the sufferer at least as much as relieving their situation.

Beyond this, however, is something much more intangible, involving an actual 'suspension' of another's agony. Williams would, I think, simply say that this operates at a level of spiritual interconnection that is simply not susceptible of measurement or proof, but that believers are encouraged to trust its possibility and nurture the dispositions that prepare us for it. But the problems do not wholly disappear by any means. Williams' direction to individuals to take up the burden of other specific individuals is the unmistakeable assumption of a spiritual authority that could be highly risky. It seems to operate almost randomly (and I think Williams rather takes it for granted that it does and should) and therefore without accountability for its effect on those undertaking it. It is alleged to work independently of any actual embodied relation between those involved in an 'exchange'. It implies that there is always a way out of a situation of pain or fear, and that refusing to 'hand it over' makes you complicit in your own suffering. The heady notion that each member of the Company – and in principle each member of the Church, and indeed of the human race – is equipped here and now to relieve the suffering of any imaginable other has the ultimate effect of making the solidarity that is envisaged curiously disembodied, a universal love that bypasses the historical and particular, and – to revert to a theme that has surfaced repeatedly in this book – bypasses the challenge of the 'labour' of solidarity. In fairness, it should be noted that Fiddes[20] draws attention to a passage where Williams seems to suggest a limit to the capacity of an ordinary human being to carry the actual *selfhood* of another. Pauline, in *Descent Into Hell*,[21] wonders whether she has overstepped a boundary in offering to 'learn the part' of another character. 'A god rather than she, unless she were inhabited by a god, must carry Adela herself, the god to whom baptism for the dead was made, the lord of substitution, the origin and centre of substitution.' But the possibility of this limit being overcome if someone is 'inhabited by a god', specifically the Christian God of trinitarian exchange and incarnational substitution, is left, tantalizingly, open, with a strong hint that this may indeed be the point to which we are moving. In Fiddes's discussion, this is a significant moment in Williams' development towards a final and theologically explicit scheme in which the practice of 'substituted love' is fully integrated into a vision of cosmic, 'co-inherent' equilibrium that embodies the divine life of interchange.

But this does not quite resolve the issue. The question remains of *what* exactly the nature of the exchange is: what is displaced and relocated in substitutionary and co-inherent love? Can we think of a sort of quantum of jeopardy, vulnerability, agony, that is simply to be outsourced, a reified bundle of emotion, even the entire bundle of emotion that accumulates in a whole life, the 'part' that another may, through the indwelling of divine grace, learn and assume? I don't think that is precisely what Williams has in mind; but the immensely powerful metaphor of exchanging burdens has pushed his insights about radical interdependence in a direction that (paradoxically) generates fantasies of control from a distance, and even of a kind of omnipotence in the face of what most insistently reminds us of our limitations – the uncontrollability of our environment and the injury that this inflicts, and the irreducible strangeness and otherness of the human other, not least in their pain.

2.
I have chosen to linger a bit further in theological territory here, and to spend some time on Williams, eccentric as he is, because his idiosyncratic scheme brings into focus both positive and negative aspects of the religious approach to solidarity. He offers a robust model of interconnection – and the obligations of interconnection –

grounded in a theology of the interconnection of the divine life itself, and thus pushes about as far as it will go the conviction that solidarity rests on a given state of affairs within reality itself. And he presents one way of glossing the language of 'responsibility' that Bonhoeffer and others utilize: our response to another's pain and jeopardy must begin from the assumption that this is both something that affects us (that it is not a totally unconnected phenomenon) and also something about which we are summoned to do something. Part of that 'doing something' is letting the sufferer know that we acknowledge them and acknowledge our implicatedness in their lives (they do not suffer alone or unwitnessed).

At the same time, his understanding of substitution and exchange highlights both the serious possibilities and the moral risks of an intensified understanding of solidarity in ways that may throw some light on the more practical questions of what action in solidarity may entail. As we have seen, saying to someone 'Give me your suffering' – in Williams' sense – may be a charged and ambivalent affair, because of its entanglement with the questions of power or advantage bound up in it, and the further danger of presenting oneself unequivocally and unself-critically as the saviour of the sufferer. This is difficult moral territory. But at the same time, there is something in the invitation that may also speak of the readiness to be exposed to risk alongside the sufferer. I am declaring that I shall think and behave *as if this were indeed* my situation, my jeopardy. This pain is not something from which I can stand apart, not something known simply as a phenomenon burdening another with whom I have no connection. There is a radical level of recognition here which may itself be of some transformative import. Williams' scheme may work almost as a thought experiment: how far could we imagine going in – let's say – carrying the cost of another's oppression, anguish, guilt, or whatever?

What is less useful in Williams' theories is the near-magical element of transferring the burden without remainder. But his complicated and not always consistent reflections on this at least illustrate some of the temptations that may be caught up in the assumption of responsibility as a dimension of solidarity. Williams can be read as illustrating the risk of what we earlier described as letting empathy do the work of solidarity. Although he does not see his 'substituted love' precisely as a *sharing* in someone else's feeling, the pattern of his thinking follows the logic of 'empathic' identification. What was yours is now mine, and so is no longer your problem. The healing or removal of the suffering has nothing to do with the work of understanding it — learning (we could say) not the 'part' but the actual language of the sufferer, so as to be able to hear it and respond to it in the work of conversation (including the distinctive kind of conversation represented by Bonhoeffer's 'helpless solidarity', a mute enduring of the company of the suffering other, without rushing to a solution that relieves my impatience, irrespective of whether or not it is actually effective for the other). In other words, Williams' theory underlines the danger of any language that seeks to appropriate the actual experience of another, and so clarifies the way in which purported empathy may simply express another distorted power relation.

Williams clearly assimilates his concept of 'co-inherence' to that of 'communion' in a more traditional vocabulary; both words refer to something more than just a deep 'togetherness', but point to an actual and foundational interdependence between agents in the world (and for Williams also between divine and human agents). Recall again the rather unexpected use of 'communion' by Joanna Bourke at the very end of her discussion of *What It Means To Be Human*,[22] where it is left without any gloss as to its meaning; but the whole of the paragraph ending with this reference to 'communion', the final paragraph of the book, gives a clue. Bourke draws together the argument of her book with a plea for us to be suspicious of strategies that 'flatten out' the world, and to embrace whatever helps us develop a subversive critique of 'identity politics'.[23] But this is not in the name of a radical or conflictual pluralism. Simple plurality does not have the last word; this is not a world of zero-sum games. We cannot live/speak without the appetite for that distinctive kind of certainty that is the affirmation of self by other, something that is in fact intrinsic to all effective exchanges of language. Yet a 'perfect' transparency, a mutuality without boundaries, would not be a mutuality at all. So we continue to negotiate our way between the respect for opacity and difficulty that Aruna D'Souza insists upon, and the hunger for a common stability, an 'anchored' sense of meaningfulness, that saves us from complacent tribalism. As Bourke puts it, we do not 'deify' other humans, or indeed other beings in general, but seek to locate them in a flesh and blood world that we share, 'with all its sufferings, joys, identifications and struggles'.[24] We affirm the shared knowledge we actually attain, but acknowledge its partiality and the unending pressure for it to be enlarged and revised. Bourke seems to understand 'communion' as the creative urge towards both crossing and holding open the space of difference. The juxtaposition of 'identifications and struggles' is telling: we are not presented with a tidy evolution towards frictionless social unity. But neither is this a landscape of disconnected *plural* enterprises. What is in view is a temporally extended process of understanding and misunderstanding, held together by a refusal to settle with any account of the environment of our living premised on wholly incommunicable, incommensurable or rivalrous pictures of hope and common good.

This mobile and critical understanding of 'communion' is an important qualification of any bland collectivism or idealizing of consensus. Like Gillian Rose's account of a communicative practice that develops through a series of critically acknowledged misrecognitions, it presents the common life of embodied speakers as a process of continuously learning how to live with the otherness of the other. The other is intrinsically neither an impenetrably alien enemy nor a disguised version of the self. Indeed, we could say that both of these fictions have the same root. If I see the other as always an enemy, I see the other as always competing for the same ground that I occupy; the central, perhaps the single, fact is my definition of that ground. When the other is reduced to the proportions of my selfhood – absorbed, assimilated – I am reassured that there is indeed no other place to stand than where I am. It is this, as we have seen, that is most radically contested by a model like that of Edith Stein, in which the necessary, irreducible alienness of the other's place/point of orientation is in fact the condition of my being able to identify a point where I myself stand. Such irreducible difference means that exchange will always be difficult and incomplete, that it will *take time*. But that taking of time allows learning; our skills as recognizing the risks of misrecognition develop – not towards an absolute mutual transparency, which would be impossible in relations between mobile and growing subjects, but towards a patient commitment to questioning and self-questioning, perhaps something like the 'apocalyptic patience' that Andrew Shanks analyses in his book of that title. At the conclusion of the book,[25] Shanks identifies the core problem we face in this as 'the impatient *will to feel innocent*'. It is, he says, a temptation for evangelist and philosopher alike, and it is essentially a variant of what other writers we have touched on – Bourke, D'Souza, Rose, Jamison, Tischner and others – see as the urge to occupy a place that is beyond question and beyond history, a place that has not evolved through conflict, imagination and labour, a place where things are *obvious*, and can only be thought of as true when they are thought of as obvious. Not a good recipe for 'conversational labour'.

So we are edged towards the rather paradoxical conclusion that 'communion' has something to do with the non-obviousness of truth – in the sense that truthfulness requires a continuously enlarging awareness of the strangeness of what is outside the ego. In more conventionally religious terms, it requires an openness to the uncontrolled character of 'grace', the unexpected and unbargained-for gift of new perception in our encounters. Anna Rowlands opens the final chapter of her study of Catholic Social Teaching, *Towards a Politics of Communion*, with a quotation from Charles Taylor: 'Communion has to integrate persons in their true identities, as bodily beings who establish their identities in their histories, in which contingency has a place.' She goes on to discuss the interpretation of the parable of the Good Samaritan offered by the radical theologian and educationalist, Ivan Illich, who challenges a blandly universalist reading of the story and insists on the particularity of this moment when compassion arises 'between a despised man and a wounded man', a man who is defined as a threatening alien and a man who has no agency or voice left because of the violence done to him. The 'scandalous fittingness' that now connects these two is both, for Illich, a reflection of the gratuitous solidarity between God and creation created by the incarnation of the divine Word in Jesus and a foretaste of the community of interdependent strangers created by the death and resurrection of Jesus. As in Bonhoeffer's theology, the realization that the stranger is a 'proper', fitting partner in solidarity, someone whose humanity is recognizable and whose condition is of immediate relevance, is what follows from the revelation that the stranger is always already embraced, whoever they are and whatever their condition, by a divine act of solidarity.

And this realization and revelation are not things that can be possessed and acted upon in a secure, unquestioned way; they need to be repeatedly renewed in the ever-changing contingencies of encounter. The history of both political and theological accounts of human society show with awkward clarity how putatively comprehensive or egalitarian language coexists with exclusivist practice until starkly challenged – from the Enlightenment rationalist untroubled by the slave trade, to the early twentieth-century liberal blithely recommending eugenics to eliminate 'inferior racial types', and the mid-twentieth-century radical oblivious to the male privilege embodied in the life of many would-be revolutionary networks. The modern history of Christian struggles over gender and sexual identity is familiar enough, alas. Societies and churches find themselves obliged to encounter not only strangers from elsewhere but strangers within, those whose voices have historically been ignored or actively suppressed. And the protests that resist such suppression are – in the perspective just sketched – acts of witness to 'communion', moments in a continuing struggle against misrecognition and the 'will to feel innocent'.

Taylor, in the same section of his book, *A Secular Age*,[26] that is quoted by Rowlands, notes the significant strand in early Christian thinking that sought to define the personal not in terms of individual agency or reasoning capacity but of 'being capable of communion'. In the light of our discussion thus far in the last few pages, we might say that this is to define the human person as capable of sustaining conversation over time. Communion is not primarily a static condition of unchanging harmony but an 'agonistic' matter, a struggle against the twin pressures of polarization and assimilation, never arriving within history at a secure settlement. And it has to do also with how we construct our histories and how we continue to re-read and re-shape those narratives. The familiar phrase in the Christian creed about believing in 'the Communion of Saints' is not just a matter of expressing confidence that we are invisibly accompanied by praying presences – though it is at least that – but a reminder that the labour of conversation goes on not only between contemporaries but with those who have spoken and interacted before us. Our 'communion' with the tradition we inherit is itself an exchange of a distinctive kind, not only a repetition, so that we neither assimilate the past to the present (thus obliterating the processes of historical learning) nor attempt to immerse ourselves completely in the language of the past (thus obliterating the specificity of the moment we actually inhabit and the unique network of relations in which we now stand). But adequately exploring this would be a longer story than there is room for here.

To return to some of the questions touched on earlier in relation to Charles Williams: his bold speculations about how substitutionary love could work backwards in time may, even for the sceptic, offer some perspectives about how we understand the past. It implies that, on the one hand, we encounter our forebears as strangers: their suffering, like their belief or hope, is simply not literally ours, and we need to recognize and respect that distance. Yet on the other hand, we are also constantly engaged in re-learning who they were, renewing them in our imagination, taking our stand alongside them *in* their strangeness rather than relegating them to another moral universe. Whether it is true (how could anyone know?) that our prayerful commitment, as Williams describes it, could somehow bring healing to a wounded past, there is some weight in the imperative of surrendering a dismissive and alienated superiority in respect of our ancestors, learning some kind of imaginative interaction with them. As we have more than once observed, Williams' ambition for an exchange without remainder of painful experiences between separate subjects highlights a stubborn difficulty in so much thinking about empathic imagination and its place in solidaristic practice. We risk lifting bundles of 'experience' out of their context as if they were commodities of some kind; we risk exposing ourselves to what we can neither comprehend nor bear (exactly how does a 'modern' subjectivity absorb or even 'carry' the state of mind of someone about to be tortured to death for their religious conviction in the way Williams narrates in *Descent Into Hell*, even granted his caution about treating this as the literal appropriation of another's feeling?). For a theologian, the relation between the present Christian subject and the faithful departed is indeed one in which there can be a reciprocal difference made: prayer for the departed and prayer *by* the departed, especially the conspicuously holy departed, is held to open the door to some deeper apprehension of and participation in the loving action of God. That is the way in which the retelling of our story and theirs becomes a vehicle for healing in ways that are hard to spell out with clarity; the conviction of a continuing shared 'labour' is a consistent feature of Christian attitudes to the dead. We are not just thinking about a 'retelling' in which one party is entirely passive. Likewise, there is a sense in which the Christian praying for another (and acting for/with another) is assuming a common identity in which the other's suffering impinges upon, even diminishes or deprives, the praying person; we might recall John Donne's famous claim that 'every man's death diminishes me.' Something like exchange, if not exactly substitution, is wired in to the Christian account of loving communion. But Williams' intricate and highly charged language about exchange sits awkwardly with the recognition that communion has to retain a consciousness of the opacity, the difficulty, and thus also the potential gift-character of the other; co-inherence is both a powerful imaginative intensifier of what communion entails in the Christian framework of reference, the imagery of the Body of Christ in particular, and a cautionary example of how overambitious accounts of empathic identification can distract from the work of actual recognition in a world of irreducible difference, 'avoiding the tendency to invent other creatures (human or animal) in our own image or to use them simply as pawns in our own ideological or material battles'.[27]

In short, it seems that a critical understanding of 'communion' may be an essential aspect of any account of solidarity that preserves the importance of difference and the 'contingency' that Taylor speaks of. The recurrent suspicion that solidarity language lends itself all too easily to a thinly moralized tribalism is not completely without foundation when we look at the weaponizations of shared identity that disfigure politics on both right and left; Taylor, just as much as someone like Aruna D'Souza, reminds us that a non-tribal solidarity begins in the readiness to explore and test connection and recognition in any circumstance that arises – which is another way of expressing Bonhoeffer's (and Dostoevsky's) language about universal responsibility. Such a solidarity presupposes what Joanna Bourke says about the apparently inescapable desire for the mutual assurance of durable common life. But this will always be a desire, not a steady state, simply because of the contingency already noted: a consolidated and finalized communal identity would inevitably entail a decisive fixing of boundaries. The creative role of this kind of desire is in how it steers us away from resting content with partial models of human solidarity, while acknowledging that non-partial expressions will remain as long as we are temporal and contingent agents. But equally, a disregard for boundaries of all kinds here and now, a principled indifference to identity as such, is no less risky. If it is dangerous for our human critical energy to settle down with defined boundaries, so too it is dangerous to imagine we can ignore the diverse grammars and traditions of humanity as it actually is. Both the aspiration to boundaryless openness and the aspiration to final communal harmony are attempts to bypass the processes of learning over time and in conversation with specific (incarnate) others.

3.
What then might it mean to 'bear one another's burdens'? Williams' intensely realist account of this is, as we have seen, fraught with both conceptual and moral difficulties; but his comment, in the *persona* of the playwright Stanhope, that it must be more than 'listening sympathetically, and thinking unselfishly' is worth pondering. We noted earlier[28] the language that Tischner uses about how the other becomes a 'burden' in the exchanges of conversation. Central to his analysis is the idea that the other's question 'dislodges' me from my position as sole focus or arbiter of meaning. I take upon me not the literal pain or need of the other but initially just the knowledge that the world can be seen and felt from elsewhere. I become aware that 'my' world is always liable to be destabilized by this. My perspective on the world is now augmented, 'weighted' we might say, by that imagined but inescapable elsewhere that the other's words embody for me. And, as Tischner observes,[29] the questioner too takes on a burden; even to begin to frame a question requires a parallel dislodging, if the question is to be heard and answered.

So the burden is, in the first place, the knowledge of a gap between the ego and the reality of the world, a gap to be recognized and negotiated, not filled. This knowledge lays upon us the obligation to listen, to receive: the first burden is the acceptance of the fact that my will and agency are neither the touchstone of truth nor the sole driver of change in the world.

But the burden is more than this alone. In acknowledging the gap between ego and world, I acknowledge what we could call the *burden of action*, the necessity for co-operation, even at the most minimal level, in negotiating a shared environment. This in turn means that the other's capacity for action becomes a matter of immediate relevance for me: I cannot enact what I desire without the agency of an other or others, and so I cannot fully *understand* my desire (in the sense of being able to utter it intelligibly and interrogate it) without the imagining of how that other agency works or is prevented from working. And so the *burden of the other's question* becomes a reality for me; as Tischner says, this is both burden and liberation, since the other's presence is at one level the opening up of a way out of the individual ego's frustration, its inability to enact its desire, its enclosure in its own distance from reality.[30] Both self and other are implicated in each other's history. The frustration of the other's desire and capacity are thus bound up with my own frustration; the release from frustration has to be a common, reciprocally configured task.

In this context, the bearing of another's burden as an ethical category involves a complex interplay of self-interest and other-directedness – or rather, as we have noted in several earlier discussions, it reshapes what we might mean by 'self-interest'. The other's lack, suffering, incapacity, disadvantage is neither a neutral fact at a distance from me nor a matter of immediate, appropriated personal affliction; it is something 'dialogically' bound up with my well-being. And that individual well-being is precisely a well-being that is both vacuous and morally corrupt if it is not kept under constant interrogation as to whether and how it converges with and nourishes the well-being of the other. The burden of action and the burden of the other's question bring with them the *burden of self-scrutiny*. How far am I retreating into a 'private' account of well-being, ignoring or minimizing the other's lack or limit? I bear the burden that is the other – the irreducible, elusive, persistent other with their alien, 'dislodging' questions – in this practice of critical candour, a practice itself enabled and sustained by exposing myself to the other's challenges. And thus I bear the burden that is the other's: what constrains and oppresses them is my agenda, not because I have successfully imagined what it is like to be the other (which may or may not be helpful in every circumstance) nor because I have by some mysterious process removed an experience (or the effect of an experience) from their psyche to mine, but because I have learned a little better to recognize what I am in a shared world, to challenge the self-evident priority of my immediate gratification, to attend in detail and intellectual courage to what constrains the humanity of another – and indeed, to echo points made earlier, what constrains the life of the non-human agent also.

This is where solidarity opens out on to communion: an act of identification becomes an act that opens up a reciprocal engagement and – potentially – enrichment, in which neither subject remains unchanged, and in which each acquires a history in which the other is constitutive. My act of identification becomes an act in which I begin to re-identify my self, as participating in a reality of mutual movement and development. And, as earlier chapters have argued, this is a rediscovery of something that is fundamental to the formation of a self of any kind, most specifically an *embodied* self. The act of solidarity as it evolves into the fuller mutuality of communion is not an imposed discipline designed to limit the damage of predatory egos in competition, but the enactment of a reality overlaid by distorted and destructive relations of power in the world, relations between persons, communities, species. Charles Williams, in his list of founding principles for the 'Order of the Co-inherence',[31] appeals to a number of biblical texts as touchstones for his vision – 'Others he saved, himself he cannot save', 'Am I my brother's keeper?', 'Let us make man in our own image', 'Bear ye one another's burdens' – as well as the quotation from the enslaved Felicitas as she faces death in the arena, 'Another will be in me who will suffer for me, as I shall suffer for him.' All of these will make some sense read in the context of the account just outlined of bearing another's burden. No one is capable of 'saving' themselves by their own action; they must be object rather than subject in the process of healing or liberation. All are answerable for the well-being of others and their access to just treatment. All human agents in some way or some degree embody the truth that the most fundamental level of reality is not an 'atomic' unity or an ultimate sameness – an anthropomorphic divine individual or an indistinct totality. All are enjoined to 'carry' as their own what the other suffers, at least in the sense that all are called to recognize that they are diminished by the diminishment of the other. And the condemned woman in the arena is – again, at least – able to give significance to her agony by seeing it as something both embraced by the divine and offered for the good of the believing community. All of this is indeed rather more than the performative empathy that Williams regards as inadequate; whether anything further is thinkable in terms of the very direct relief of another's pain through 'substitution' is impossible to assess in any academic mode. All that can be said is that such a process, as Williams describes it, brings some serious problems, conceptual and spiritual, into focus. Tischner's analysis of the burden of the other seems to offer a less problematic account, if only because it underlines so strongly the importance of actual attention to what the other endures – and so the impossibility of any resolution that simply reifies this and treats it as somehow transferable to another subject; it would be hard to say of Williams' schema that it really allows us to say that the other becomes part of my 'history' and vice versa.

It makes sense to see the bearing of the other's burden as a dimension of solidarity in its most robust sense. But a solidaristic response to suffering is not primarily a deep internal feeling of identification with another's pain but a recognition that we cannot understand that alien pain unless we recognize it as *our* issue, our privation or frustration – and so as something summoning us to take up the burden of work, both the work of listening and the work of shared construction of some new state of affairs. Bearing burdens is a matter of 'intelligence'; not in the sense of conceptual ingenuity or penetration but simply as the outcome of thoughtful attention and the capacity to grasp one's own limit or need as well as the other's. An unintelligent solidarity would be the kind of identification that presumes I can stand in the shoes of another or claim that I speak from within their situation without any history of probing self and other, any practice of attention or self-scrutiny, any questioning around the relations of power and advantage that characterize a situation. The 'performative solidarity' mentioned in the Introduction is one expression of this unintelligent identification; it may be relatively harmless, and it is undoubtedly well-meaning, but it helps to give solidarity precisely the bad name that many modern commentators take for granted, labelling it as innately unreflective, sentimental and potentially tribal. If there is always work to be done in realizing solidarity, this is a confirmation of the fact that what we are talking about is a negotiation between genuinely and lastingly different subjects/agents. Hence the suggestion here that the language of 'communion' is so essential an element as a critical balance for the pressure towards identification. And as I have been trying to argue in this chapter, Charles Williams, for all the tangles of his exposition does leave us with clearly distinct subjects at work in the processes of co-inherence.

4.
Solidarity without labour becomes nothing but a shared passivity, a shared privation. Sarah Perry's subtle and intricate novel, *Melmoth*,[32] explores the difference between active witness and a passive solidarity in despair, in a way that illuminates the point from an unexpected angle. The novel deals with the experiences of a series of individuals from different contexts and historical periods. Each of them is guilty of some disastrous act of betrayal that has in one way or another ruined or destroyed the lives of others – including others that they love, or else has represented a fundamental denial of some commitment central to their integrity. Each of them speaks of being haunted by a ghostly presence who offers consolation and company in their guilt, and actively lures some of them into their acts of betrayal by promising loving consolation afterwards. This figure is 'Melmoth' – Perry's variation on

the theme of 'Melmoth the Wanderer', the central character in Charles Maturin's 1820 Gothic fantasy of that name,[33] who travels across the centuries trying to persuade others to take on the contract by which he has sold his soul to the devil. In Perry's version, 'Melmoth the Witness' is a woman who has seen the resurrection of Jesus but then denied it, and is condemned to an eternity of wandering the earth, seeking out those who are guilty of some comparably conscious and willing denials of the truth. She offers them 'no hope…but a loving companion in your despair.'[34] Those whom she haunts are deeply tempted by the possibility of simply surrendering a tormenting hope that they believe to be unrealizable – the possibility of, in effect, accepting the 'damnation' they think they have earned. The alternative is another kind of witness, not the unsparing, timeless gaze of Melmoth, but the actual human witness of those with whom some kind of reconciled future is – in spite of everything – imaginable. But this means finding the courage to re-enter history, relationship, converse, the world's unfolding history. The novel's concluding pages remind the reader of how difficult this would be, in the words of direct appeal from Melmoth: 'I know what you cannot confess…I know what a fraud you are…how weak, capricious, cruel!…And don't you know you were born to sadness, as surely as sparks fly up from the fire?…I have walked to you on bleeding feet: who else could want you like this?'[35]

Active witness is the declaration that betrayal is not the last word and that the betrayer – even the one who betrays in full awareness of their violence against the truth – may still be brought back into the connections of time and speech and relation. Our apparent instinctive urge to withdraw into a self-condemned isolation, accepting a fixed destiny of misery, is deep-rooted, offering a kind of peace in its finality, along with the ersatz consolation of the presence of other terminally isolated and self-hating souls. Perry is sketching a persuasive picture of hell (it is significant that Melmoth's initial betrayal is the denial of the resurrection, and so of the 'harrowing of hell'). Perry's potent final image of walking to the sinner on bleeding feet, and the challenge of 'who else could want you?' leaves the reader to decide, like the characters in the novel, whether they are indeed able to be desired by anyone, or whether they are beyond grieving for, beyond anyone's wanting, unmissed. Casting the theme in this way echoes another recent engagement with the themes of human redeemability and enduring dignity, the idea of 'grievability' developed by Judith Butler.[36] For Butler, the ascription of human dignity is bound up with the recognition that a life lost is a life to be mourned; the starkest possible sign of dehumanization directed towards another, individual or collective, is the denial of this, something characteristic of mass warfare but also of mass incarceration, mass poverty or homelessness or any general disvaluing of certain kinds of human life. Grievability is a way of acknowledging the precariousness of human life, but not simply as a neutral or biological fact: to say that a human life is 'precarious' is to say that it is involved with other lives, it lives from other lives, is in the hands of other living beings, is exposed to others. Sustaining the life of the other is a social matter, and the implied dispensability of some lives is the clearest indication there could be of social refusal and exclusion. But destroying the other is also destroying the self: I am not naturally exempt from precariousness, my life too is in other hands, and sometimes in the hands of strangers. The repeated question – the fundamental moral question – about whose life is being treated as grievable is one that will properly go on unsettling any definition of who the 'we' are who have obligations to a 'they'. And this is not only a point pertinent to war or pandemic, poverty, migration, penal policy or the stigmatizing of those living with HIV; it is also to do with the collective human 'we' that habitually fails to grieve for the rest of the living world, the non-human world, in whose hands we also sit. Picking up the language used earlier in this chapter, we could say that grievability is built into 'communion' as we have been defining it: the language of communion too tells us that 'we' is always an unstable construct because we cannot know in advance what new lives we shall encounter in whose hands we shall find ourselves, and whose lives are placed into our hands. Properly grasped, communion can never be a tribal notion if its indefinite extension in both time and space is recognized; and this translates into an indefinite account of grievability – another way of rendering the theme that keeps returning here, of what 'unlimited responsibility' actually means.

Grievability is obviously connected with 'desirability': if we mourn a loss, we confess a need. And throughout this reflection we have in one way or another been connecting solidarity with need, not only with some sort of other-directed benevolence. There is as much of a risk in adopting an uncompromising idealizing of selflessness as there is of canonizing unexamined self-interest. The 'abjection' before the other that Gillian Rose diagnoses so sharply is in practice another way of refusing the labour of shared discovery and shared intervention in the world. It is true that we must indeed decisively overcome the fiction of a self-evident self-interest and reimagine the self in its relativity and dependence, even in some sense its 'insubstantiality' (i.e. the fact of its formation in time and interaction, its status as a unique continuity of converging energies rather than a simple monad whose identity is timelessly fixed). But this disowning of a mythical monadic self is not the same as the denial of a position from which to speak, that 'zero point of orientation' that we have noted from time to time, with its irreducible relatedness to the narrative of our speaking selves and the irremovable inscription of past time in our bodies. 'Abjection', the plain denial of inhabiting a position with both perspectives and interests, turns away from responsibility. Our positionedness in the world is not a place of impregnable certainty and privilege, but it becomes one pole among others of the collaborative labour needed in order to 'do justice' to and in our environment, a justice that is not done if we do not do justice to what we actually are as subjects – a venerable Aristotelean, Augustinian and Thomist insight. If this is the pattern within which we act as moral subjects, it follows that each subject is 'desirable', in the sense that what is distinctive is *wanted* for the honouring and healing of the world we share. And if that is the case, then there is an imperative to work towards the reintegrating of those who are responsible for betrayal and refusal. As has often been said, the moral imperative to resist or overthrow oppression is for the good of the oppressor as well as the oppressed. The world of 'Melmoth' is one in which solidarity can never be transforming; it is only the mutual recognition of failure and the false consolation of seeing one another as equally lost and isolated – a recognition with no moral consequence. This cannot be a solidarity of labour or shared intelligence; it is in fact a distortion of the foundational mutuality of the finite world, a retreat from the real.

This chapter has ranged widely, from idiosyncratic theological speculation to recent fiction and feminist philosophy, but I hope that some connecting threads will be reasonably clear. Charles Williams' distinctive account of substitutionary love prompted some examination of the ambiguities of a solidarity that appeared to minimize the specific locatedness of human need or suffering, but also challenged us to think through what was entailed in the injunction to bear one another's burdens. And this led into a discussion of what is involved in regarding the other as a 'burden' in a more general way, and of the habits and practices of interrogation that made sense of this. The solidarity envisaged in this framework was contrasted with the pure solidarity in guilt and suffering memorably evoked in Sarah Perry's fiction, with its implied denial of 'grievability' to the guilty; Judith Butler's analysis of what it means to regard both our human and our non-human environment as a proper subject for grief in the event of loss brought us back to the way in which solidaristic thinking and practice affirms that every subject is in some way 'wanted' for the collaborative project that is our human history as agents within a wider network of living reality.

In the final chapter, we shall be returning to some questions around the nature of shared work, but also to some questions prompted by Judith Butler's reflection on mourning and those who are not mourned, questions particularly connected to the recent experience of the Covid-19 pandemic and other contemporary global crises. We shall also be attempting some tying together of the philosophical and theological motifs that have pervaded this book, with a view to sketching, even if very roughly, something of the anthropology we need to equip a broad front of resistance against the stubborn and none too coherent blend of functionalist collectivism and libertarian ambition that seems to shape so much of our cultural and political world at present. If the preceding pages suggest anything, they should point to the existence of some intellectually serious alternatives to such mythologies; and the final chapter of this essay is meant to crystallize something of that challenge a bit more directly.

CONCLUSION

1.
This book began with a question about what it is that prompts people to reach for the language of 'solidarity' rather than just 'support' or even 'sympathy' to express serious moral concern for some other group. The various texts, writers and arguments we have discussed here converge at least on this: serious moral concern for the other is regularly bound up with a sense of belonging in a shared situation, in which what confronts the other is intelligibly similar to what confronts the self. I recognize the fragility of the other as like my own; I understand that the jeopardy of another might be mine. It therefore becomes important to examine and understand the ways in which human beings have educated themselves not to recognize this shared jeopardy, the strategies adopted by various groups designed to minimize recognizability, even where this entails educating people not to trust their own immediate perceptions. Animals or 'deficient' humans (of another race or gender) may *look* as though they are suffering as we might, but we know that they can't be. As we observed earlier, those others are no longer the owners of their experience; it is definitively interpreted for them by the fully rational observer. The political consequences of this are obvious, perhaps most dramatically in the history of colonially directed enslavement.

But this is only part of the story. In analysing some of the intricacies of what we mean by 'empathy' it becomes clear that we are not talking simply about one atomized subjectivity considering the plight of another atomized subjectivity. To be a subject at all – and, importantly, to be a *body* in the full sense of a self-directing organism – involves being seen, being known, being acted upon.

We do not begin with a naked self-awareness that is gradually and speculatively enlarged to accommodate others. We slowly disentangle self-perception from a complex, interactive psycho-physical pattern of response to an environment, and we learn to articulate what is happening in us because we are addressed and engaged. Language itself shows us that we are always 'reading and being read'; language is one obvious sense the vehicle of solidarity, and solidarity is typically the solidarity of *speakers* – that is, of reflective users of symbols, gestural as much as verbal. Our selfhood is always being constructed in this kind of interaction, in which I am confronted not only with the difficulty of recognizing an other, especially a cultural or ethnic other, but by the difficulty of recognizing myself, the difficulty, that is, of making a coherent story of my own learning and perceiving. I recognize and misrecognize, succeed and fail in communication and understanding, and continue the effort, in the faith that I am discovering a communality with the other that lies deeper than the obvious forms of sameness.

In this light, the question of human rights, what is due to human beings as such, becomes something other than an issue about individual claims. If the finite world is a pattern of interactive construction, the mutual making of identities, each agent has a distinctive place from which to act, a distinctive accumulation of gift or energy to give; and this distinctiveness is literally embodied in physical distinctness, physical difference and diversity of skill or endowment. The idea of 'right' needs to be rendered freshly in terms of the liberty to enact this distinctiveness in relation, in mutuality; the denial of right is the denial of an agent's capacity to do what only they can do in the interactive pattern of world-making. This is not, as should be clear, a matter of the liberty of 'self-expression' in the more vacuous modern sense. The 'self' is precisely what is being formed and negotiated in mutuality. But this model at least avoids the Sisyphean task of constructing some kind of comprehensive list of abstract entitlements whose sum total constitutes the ideally 'just' situation. To put it (perhaps too) epigrammatically, the central element in human right/s is *the right to be 'imagined'* – the expectation that one's perspective and desire and liberty to speak are taken with maximal seriousness by any responsible other. And this also nudges us in the direction of a model of human right that is in some way prior to the specifics of any one human society; it is more than a set of binding legal conventions but the recognition of an abiding state of affairs within which the 'language animal' (to borrow Charles Taylor's evocative term) lives.

With these general considerations in mind, we examined the evolution of solidarity language in European thought, from its sociological and descriptive origins to a more ambitiously metaphysical and normative usage in Catholic Social Teaching. Although its strongly anti-capitalist resonances in early twentieth-century German Catholic thinking were largely muted in later papal teachings, the idea that 'solidaristic' values were an essential part of a just society became more and more explicit, grounded in a theological picture of human interdependence and a critique of individualism. The balance between what we have called solidarity as condition and solidarity as value or imperative is handled with some assurance in the social encyclicals especially of Pope John Paul II, but the themes continue to be explored – even where the actual vocabulary of solidarity is less front-and-centre – up to and including the magisterial pronouncements of Pope Francis. It is clear that actions expressing solidarity are expressing not simply an ideal to be attained or a method for achieving other social goals, but that a society marked by solidarity is one that lives in accordance with the Creator's purpose and manifests what is abidingly fundamental in human affairs and human 'nature'.

The critical potential of solidarity language becomes clear when we see how it has been used in the context of different kinds of totalitarianism. Jan Patočka's sophisticated phenomenological account of the formation of self and 'soul' implicitly warns against what we might call a pre-critical exaltation of solidarity by noting the significance in cultural history of the 'religious' moment that breaks through the conventions of inherited group identity – the religious as opposed to the 'sacred', understood as the unchallengeable grounding of existing relations. It is this moment that makes us strange to ourselves, and so liberates dimensions of human imagination that have hitherto been muted or unrecognized. And at the summit of such experience stands the breakthrough that Patočka calls the 'solidarity of the shaken', the profound sense of convergence between those who have lived through a radical and violent dissolution of pre-existing sources of shared meaning, and out of that trauma offer the possibility of a new social imaginary shaped by egalitarian, innovative, self-critical practices. Jozef Tischner's development of the idea of solidarity in the Poland of the 1980s has points both of convergence and of tension with Patočka's vision – not least in their respective valuation of 'labour', which for Tischner becomes the primary vehicle for understanding and practising solidarity. For him, work and conversation are bound together as embodying the solidaristic vision; and the ideal of solidarity is interpreted firmly and consistently in terms of *fidelity*. The just society is one in which what we owe to one another is faithfulness in adversity, but also faithfulness in telling the truth. Concealment is a form of betrayal, making shared labour impossible. By concentrating on these aspects of solidarity, Tischner is able to sketch a model of solidarity that does not depend on the unification of a group in shared opposition to a common enemy, and is realized in a pattern of dialogue in which each participant begins from the recognition that the other has something of which they themselves are in need. And the primary driver of solidaristic action and witness is 'conscience', the recognition of the fact that we carry the 'burden' of each other's situation, and that this burden is denied when someone tries to evade their involvement with the other and to intensify the burden of pain or disadvantage that the other carries – a refusal that ultimately disables and destroys the one who refuses, as well as their victim.

Tischner's theological background occasionally shows through both in his philosophical and his more overtly political writing, but it is not generally presented in a systematic way. This contrasts with another great critic of totalitarian politics, Dietrich Bonhoeffer, whose analyses of 'substitution' or 'representation' and 'responsibility' are firmly anchored in reflection on the mystery of the incarnation – God's act of 'solidarity' with human chaos and lostness. The presence of God in the humanity of Jesus of Nazareth establishes that God is faithfully present where there is apparent Godlessness or meaninglessness; the other to be loved and served is one who has already been affirmed by God, one with whom God through Jesus Christ is identified. The individual Christian's actions in solidarity represent the same identification with the vulnerability of the other – not an identification with their experience as such but a sharing of the jeopardy in which they stand and an acceptance of complicity in the entire sinful system that makes them suffer. As Christ represents humanity by standing where sinful and suffering human beings stand, so we seek, not innocence and righteousness, but fidelity to the place where suffering is happening and to the compromised world of imperfect decisions, shadowy motivations and the like in which humans live. Faced with the world's suffering and the manifest and atrocious injustice under which our fellow human beings live, we shall regularly find ourselves 'helpless' to articulate solutions and can only stand faithfully alongside, in the confidence that our incapacity will at least make room for God's action in God's time. Our solidarity depends on God's eternally pre-existing solidarity; and so our practice of solidarity is one of the crucial ways in which we are reminded that we are not God. And our mutual dependence as finite (non-divine) agents is made concrete and historical in the Body of Christ, the *sanctorum communio* so basic to Bonhoeffer's thinking, in which each serves the other's capacity to serve the capacity of someone yet other to them. Our own 'self-dislodging' is undertaken so that we may stand as guarantor in the self-dislodging risk that the neighbour undertakes for *their* neighbour – and so on, ad infinitum. In this sense, we love the selfless potential in the other as we love our own potential for this; we do not simply and blandly love a given, monadic self-identity when we love ourselves or our neighbour. We love in the hope of active, 'substitutionary' solidarity.

The theological underpinning of this is elaborated by Charles Williams, with an intense and often problematic realism. In the 'co-inherence' of the believing community, the Body of Christ, what is actualized is the universal truth of the universe (as articulated by Heraclitus) that everything lives from the life – and death – of everything else. But if this is more than a vague fellow-feeling, it must surely mean that it is possible for us deliberately to undertake not only a Bonhoefferian act of entering the other's position of jeopardy, but the actual jeopardy itself, lifting from another the burden of their fear or agony. This practice of 'substituted love' is fraught with complexities, and Williams is never wholly clear about what it entails, except that we may be confident that, if we willingly declare that we shall 'stand in' for another within the co-inherent 'Mystical Body', a difference will be made. One of the problems arising is that this seems to assume an active–passive relation between the one who offers and the one who receives the substitution. And although this is qualified by the fact that someone passive in one setting will ideally be active in another, it configures the process of substituted love as essentially a binary of agent and recipient; there is little here of the conversational and co-operative flavour of Tischner's account, the necessary labour of attention and discovery and allowing the other to define themselves. But the challenge to think of what more is involved in solidaristic love than benevolent and unselfish feelings is a real one; and bringing Tischner's account of the 'burden of the other' into play in dialogue with Williams helps to clarify some of what can and can't usefully be said. Central to Tischner's account, so I've argued, is the recognition that the other's loss is my loss – not the *same* loss, but a privation within the shared relationship that makes both of us who we are. This takes us back to themes opened up in earlier chapters, about the necessary time-taking of recognition, the acknowledgement of real difference as a condition of the mutually constructive model of relation that some thinking about solidarity emphasizes, the respect due to (the 'right' recognized in) the distinctive history and position of the other, and so on. It prompts a reworking of the idea of 'communion' as exchange between points of irreducible difference; we have to learn to balance aspirations for transparent intelligibility with the reality of constantly shifting patterns of exchange – the accumulation of 'conversational' learning and development, in which conflict is neither avoided nor canonized. And this in turn is linked to the notion of active and transforming *witness*, as opposed to a sentimental and self-focused form of empathy.

In the last two chapters particularly, we have been reminded regularly of a number of significant theological themes raised by the discussion of solidarity. The notion of humanity as made in the divine image has been in the background of several approaches, but it is used in a variety of ways. Most simply, it is an affirmation of the universal value to be ascribed to human agents; they exist as a consequence of the gratuitous love of God in creation, and their exercise of love and intelligence, however expressed or embodied, reflects the initiative or creativity of divine life. More specifically, in the context of Charles Williams' ideas about co-inherence, the interdependence of human/finite existence is seen as mirroring the interdependence of divine life – the trinitarian pattern of agents whose identity is constituted by their mutual relationship. As Fiddes argues in his study of Williams, this openly trinitarian rationale for interdependence is only made really explicit in Williams' later works; and it is significant that the word 'co-inherence' itself (*perichoresis* in Greek) is used in the context of both trinitarian and Christological speculation. It is a way of insisting that the ultimate active and transcendent unity upon which the universe depends is itself irreducibly plural in constitution, not a unity of impenetrable self-identity or of sheer numerical singleness but a circle of mutual definition, reciprocal 'life-giving' of some kind. But we should also note that there is an 'imaging' of God's action envisaged by Bonhoeffer in rather different terms, the sharing of Christ's representative adoption of the desolate human condition in a free act of love. We are summoned and enabled to become more fully 'incarnate', more fully present in the world, embracing in Christ the need of the neighbour and liberating the neighbour to become a liberator in turn.

The importance of this theological hinterland is that it repeatedly points us back to the question of why and how we are engaged in the 'moral imagining' of others in the way we are. Even if we accept in one form or another the thesis of our innate dependence on the other's act and perception for our own self-formation, there remains a further step to the acknowledgement of a summons to stand with or for the other in the labour of solidarity as we have outlined it. Tischner's analysis of what he calls the 'agathological' element in our consciousness of the other's reality is relevant here: the attempt to define myself in action solely in my own terms, or in reference to my supposed individual interest, is manifestly a revolt against the real or the true, given what has already been said about our inescapable implication in each other's reality. Thus we cannot *intelligibly* ignore the need of the other; we cannot rationalize any such moral policy as grounded in a common truth, and so we cannot *talk* about it. The moral world collapses around us. A radical moral individualism would be incapable of producing anything in the way of shared work; ultimately it would be inimical to speech itself. The complex bundle of responses to the world that we call moral involves an 'honouring' of the difference of the other and a 'dislodging' of the assumed superiority of the ego's immediate demands, if we are to be faithful to the truth that common work requires if it is to be effective. But at the same time, it remains possible to refuse this intelligibility. 'Obedience' to the pattern of mutuality is something that will make full sense when we acknowledge that what we are is maintained by the gift of the other – not just the gift of the finite other with whom at this or that moment we are in negotiation or conversation, but the gift that is at work in each and every instance of finite life-sharing or life-enabling: creation – in a familiar theological dictum – not only being made by God but being made to make itself. Our conformity with this pattern, a conformity that is emphatically not a conformity to an externally imposed norm but the living-out of what is fundamental to the nature of our self-formation, is what moral life consists in, what 'conscience' directs us to, a structure of active fidelity to the truth and so to the common good.

And for Bonhoeffer – in this as in other ways complementing Tischner – this active fidelity is most fully released in and through fidelity to the form of Christ's action of representation and responsibility: a letting-go of any fantasy of self-protected, self-justifying and self-serving rightness in order to become open to the active presence of grace, the Spirit forming the reality of Christlike action in us, overcoming our own compulsive reversions to self-interest, to what Bonhoeffer calls the state of being 'in Adam', rehearsing the illusions that captured and corrupted the first human agent in the biblical story. So far from solidaristic action being, as its critics suggest, a piece of moral self-indulgence, making a grab for absolute innocence by means of an unconditional identification with the victim, it is, in the Bonhoefferian perspective, an acceptance of shared ambiguities, hidden complicities and compromises, constantly renewed trust in a restoring and reconciling agency outside our control or manipulation. We seek to act in 'righteousness'; but this is not an individual examination score in correctness, rather a repeated self-questioning as to how far we are aligned to what the world, the other in all its forms, asks of us as a truthful or adequate response. The 'imperfect solidarity' of Aruna D'Souza is what we work for, situation by situation, crisis by crisis, accepting that we shall be involved in various kinds of misrecognition and the unresolved tensions of ill-distributed power. Solidarity as unconditional identification with the innocent does no justice either to us or those with whom we want to identify; solidaristic care and effective action, even 'substituted love', if we want to use that language, do not depend on the other fulfilling a set of criteria for being taken seriously or being pitied or being 'grievable'. They are to be taken seriously as morally imaginable others, to be pitied or grieved, simply as organically human partners in the world construction of speech and symbolic exchange. No one has to *earn* the right to be affirmed by the solidarity of others. A theology of creation, incarnation and grace ought to be the seedbed for the practice of a solidarity that sees first the shared jeopardy, the shared damage, that another's pain embodies. A practice rooted in conscience, as Tischner defines it.

2.
Implied in all this is the fact that a solidarity that has any claim to be a transformative and genuinely radical practice takes time. It is obviously more than a simple gesture of identification; it requires learning – the learning of another's language to some degree, the learning of what is and is not possible to achieve by shared work

in a given situation, the learning of one's own limits and need. Richard Sennett's book on co-operative work, mentioned above in the Introduction, provides some invaluable insight about the ways in which co-operative practice in the workplace has altered over the centuries, noting how the technological innovations of the early modern period both unsettled more apparently organic models of co-operation and created fresh vehicles for it. On the one hand, production of complex artefacts was more likely to be shared among a differentiated and physically separated group of workers. On the other, the advances in what was technically possible created an experimental environment in which wider participation and genuine dialogue could flourish; hierarchies were broken down, as new voices entered the discussion. 'Experiment invites the dialogic conversation,' Sennett writes,[1] 'the open-ended discussion with others about hypotheses, procedures and results'; and he quotes Mikhail Bakhtin to the effect that such dialogue both reinforces faith in our own experience and (helpfully) distances us from what we seek to understand. What we are examining together – even if it is an apparently definite material object or configuration of objects – is something that is neither mine nor the other's, but is an indeterminate something hovering between us, waiting for the definition that can only come by means of our co-operation. Although in some respects early modernity disturbs the tightly collaborative mutuality of medieval labour, the early modern workshop is also a liberating phenomenon, especially at a time when meaningful participatory ritual in social and public life had increasingly turned into spectacle.

It is in later modernity that co-operative patterns are more deeply weakened and compromised, as competition becomes more uncontrolled and civic bonds and residual rituals are sidelined by the obsessive maximization of profit in an undifferentiated time continuum with no natural rhythms. Sennett sees this as issuing in the 'Uncooperative Self' of contemporary capitalism and its markets, for whom co-operation has ceased to be a value in itself.[2] In a concluding chapter, he notes[3] that a certain kind of solidarity has overtaken co-operation as a strategy for resisting social fragmentation, a 'destructive solidarity of us-against-them'. What this does not address, he argues, is the dissociation of 'power' from 'authority' in the contemporary world, represented by the distance between elites and working communities (and conspicuously evident in the pattern of appointment to the new US administration); while those communities struggle to maintain cohesion, decisions are made at a vast distance from them by individuals and collectivities to whose workings they have no access and which are not accountable to any public scrutiny. In the societies of the North Atlantic world, people 'have less and less a fate to share in common'.

Sennett's analysis is persuasive; but part of the motivation for writing this book has been to see if we can reconnect solidarity and co-operation, especially by way of something like Tischner's foregrounding of 'faithfulness' in the context of work, and the conversational character of labour. The problems Sennett very reasonably identifies in solidarity language reflect precisely the static and abstract solidarity of 'identification' rather than the mobile and imperfect conversational alliances that have featured in some of the discussions summarized here. The solidarity that we have outlined here, a solidarity that is both a given and an agenda, is only intelligible as an inclusive project, always committed to questioning its failures or limitations in the name of a deeper receptivity to the challenge of the other. As we have noted more than once, this does not mean a commitment to the erosion of historical identities for the sake of global homogeneity; nor does it deny or sidestep the reality of conflict between identities. The possibility of solidarity in action routinely involves the protracted discovery of where convergence is imaginable and where it is not in the short or medium term. To echo Joanna Bourke once more, our action is made intelligible by the persistent *hope* of mutual intelligibility, even when it involves a recognition of the depth of existing misrecognitions.

What should concern us is a rhetoric that assumes a radical mutual unintelligibility. This is, ironically enough, what current discourses of solidarity can encourage: where solidarity has become a matter of declaring identification, then, as we noted in the Introduction, it is more tempting to absolutize oppositions. Solidarity becomes a declaration not of commitment to collaboration and learning but of unconditional affirmation. And this in turn can lead to a situation in which my affirmation of solidarity with a group or a cause becomes inseparable from the affirmation of my own moral worth, so that a challenge to it appears as a refusal to treat me with moral seriousness. Nuance, difficulty, respect, realism and a good deal more, all these disappear in a static map of incompatible loyalties.[4]

This is the solidarity that Sennett invites us to be wary of, whether it wears the colours of left or right. It is inimical to co-operative practice, to Tischner's conversation of labour. Its current popularity reflects two broader aspects of our cultural and political circumstances. The first is an aspect of the theoretical discussions we have looked at, an aspect touched on here and there in earlier chapters – the relative devaluation of *work* in some twentieth-century philosophies. We have seen how thinkers like Arendt and even Patočka – though in very different ways – suggest that there is a radical gulf between the sheerly mechanical problem-solving of human agents and the real exercise of creative intelligence. Not the least important aspect of Sennett's work[5] is his refusal to accept such a gulf, inviting us to think through material craft and skill not only as inherently intelligent practices – even in a sense 'intellectual' practices, to the extent that intellect in pre-modern philosophies entails an entry into the rhythms and energies of what is not the individual self – but also as inherently collaborative and *linguistic* practices, depending on social trust, faith in mutual intelligibility, readiness to learn, and acceptance of the time to be taken in such a process. As John Hughes's masterly discussion of *The End of Work* argues,[6] we have become captive to a utilitarian model of labour as an essentially sub-intelligent activity in which granular practical issues are resolved and basic needs met. Both traditional religious and Marxist discourses offer resources for thinking more seriously about this, according to Hughes, and any critique of social injustice that does not address this fundamental matter is going to be superficial.

But this immediately highlights the second factor that keeps us from thinking seriously about 'conversational' labour, the actual character of modern work. In the modern globalized economy, labour is systematically reduced to separable tasks, in principle capable of being performed anywhere by anyone, and so of being assumed in due course by appropriate mechanical 'agents'. Co-operative practice in the working place – any kind of working place, not just the traditional manufacturing shop floor – is routinely undermined by this climate of assumptions. Work is a matter of properly operational functions, specified in advance. The perfectly proper business of maximizing efficiency by automating what can be automated has created a default position in which the paradigm of work is the closely defined and bounded operation with closely defined and bounded outcomes. The worker is not expected to be engaged in any kind of Tischnerian or Sennettian dialogue about the best operational strategies or the overall place of a goal within the wider social scene. Is there any point in talking about the 'conversation of labour' when labour is so reduced and one-dimensional a thing?

The salient point is that, in a climate like this, what it actually means to learn within a collaborative process, to test, miscalculate, adjust and partly realize what is needed to achieve some shared good, is not going to be a priority – whether it is to do with the most local questions of practical operating in a production plant or with the 'production' of governance by supposedly democratic procedures or the delivery of effective aid to struggling and disadvantaged economies. The term 'co-production' may have become an irritating bit of jargon in recent years, describing the aspiration towards the fullest and most equal possible collaboration in some kinds of working environment, not least the 'creative industries', but it points to something extremely important. The experience of shared responsibility for an outcome is itself part of a good outcome, insofar as it generates a realistic combination of self-trust and trust of the other. Social and economic patterns that do not allow for this kind of joint and mutually informing activity may produce results that will satisfy certain abstract criteria but they will undermine the capacity of those involved to build a common culture in the process of shared work, and contribute to the alienation of groups and individuals from public life in general. The deep suspicion of institutions, leadership, political mechanisms and 'specialists' is closely bound up with this alienation; and it is part of the appeal of the sort of solidarity deplored by Sennett that it offers an apparently robust and active account of 'belonging' that is absent from most of our large-scale collectivities.

The language of solidarity can indeed be dangerously empty if it is only about a declaration of imagined identity; the hard work is in the *constructing* of an identity that is commonly owned – not the imposition by one party of the ideal that they bring to the encounter (a characteristic failing, for example, in the world of aid and development, whether administered by governmental or non-governmental agencies), and not the tactical co-belligerence of two groups that remain unchanged by the encounter. In the perspective of much of what this book has discussed, the process of identity construction is energized by the conviction that there is always work to be done in 'excavating' the lost, contested, almost unimaginable common human project in which all human agents find their most lastingly definitive identity. And this book has also noted the ways in which a theological perspective grounds this identity in diverse ways – as the common image of God in humans, as the interweaving of divine gift in the organic unity of the community as 'body', in the fact of divine embrace or affirmation as an always already given truth about the stranger and even the enemy. Noting this may at least be a reminder of the truth that there is (*pace* Tischner at his most optimistic) nothing self-evident about the imperative to co-operation. But whether or not the theological framing is accepted, the solidarity that emerges as morally and imaginatively credible in the various analyses that we have traced here is one that is determinedly active, and oriented to realizing a fresh level of human interdependence, a level less distorted by an absolutizing of local loyalties and by unchallenged inequalities of power and resource.

Taking such solidarity seriously is an urgent matter at present, not only because of the sour climate of competing absolutisms that dominates so much online and offline debate, but also because of one overwhelming fact about our global situation – an elephant in the room throughout the preceding discussion. The environmental crisis that we confront is something that is not confined to one region, one ethnicity, one class; it is indifferent to our tribes. We are, as it were, forced into a common identity as vulnerable to the upheavals and privations that will follow on the likely consequences of accelerating climate change. As usual, it will be those already living with deprivation who will be in the front line – those in threatened regions who have limited power to move and resettle, those whose national economies have little space either to reshape themselves in more eco-friendly modes or to cope with large-scale natural disaster and environmental degradation, those whose habits of food production are under threat from environmental change, those whose access to safe water supplies is already precarious or minimal. But in the medium term, this will not be a disaster for distant others. Both directly (in the form of extreme weather) and indirectly (in the form of dramatically increased displacement of populations), it will be at the doors of the prosperous sliver of the world's population whose consumption has helped to drive the crisis. There is an unmistakeable existential 'solidarity' here, a given, shared situation that ultimately equalizes our human fates. And in the face of this, we continue to fail in enacting a collaborative solidarity, a commonly owned project of mutual life-giving or life-securing.

More than this: a recurrent theme in what we have been examining is the possibility of understanding our solidarity with the non-human world. Mutuality is not something relevant to humans only: we live from the life and death of non-human organisms. And our standard mode of operation in the 'developed' world for the last couple of centuries has been to regard this relationship as dramatically one-sided. The goods of the earth are there to provide life for us, but any obligation to conserve non-human life except as a resource for ourselves has been – to put it mildly – elusive. It is perhaps a stretch of the imagination to speak about a 'conversation of labour' with the non-human environment. But this is not nonsense: learning the intelligible patterns of the embodied life around us, learning what threatens it or enhances it, is at the very least analogous to conversation, analogous to the process by which we create an identity that is new, in which we and other material substances or agencies may find a co-operative mode of living together. A solidarity that does not extend to the whole organic world is still bound to a 'tribalism of the human', an assumption that human good is in the last analysis separable from the well-being of the whole finite order. That illusion has been fostered by some religious language, undoubtedly; but it is also profoundly at odds with any coherent understanding of the relation of creation to creator, and we have noted some of the ways in which this perspective has surfaced in accounts of the solidaristic vision.

Solidarity as a context for learning is manifestly a commitment to self-questioning – which is why it is ironic that (to refer back to a point made at the beginning of this study) it can be a kind of bid for 'innocence'. The urge to declare solidarity can be a decisive rejection of being held to account for any involvement in the guilty history that produces a situation of suffering and injustice: I am determined to stand with the victim not the perpetrator. In one way, this is intelligible and even positive. To say, 'Not in my name' or to refuse to collude with or excuse the violence of a perpetrator – in cases of abuse, say – is a proper reaction, a significant moment of moral discrimination. The difficulty arises when it stops at the declarative level. Even if I rightly seek to stand apart from a specific act of violence or corruption, a commitment to solidarity will involve questioning myself – about the limits of my capacity or willingness to pursue work for a more just future in a world of difficult and not always morally clear policy-making that takes time and negotiating patience, and also about the areas elsewhere in my life where I am involved in as yet unexamined imbalances of power that stand in the way of honest conversational labour; what voices I am not ready to listen to. So far from solidarity assuring my innocence, it will acquaint me with my actual and potential guilt; not necessarily in the sense of some individualized reproach that becomes another ego-centred drama (remember the irrelevance of 'white grief' to the struggles of non-white communities), but as a fact of my existing involvement, whether I like it or not, in a history of unjust or abusive patterns. Facing this involvement without evasion, without panic, and without using it as a springboard for yet another campaign to prove myself innocent or righteous is one aspect of a truth-telling

CONCLUSION

that can be restorative and transforming. It does not have to be the obsessive self-castigating and disowning of the past that is such a cause of worried anger for some on the political right who fear an endless and compulsive cycle of moralized self-loathing.

3.

The spring of 2020 saw the beginning of an unprecedented social disruption in most global societies as the Covid-19 pandemic took hold. The eighteen months or so during which various levels of restriction so conspicuously affected public (and often private) life witnessed some rather abortive pleas for a reconsideration of social priorities, especially a reconsideration of what jobs in society most deserved reward. It would be nice to think that the collective trauma of that brief but intense experience had led to some serious ongoing collaborative work between states around the protection of citizens, and some fresh imagining of what counts as a desirable – even an 'honourable' – life. No such development is there to be celebrated as yet, and it is wise not to hold our breath. But looking back at the pandemic, there are themes emerging that make it almost a parable of what solidarity might be, where it may fail, and why it matters.

Negatively, one of those themes was, sadly, the reluctance of government in advance of the pandemic to work at credible and effective cross-frontier protections and conventions, even though qualified bodies had not only given warning but offered strategies to minimize damage.[7] The reality of shared jeopardy remained at the theoretical level and failed to outbid the traditions of national competition and isolation (a phenomenon that, of course, persisted in much of the official response during the period of lockdown). But at the same time, appeal was constantly and eloquently made to a model of reciprocal responsibility: citizens were reminded of the fact that not only were they as individuals at risk but *they also constituted a risk to others*. Young people were warned that unthinking contact with older relatives could be a death sentence for the latter. Despite a bit of rather unreflective rhetoric in some quarters (including religious circles) about the humiliating character of a message of self-protection, the fact was that much of the official language about public security appealed to the priority of care for the more vulnerable neighbour. And the often-repeated mantra that 'no one is safe unless everyone is safe' was a powerful statement of one dimension of solidarity, and a rationale for common action, even if only in the form of compliance with public safety mandates. We were presented to ourselves as involved with one another in ways we had not chosen and could not control, and exhorted to act intelligently and co-operatively, since there was no good outcome for the other that was not also a good outcome for oneself – and vice versa. What is more, the insistence that we were not only *experiencing* jeopardy ourselves but also a potential *cause* of it for others took the entire discourse out of the realm of competitive bids for innocence or moral neutrality. The self imagined by government regulation during the pandemic was very definitely a 'solidaristic' one, a self always already engaged, not 'innocent' but in some ways dangerous, a self charged with the good of the neighbour as something inseparable from one's own.

It was an instructive period – if not, in retrospect, an encouraging one. With the wisdom of hindsight, we can see that the appeal to the absolute authority of 'the science' perversely helped to undermine the authority of actual evidence-based policy, and that the extreme centralization of the decision-making process often left not only local communities but regional devolved governments confused and critical. It is unquestionably the case that emergencies require unusual levels of centralized control; perhaps what has been lacking has been an entrenched habit of consultation before such decisions become urgent, so that a degree of trust will have been built up. That being said, it remains significant that the appeals just mentioned were possible and even persuasive. 'No one is safe unless everyone is safe' might well sum up a good deal of the thinking about solidarity outlined here; and it echoes the way in which a writer like Aruna D'Souza foregrounds *care* as a priority, ahead of the more obvious kinds of emotional engagement that might attract or satisfy our self-dramatizing habits. In a situation of pandemic disease, no one actually knows the extent of their potential dangerousness to others, no one knows the extent of their own jeopardy. In such a situation, the acknowledgement of 'indeterminate' responsibility for the neighbour is clearly a priority; and this clarifies what we have recognized as the challenging and not always straightforward injunctions about 'unlimited' responsibility that we have explored in some approaches to solidarity, as well as underlining the need and possibility of learning more about one's own complicity, conscious or not, in the process of discovering what work can be done in co-operation. It also serves as a reminder that solidarity is in its essence to do with creating safety – not static and heavily protected security but mutual confidence based on the knowledge that when one party is at risk or takes a risk, the other does what can be done to assure them of their fidelity. We are brought back once more to Tischner's vocabulary: fidelity belongs with the demanding truthfulness that solidarity requires in order that the work undertaken together may have a steady and dependable environment in which to unfold (meaning that tension and conflict should not have the last word).

Picking up an insight suggested by Bonhoeffer's theology of representation and responsibility, we might add that this imperative to act in the name of care and safety is not something that is given as any kind of 'reward'. While – as we saw earlier – it is bound to the love we owe to the other's capacity to give and to forget self-concern in that giving, we do not confer care on the other in proportion to their actual record as manifest and deliberate givers of life. We do so in the light of the acknowledgement that we are already interconnected with them, that the gift they give may, practically speaking, be more or less independent of their individual will, and that what is owed to them is owed simply in virtue of their status as indispensable elements in the network of finite life. Theologically speaking, this rests on the conviction that every finite agent is a unique crystallization of the infinite self-diffusing good that is the source of all. But even a relatively 'secularized' version of this can make some sense of the idea that, in an inescapably interdependent world, care cannot be seen as conditional, as an optional policy for individual benevolence; it is an appropriate, a 'just', response to the indeterminate or inscrutable web of agency in which our own identity and flourishing are located. In this context, we might say, ambitiously, that solidarity is an embodiment of *grace*: it is action that is simultaneously supremely 'apt' to the reality towards which it flows, and also unforced, non-mechanical, gratuitous. It is given in virtue of what another finite subject is rather than what it does. It is equally both 'just' *and* out of what we might think of as proportion. And all this takes us back to our opening discussions of the dangers of setting conditions for recognizing what counts as human, what we shall judge to be worthy of our attention or compassion. It is the fact of material partnership within the network of finite interdependence that grounds the unrestricted claim of 'solidaristic' co-operation, active compassion, love (in a sense different from simple individual affection or affinity, a sense that has something to do with utterly attentive fidelity to what is non-negotiably the case, a 'contemplative' faithfulness).

Solidarity as a moral and political theme is always, I have suggested, on the frontier of theology in these and other ways, inviting us to recall the language of irreversibly given human dignity, gratuitous mercy, the magnetic drawing of unchanging and unconditional self-giving, the communal enactment in liturgy and sacrament of all these things. The word 'liturgy', of course, means public or common work: there is more to be said[8] about religious and specifically Christian liturgy as a realization of solidarity in its most resourceful sense. The innate egalitarianism of being fed together with the same food, the disproportion between what is given and any idea of claim or earning, the weaving together of meaningful labour (the bread 'which human hands have made') with the prayerful re-enactment of the supreme moment of divine 'representation' of the mortal and devastated human condition we share – all of this is quintessentially a rite of solidarity grounded in the enacted, incarnate solidarity of God with creation; a conversational labour, and a labour of 'art'. If solidarity is to be sustainable, it will need ritual self-representation. One of the difficulties of our cultural setting is that we not only (as I've said earlier) lack settings in which we learn how to sustain the 'conversation of labour', we also lack a credible and socially accessible language of symbolic representation and renewal that holds us to our commitment and secures a language in which to speak about it. Richard Sennett, whose work deals extensively and effectively with ritual, writes[9] of how effective ritual manages the differentiation of exchanges, balancing the imperatives of co-operation and competition so as to avoid sterile confrontation and mutual silencing. Solidarity, it seems, needs some kind of ceremonial and celebratory articulation, a public drama of 'rebalancing' in which we are urged to imagine ourselves afresh as standing on common ground with common needs; and we currently live in a culture where even religious ritual can be assimilated to something other than itself, becoming one or another kind of performance generated by professionals for spectators, rather than a work that is both shared and differentiated.[10] Such rituals of solidarity as we have (sporting and political) tend to be passionately identitarian and conflictual. The exception is probably the large-scale rock concert, a context in which stars regularly gesture to inclusivity and non-confrontation as shared ideals. Events like this are by no means insignificant in influencing the temperature of moral culture, and it is a mistake to belittle their impact. But they are still dependent on an immense marketing operation and a systemic disconnection between providers and consumers, to a degree that makes it difficult to see them as 'liturgy' in the sense of something involving differentiated agency and genuine shared ownership.

More interesting from this point of view are ambitious community-based dramas – the 'Redcrosse' play designed for a St George's Day celebration in a multicultural community,[11] or the monumental Passion play directed by and starring Michael Sheen, performed in the streets of Port Talbot in 2011. Both looked for inspiration to the medieval 'mysteries', adapting and 'indigenizing' traditional narratives and involving non-professionals from the locality in both conception and performance. Both looked to embody a solidarity that became visible not so much in the common affirmation of a fixed identity but in a questioning exploration of the variegated experience and history at work in the hinterland of a community's contemporary life, aimed at deepening and enriching rather than defending a shared culture. A liturgy is indeed a process of labour, of production: its 'work' is to conduct a community from one position to another, verbalizing and dramatizing one set of roles and imaginative co-ordinates, exposing tensions and unfinished business, questioning and unsettling those co-ordinates, proposing alternatives, articulating the possibility of change, dramatizing new roles. On such a basis, these examples have a genuinely liturgical character. And it is not accidental that they are variants of 'sacred' narratives that are traditionally linked with practices that represent transformation or redemption in dramatic form, sacramental practices in the broadest sense.

All this deserves fuller discussion; but the main point is that we have some specific examples to flesh out what rituals of solidarity need to embody if they are not simply to reproduce existing divisions and existing imbalances of productive power and managing control. The critical solidarity that we are trying to characterize here is a process that enacts – sometimes literally dramatizes – the fundamental interdependence within which we exist. As such, it is bound to probe the habits and myths that seek to evade the recognition of this interdependence, whether by absolutizing our self-determination or denying to others their liberty to narrate their history and bring it into dialogue. It is systematically suspicious of any reduction of its scope to a prematurely defined communal good in which imbalances of power are not addressed, and so should not be a way of sidestepping necessary confrontation. But it will understand such confrontation as an act of faith in the possibility of continuing some sort of shared work, the construction of a culture of mutuality, the reciprocal assurance of faithfulness in times of jeopardy. It will resist anything that reduces its scope to empathic reaction only, but will involve imaginative projection and the suspension of a self-centred emotional focus. It will look for clarity about self and others; it will seek to 'see justly'.[12] And this struggle to clear our perception of self-reference and acquisitiveness is where the language of rights most intelligibly belongs.

Speaking of justice and clear vision in this way assumes that there is something to which we are commonly answerable, independent of our local needs and agendas; solidarity has – to this extent – a metaphysical hinterland. Not that we can lay hold of a definitive account of how we map the human place in the interweaving of the finite order; but we act, we work/converse, together in the trust that all who are engaged are engaged in a single, diverse and connected project of mutual 'creation', whose final aim is a maximal freedom of exchange, a mutual life-giving, extending into the non-human realm in the processes of listening and attuning to the patterns of natural growth, movement and flourishing. And such a framework has at its centre the conviction that the distinct personal subject is never an isolated, self-creating agent, but a reality that is formed in response and interaction; the metaphysics of solidarity is also a metaphysics of the irreducible relationality of personal/psychic identity – though it is clear that it ultimately entails a more comprehensive assertion of relational interdependence in all finite substance and agency.

Inimical to solidarity are habits of representing individual agency as self-defining and self-sufficient, and also of reducing the reality of what or who we encounter to what they can do unilaterally for *us*; habits of addiction to prescribing for the other the nature of the good that is to emerge from shared work; disparity or disconnection in what is said about the character of human flourishing; and – not least – the passionate 'will to feel innocent' diagnosed by Andrew Shanks. But for solidarity in its full sense to characterize political life – at local, national or international level – requires us above all to think again about the nature of work as a form of constructive *linguistic* activity in which the refining and extension of communication are at least as important as the achieving of a particular local outcome. As we have seen, 'liturgical' action, structured communal drama, is an acknowledgement of this. A solidarity that is to remain critical and creative in its engagement needs to build into its workings a ritual representation of its grounds and goals that will remind us of the context into which we are born and which we have not planned and scripted, the context that teaches us how to recognize ourselves as much as each other and also how to interrogate precisely the language that makes us recognizable to each other, scrutinizing what imbalances and exclusions are still at work.

This book has been written with the aim of evoking the larger and less anxious world that critical, labouring solidarity both assumes and creates. Communion is not an easy or cheaply consoling variety of warm togetherness, and its demands are serious and, yes, alarming; something *dies* in solidarity. The uncriticized, unchallenged claim of the solitary ego cannot survive in a deepening practice of communion and mutual recognition in common work for the fuller humanizing of our relations with one another and the world. But this is not a straightforward once-and-for-all act of dramatic renunciation. It needs learning, probing, testing and renewing. In a recent and very interesting book about the religious imagination of younger people at the present time, Lamorna Ash writes of her slightly younger self, 'Nothing in me was willing to be undone back then.'[13] She goes on immediately to add, 'To be kinder to my younger self, perhaps her identity was not stable enough yet to be undone.' The balance of the two statements crystallizes very acutely the tension between the seriousness and urgency of the imperative towards solidarity and the patient recognition that absolutist demands are less likely to move things on constructively. The decentring of the self paradoxically requires maturity and a measure of self-awareness, a freedom from anxiety that takes time to learn. We are not faced with any straightforwardly non-fatal options, but we should be realistic about the chances of any triumph for idealized selflessness in a culture where the sense of self is radically insecure. In this discussion, I have tried to see what might be involved in doing justice to the continuing reality of constructive, even nourishing distance and difference; solidarity is not about a mystical sinking into otherness. But it is a 'dislodging', a new imagining of what it is to be a self, to be *my* self, in that elusive relation we have been calling communion. The question is whether our understandable fear of this drastic rupture in the selfhood we take for granted is more or less rational than the fear we *ought* to feel at the erosion and shrinkage of the world that is promised by the refusal of communion.

ACKNOWLEDGEMENTS

As noted in the Prologue, much of the content of this book has been developed in lectures to various audiences over ten years or more, and I want to express my abiding gratitude for invitations to lecture, for hospitality of all kinds, and for so many transformative conversations about the issues touched on here, and a good many more.

Delivering the Tanner Lectures at Harvard in 2014, I was generously welcomed by Homi Bhabha, and provided with a stellar panel of respondents – Amy Hollywood, Richard Kearney, Emma Rothschild, Regina Schwartz, David Tracy and Nicholas Watson. Informal conversations with Michael Sandel and Elaine Scarry added still more intellectual nourishment to the visit. The Payton Lectures at Fuller Seminary in 2016 involved conversation with large groups of faculty and graduate students too numerous to list. At the Pontifical University of St Thomas Aquinas (the Angelicum) in Rome in 2022, Fr Thomas Joseph White OP and Fr Simon Gaine OP were unfailingly kind and affirming hosts, and a class of mostly Polish and Irish students proved a complete joy to engage with, in and out of the classroom, in the course of a series of lectures on the role of solidarity in Catholic Social Teaching and its wider theological implications. At Yale Divinity School in 2024 for the Taylor Lectures, Greg Sterling and Andrew McGowan made me very much at home over a week of intensive but rewarding work; and it was a privilege and delight to renew friendship with David Kelsey. In Oxford, the Electors to the Bampton Lectureship, particularly Jane Shaw, did all that could be done to support and encourage; and I must also thank John Vickers and Jan Royall for kind hospitality during the period of the delivery of the lectures, and Mark Jordan, visiting from Harvard, who offered a probing and sympathetic public response. Andrew Karpinski offered invaluable comment and insight on Jozef Tischner, the subject of his own current research and has been a major source of information and material for a lecturer with a painfully minimal grasp of Polish. Thanks also to David Cockburn for the invitation to the 2024 meeting of the Welsh Philosophical Society, and to all who shared in discussion at Gregynog Hall. My hosts in South Africa in November 2024 deserve special mention – and particularly Robert Bosloo, John de Gruchy and Marnus Havenga; and conversation with Ernst Conradie and Pumla Madikizela concentrated my mind in all sorts of helpful ways. I am very grateful.

Thanks too for exchanges over the years with a wide range of research students, colleagues and friends in all sorts of settings: among them Maria Balaska, Ragnar Mogard Bergem, Judith Butler, Howard Caygill, Hannah Critchlow, Damian Freeman, the late Kenneth Leech, Patrick McCormack, John Milbank, James Mumford, Adrian Pabst, Jacqueline Rose, Anna Rowlands, Andrew Shanks, Richard Sennett and Mary Zournazi. Working alongside Laura McAllister and other colleagues on the Independent Commission on the Constitutional Future of Wales between 2021 and 2024, as this book was taking shape, renewed my conviction that a positive renewal of political energy and intelligence, in a genuinely collaborative spirit across wide ideological divides, was still very much possible. The Commission, along with the ongoing work of the Bevan Foundation and the Wales Peace Academy/Academi Heddwch Cymru (led with such energy and inspiration by Mererid Hopwood), consistently offered hope at a time of much polarization in national and international contexts.

Liza Thompson at Bloomsbury has been an editor after any author's heart, sympathetic and constructively critical, full of ideas about material that might be looked at to enrich or qualify an argument, consistently encouraging but equally capable of being quite clear about what doesn't make sense. I have been very lucky to have her guidance, and I'm pretty certain that in the few cases where I have neglected this, I shall live to regret it.

And finally, as always, deepest gratitude to my family for their patience and love.

ENDNOTES

PROLOGUE

1 See Michael Battle, *Reconciliation; The Ubuntu Theology of Desmond Tutu*, Cleveland OH, Pilgrim Press 1997 for an overview of Tutu's use of the idea.
2 'May the Real Ubuntu Please Stand Up?' *Journal of Mass Media Ethics* 30.2, pp.125–47.
3 Edinburgh, T. and T. Clark 2000.
4 *Faith in the Public Square*, London, Bloomsbury/Continuum 2012.

INTRODUCTION

1 In a rather more surreal touch, some participants at the 2024 Republican Convention in the USA elected to wear bandages over their right ears in imitation of Donald Trump, whose ear had been injured a few days earlier in an assassination attempt.
2 We shall be coming back to the way in which the language of human rights is now a locus of last resort for the 'sacred' (the imaginatively unchallengeable, the level where the spade is turned) in popular modern moral discourse.
3 Howard Jacobson, *New Statesman* 14–20 June 2024, p.25.
4 For a detailed discussion that antedates the Black Lives Matter actions of 2020 and afterwards, and that also offers a finely nuanced overview of the development of solidarity language, see David Roediger, *Class, Race and Marxism*, London, Verso, 2017.
5 London, Bloomsbury 2022 (second enlarged edition).
6 See esp. pp.215–19; she discusses the bizarre history of how a seven-month-old story of terrorist attacks in Kenya, largely ignored at the time, was revived in the wake of the 2015 terrorist attacks at the Bataclan Concert Hall in Paris, as a belated effort to express interracial solidarity. 'Solidarity is nothing but self-satisfying if it is solely performative. A safety pin stuck to your lapel after a referendum about the EU that turned into a referendum on immigration is symbolic but it won't stop anyone from getting deported' (p.219).

7   Ibid., p.221.
8   *Together: The Rituals, Pleasures and Politics of Cooperation*, London, Allen Lane 2012, quoting from p. 279.
9   Ibid., p.39.
10 As readers of a certain age and background will know very well, you sing it to the tune of 'John Brown's Body.'
11 See, for example, John Johnston, *The Allure of Machinic Life: Cybernetics, Artificial Intelligence, and the New AI*, Cambridge MA, MIT Press 2016. The word 'human', Johnston suggests, might be seen 'less as the defining property of a species or individual and more as a value distributed throughout human-constructed environments, technologies, institutions and social collectivities' (p.141; quoted in Ilia Delio, *The Not-Yet God: Carl Jung, Teilhard de Chardin, and the Relational Whole*, Maryknoll, New York, Orbis Books 2023, p.153). More on AI later; and no, I am not sure either what this actually means for the individual victim of militarized rape in South Sudan, the homeless ex-soldier in Leeds or San Francisco, the child in a boatload of refugees in the English Channel…
12 See, for example, pp. 34–42 below.
13 The magisterial recent book by James Davison Hunter, *Democracy and Solidarity: On the Cultural Roots of America's Political Crisis*, New Haven and London, Yale University Press 2024, is a detailed analysis of the erosion and fragmentation of what he calls 'boundary work' – that is, the cultural labour of managing difference without social collapse, the *Durcharbeiten*, 'working through', of tension – a term borrowed, significantly, from psychoanalysis – so as to nudge us back towards an intelligible solidarity. He identifies the ways in which, by continually seeking primarily *political* or legal solutions to such tensions, we avoid this cultural labour, failing to grasp the priority of culture over politics. Hence the 'culture war' problem, reflecting the displacement of a proper understanding of culture itself.
14 A way of putting it that leaves open for now the question of whether we need to think of a long spectrum of recognition extending in some measure to parts of the non-human organic realm.
15 See Vladimir Lossky, *The Mystical Theology of the Eastern Church*, Cambridge, James Clarke 1957, p.122.

ENDNOTES

CHAPTER 1 RECOGNIZING STRANGERS: WHO COUNTS AS HUMAN?

1. Raimond Gaita, *A Common Humanity: Thinking about Love and Truth and Justice*, Melbourne, text Publishing 1999, p.57.
2. Ibid., p.58.
3. See his seminal essay, *The Struggle for Recognition: The Moral Grammar of Social Conflicts*, Cambridge MA, MIT Press 1995; also the discussion of this in relation to Gillian Rose's philosophy by Andrew Brower Latz, 'Towards a Rosean Political Theology of Recognition', in Joshua B. Davis (ed.), *Misrecognitions: Gillian Rose and the Task of Political Theology*, Eugene OR, Cascade Books 2018, pp.47–66, esp. pp.49–52 for a brief but usefully critical discussion of Honneth, noting the limitations imposed by his focus on group conflict over recognition. The issue of the radical refusal of recognition to the specific subjecthood of the other, the issue foregrounded in this chapter, opens up a rather more fundamental problem.
4. Joanna Bourke, *What It Means To be Human. Reflections from 1791 to the Present*, London, Virago 2011.
5. Bourke, op. cit., pp.45–6.
6. Ibid., pp.260 to 274.
7. Ibid., p.262.
8. For an overview setting this debate in its longer historical context, see Anthony Pagden, *The Fall of Natural Man: the American Indian and the Origins of Comparative Ethnology*, Cambridge University Press 1982. Roger Ruston, *Human Rights and the Image of God*, London, SCM 2004 (especially Part 3), also locates the debate against the background of earlier theological discussion about the rights of 'barbarians' (pp.81–7), while observing (p.85) that 'The moral unity of the human race, a fundamental principle of the debate about the Indians, is bought at the price of permanently excluding the non-human inhabitants of the earth from the sphere of justice and right.' And the stress on freedom and rationality as marks of the divine image means that if such freedom and rationality are deemed to be absent, there is no redress for 'deficient' humans.
9. On this, see for example Rebecca Anne Goetz, *The Baptism of Virginia. How Christianity Created Race*, Baltimore, Johns Hopkins University Press, 2016.
10. See Roger Ruston, op. cit. 253–9.

11 See below, chapter 6, pp.162–3 for Jozef Tischner's relevant arguments about what can and can't be an 'object' for the intelligence.
12 The idea that enslaved Africans could be regarded as literally a different species from the 'white race' had a good deal of traction in the eighteenth and nineteenth centuries, and fed into the nineteenth-century arguments between racial 'scientists' and religious believers about monogenism – the single origin of all human beings. On one vocal eighteenth-century proponent of the 'different species' thesis, see Catherine Hall, *Lucky Valley. Edward Long and the History of Racial Capitalism*, Cambridge University Press 2024; on aspects of the monogenism debate, see David N. Livingstone, *Adam's Ancestors. Race, Religion, and the Politics of Human Origins*, Baltimore, Johns Hopkins University Press 2008.
13 Bourke, pp.29–43.
14 Ibid., p.382.
15 Ibid., p.385. The risks of a 'flattening' account of solidarity, in which actual difference is erased by a dominant partner, were put to me forcefully in a seminar at the University of Stellenbosch in October 2024, and I am grateful for the points made in that context.
16 Ibid.; the book's final sentence on this page tellingly brackets 'community' with 'communion'.
17 Darwin's treatment of this in *The Expression of the Emotions in Man and Animals* (London, John Murray 1872; and see the edition of 2009 from Oxford University Press with introduction and commentary by P. Ekman).
18 For example, the work of Adam Waytz; see his contribution to the *Oxford Handbook of Social Exclusion* ('Social Connection and Seeing Human'), Oxford 2013, pp.251–6, and (with N. Epley and J. T. Cacioppo), 'On Seeing Human: a Three-Factor Theory of Anthropomorphism', *Psychological Review* 114 (4), pp.864–6.
19 Bourke, op. cit., pp.61–2.
20 Below, pp.44–8 and chapter 2, pp.65–7.
21 We shall be returning to this in discussion of thinkers such as Edith Stein in Chapter 2; see also Maurice Merleau-Ponty, *The Phenomenology of Perception*, tr. Colin Smith, London, Routledge and Kegan Paul, 1962, especially Part One, Chapter 3 and Part Two, Chapter 4.
22 Ibid., pp.7–8; and the whole issue is discussed at length in ch.5, pp.71–92.

23 Bourke, op. cit., pp.108–14.
24 Kazuo Ishiguro's 2021 novel, *Klara and the Sun*, is a notably good example; it works with some of the same emotional repertoire that is more melodramatically presented in Steven Spielberg's 2001 film, *A.I.* More recently, the 2023 Gareth Edwards film, *The Creator*, develops further elaboration of the theme; and, famously, the *Matrix* franchise has for over two decades pursued an ambitious thought experiment that has sparked some serious philosophical interest.
25 The burgeoning philosophical literature is – unsurprisingly – inconclusive. Daniel Dennett's magisterial *Consciousness Explained* (Boston, Little, Brown and Co. 1992), along with the later *Content and Consciousness* (London, Routledge 2010), provided a nuanced and comprehensive version of the 'epiphenomenon' approach that has proved very influential. David Chalmers, *The Conscious Mind. In Search of a Fundamental Theory* (Oxford University Press,1996), is the weightiest proponent of the counter-argument favouring a non-mechanical account.
26 New York, Coward, McCann and Geoghegan.
27 Conveniently reprinted in Douglas R. Hofstadter and Daniel C. Dennett, ed., *The Mind's I. Fantasies and Reflections on Self and Soul*, London, Harvester Press 1981, pp.108–13.
28 Ibid., p.108.
29 Ibid., p.112.
30 Ibid., p.110.
31 Ibid., p.112.
32 Ibid., p.113.
33 Ibid., p.115.
34 See, for example, William B. Hurlbut, 'Neurobiology and the Psychology of Desire', pp.101–19 in Pierpaolo Antonello and Paul Gifford, ed., *How We Became Human: Mimetic Theory and the Science of Evolutionary Origins*, East Lansing, Michigan State University Press 2015; the phrase cited is from p.102 of this article.
35 Wittgenstein's treatment of the issue in *Philosophical Investigations* (3rd edition, Oxford, Blackwell 2003, esp. pp.82–9.) remains the *locus classicus* for interrogating the idea that 'pain behaviour' is in any obvious sense a *piece of evidence* for assessing another person's state of mind, the 'trace', as it were, of an underlying experience, in respect of which we should need to decide whether these signs genuinely represented what they seem to represent and so could

be accepted as evidence for the intrinsically unreachable interior feelings of another. The contrast with the theatrical context is clear. The actor representing a person in pain (or the robot programmed to simulate pain) is deliberately reproducing the phenomenon of pain by representing the 'unplanned' expression or embodiment of a subject's state; they will be following a cultural convention that counts certain actions as credible representations (so that, in something like Japanese Noh drama, the convention may be highly stylized rather than directly imitative). But what I have called the 'unplanned' behaviour we encounter outside the theatre or laboratory is not normally judged according to these cultural conventions of credibility, and we should be surprised and uncomfortable if it were so – despite the fact that, as we have seen, some have apparently found no difficulty in interpreting away the signs of pain or distress exhibited by those judged to be 'substandard' humans, or 'mere' animals...

36 'Just try – in a real case – to doubt someone else's fear or pain' (Wittgenstein, op. cit., p.86).

37 See, for example, a brief and pungent essay, 'Computers Can't Do Math' by David Schaengold in *Plough Quarterly* 48, Summer 2024, pp.24–32, noting that 'Computers have no target beyond the counters they actually have. What they can count *simply is* what they can represent' (p.30). Thus there may be numbers that a computer cannot represent, and no single system can guard against this, or 'notice' the inconsistencies or plain nonsense that will emerge, in the way that a human observer will in virtue of their conceptual fluency.

38 Bourke, op. cit., p.104.

39 See, for example, his groundbreaking discussion in 'Declining Decline: Wittgenstein as a Philosopher of Culture', in *This New Yet Unapproachable America* (the 1987 Frederick Ives Carpenter lectures at the University of Chicago), Living Batch Press, Albuquerque, New Mexico 1989), pp.29–75, especially pp.51–2, 56–7. In the background is his magisterial treatment in the concluding section of *The Claim of Reason. Wittgenstein, Skepticism, Morality and Tragedy*, Oxford University Press 1979 (see particularly pp.420–2, 450–8).

40 *This New Yet Unapproachable America*, p.48.

41 Ibid., p.58.

42 In addition to Rorty's classic essay of 1979, *Philosophy and the Mirror of Nature* (Princeton University Press), the lectures printed as *Contingency, Irony, Solidarity* in 1989 (Cambridge University Press) are relevant on this.

43 For a shrewd critique of Rorty, spelling out some of this political unease and also charging him with reintroducing a philosophically primitive gulf between the practice of language and what is Really There, see D. Z. Phillips, 'Reclaiming the Conversations of Mankind', *Philosophy* 69 (1994), pp.35–53. Phillips has some interesting critiques of Cavell also (as in the chapter on 'Cavell and the Limits of Acknowledgement' in Phillips, *Philosophy's Cool Place*, London and Ithaca, Cornell University Press 1999, and 'Winch and Romanticism', *Philosophy* 77 (2002), pp.261–79).

44 Phoebe Caldwell's innovative work with young people living with severe autistic conditions is significant here; see especially *Finding You Finding Me* (London, Jessica Kingsley Publications 2006) and (with Jane Horwood) *From Isolation to Intimacy: Making Friends Without Words* (London, Jessica Kingsley Publications 2007), particularly ch.6, with its careful discussion of the limits of applying a 'theory of mind' to the phenomena of autism. She invites us to think of autism not as a case of plain incapacity to understand the interiority of another, connected with some malfunction of mirror neurones in the brain, but as a deficiency in a wider environment where neurodiverse forms of absorbing stimuli and information are not acknowledged by others, and so not 'fed back' to the neurodiverse subject. Therapeutic care and intervention thus begin with a learning *by the therapist* of the body language of the neurodiverse subject.

45 'Losing Your Concepts', *Ethics* 98.2, pp.255–77. See also her paper, 'The Importance of Being Human', in *Human Beings*, ed. David Cockburn, Cambridge University Press 1991, pp.35–82.

46 'Winch and Romanticism', esp. pp.264–5, 276. He associates Cavell with this approach, underrating, I think, the subtlety with which Cavell handles the complicity between scepticism and Romanticism touched on above.

47 Below, chapter 2, esp. pp.51–9.

48 Gaita, *A Common Humanity* p.263.

49 Gaita, op. cit., p.262.

50 Above, p.12.

CHAPTER 2 UNDERSTANDING STRANGERS:
EMPATHY AND ITS PARADOXES

1   *Zero Degrees of Empathy. A New Theory of Human Cruelty and Kindness*, London, Allen Lane 2011; quotation from p.132.
2   Ibid., p.8 (italics in original).
3   Ibid., pp.11–12.
4   Particularly in ch.2, 'The Empathy Mechanism: The Bell Curve.'
5   Ibid., pp.26–7.
6   *Empathy: A History*, New Haven and London, Yale University Press 2018, ch.9, esp. pp.269–76.
7   Baron-Cohen, op. cit., pp.58–9.
8   Ibid., p.9.
9   pp.11–12.
10 Ibid., p.132.
11 Aruna D'Souza, *Imperfect Solidarities*, Berlin, Floating Opera Press 2024.
12 This is connected with the point made above (pp.48–9) about the problematic effects of imagining that the ideal state of 'knowledge' of another subject is a matter of indubitable access to their inner lives.
13 The reference is to the work of the Filipino artist, Stephanie Syjuco.
14 Dylan Robinson, *Hungry Listening: Resonant Theory for Indigenous Sound Studies*, Minneapolis, University of Minnesota Press 2020.
15 D'Souza, op. cit., p.37. This, for D'Souza, is where we are confronted with a claim of solidarity independent of fellow-feeling and of any requirement for someone to prove their credentials as deserving of care. Cf. p.53 for a quotation from Édouard Glissant on the way in which the 'Western imaginary' requires me to 'measure your solidity with the ideal scale providing me with grounds to make comparisons and, perhaps, judgements'. The convergences with Joanna Bourke's discussions, summarized above in chapter 1, are obvious.
16 Ibid., p.83.
17 Ibid., p.81.
18 Lanzoni, op. cit., chaps. 7 and 8.
19 Ibid., p.215.
20 Roman Krznaric, *Empathy; A Handbook for Revolution*, London, Rider/Random House 2014, does not avoid this trap, especially

with an awkward chapter on 'Experiential Adventures'; the goal – breaking the boundaries of one's comfort zone in order to understand strangers – is praiseworthy, but the register of the language is uncomfortably focused on individual transformation, with a corresponding naivete about how imbalances of power might be challenged and changed.

21 Minneapolis, Graywolf Press 2014.
22 Jamison, p.22; worth noticing that her use of 'care' is not the same as D'Souza's. 'Care' here is very much a self-focused phenomenon, reminding us of the complexity and diversity of how we use the vocabulary of moral and emotional engagement with what is beyond the self.
23 Ibid., p.23.
24 Ibid., pp.156–9.
25 Ibid. p.226.
26 Matthieu Ricard, *Altruism: The Power of Compassion to Change Yourself and the World*, New York/Boston/London, Little Brown and Company 2015, pp.56–64.
27 Lanzoni's chapter 9, on 'Empathic Brains' is a very judicious discussion of this.
28 Jamison, op. cit., p.23.
29 Ibid., p.130.
30 Lanzoni, op. cit., p.276.
31 Ibid., p.279.
32 Selected chapters published as *Zur Problem der Einfühlung*, Halle, Buchdruckerei des Waisenhauses 1917. For a critical edition, see vol. xx of the standard collection of her works, Freiburg/Basel/Wien, Herder 2008. ET from the earlier edition by Waltraut Stein, *On the Problem of Empathy*, Washington DC, Institute of Carmelite Studies 1989 (a new translation utilizing the critical text and clarifying some of the obscurities in this version would be welcome).
33 *On the Problem of Empathy*, p.6.
34 There is a helpful summary and discussion in ch.9 of Alasdair MacIntyre, *Edith Stein: A Philosophical Prologue*, London/New York, Continuum 2006, pp.75–87.
35 *On the Problem of Empathy*, pp.10, 16. It is instructive to compare this with the phraseology of Adam Smith in his *Theory of Moral Sentiments*, where he proposes understanding sympathy as putting

oneself 'in the case' of another. For some fascinating discussion of this, see James Chandler, *An Archaeology of Sympathy. The Sentimental Mode in Literature and Cinema*, Chicago and London, University of Chicago Press 2013, esp. pp.171–5, 302–3. As we shall see, Stein draws the line between empathy and sympathy in a different place from Smith.

36 *On the Problem of Empathy*, pp.40 ff.
37 Ibid., p.43.
38 Ibid., p.47.
39 Ibid., pp.61–4.
40 MacIntyre, op. cit., p.83.
41 See Fanny Howe, *The Wedding Dress: Meditations on Word and Life*, Berkeley, Los Angeles and London, University of California Press 2002, pp.47–8: '[Stein] suggested that emptiness – space – teaches us to mistrust the location of the "I" inside us, since it exists as a "zero point of reference," being both at the source of the physical body and on its periphery where it, too, becomes empty…[T]his emptiness (Zero) contains something that wants to be found in the way it surrounds a person.' Thank you to Romana Huk for this reference.
42 Cf. Stanley Cavell, 'Notes Mostly About Empathy' in *Here and There: Sites of Philosophy*, Harvard University Press 2022, pp.164–80, esp. p.175: '[W]e may actually stop to ask what our own feelings are imagined to be *in response to* another's anger or pain.' That is to say, we need to understand that our being seen must become part of our adequate seeing of ourselves; seeing/knowing myself is not a matter of clear, solid connection with my state of mind as opposed to the uncertain connection I have with the minds of others.
43 Stein, op. cit., pp.66ff.
44 Above, p.46; cf. Stein, op. cit., p.112 on how human action 'bids for understanding' – asks to be read, we might say.
45 Stein, op. cit., pp.59, 76–7.
46 Maurice Merleau-Ponty, *Phenomenology of Perception*, London, Routledge and Kegan Paul 1962, p.193; the whole of this chapter ('The Body as Expression, and Speech') is worth reading in tandem with Stein's thesis.
47 Stein, op. cit. p.59.
48 Merleau-Ponty's treatment of this in *The World of Perception*, London, Routledge 2004, ch.4, is pertinent here. See also the

important essay by Richard Holton and Rae Langton, 'Empathy and Animal Ethics' in Dale Jamieson (ed.) *Singer and His Critics*, Malden, Mass., Wiley Blackwell 1999, pp.209–32.

49 Stein, op. cit., pp.109–12. There is a convergence here with some of the concepts used by Jozef Tischner around the inescapably 'axiological' character of human behaviour; see chapter 5 below, esp. pp.163–4.

50 Ibid., p.116.

51 See Gillian Rose, *Mourning Becomes the Law: Philosophy and Representation*, Cambridge University Press 1996, pp.61–2, 72–6; and cf. Rowan Williams, *Solidarity: Necessary Fiction or Metaphysical Given* (the third Gillian Rose Memorial Lecture), Kingston-upon-Thames, CRMEP Books 2023.

52 Stein, p.111.

53 As in Edith Stein, *Finite and Eternal Being*, tr. Kurt F. Reinhardt, Washington DC, Institute of Carmelite Studies 2002, pp.359–78, 447–64.

54 *On the Problem of Empathy*, pp.14–15.

55 Stein, op.cit., pp.20–3.

56 Or at the very least, thinking back to the quotation from Cavell above (n.42), my perception of my mental and psychic processes is augmented by learning how they appear as responses to actions by others.

57 See, for example, ch.3 of Gillian Rose, *Mourning Becomes the Law*, and also the very complex argument in ch. 6 of *The Broken Middle: Out of our Ancient Society*, Oxford, Blackwell 1992.

58 Cavell again, *Here and There*, p.174 on the desire 'for a passage past a standing barrier to the knowledge of the other' and its connection with 'the demand for taking on the other's introspection'.

59 Paul Bloom, *Against Empathy: The Case for Rational Compassion*, London, Vintage 2016. For a (particularly insightful) further discussion of the complexity of the relation between empathy and ethical decision, see Holton and Langton, 'Empathy and Animal Ethics', (above, n. 48); and, for a less philosophically-oriented discussion, Sarah Songhorian, 'The Contribution of Empathy to Ethics', in Maria Baghramian, Meline Papazian and Rowland Stout, *The Value of Empathy*, London, Routledge 2021, pp.122–43. Sophie-Grace Chappell's brilliant *Epiphanies: An Ethics of Experience*, Oxford University Press 2022, includes (especially pp.362–82) a lucid critique of vague appeals to empathy converging with much of what is argued here.

60 Ibid. ch.5.
61 Ibid., p.163.
62 Ibid., ch.3. The tactics of charity advertising make an intriguing study; many major development agencies have faced substantial moral questions about what images can and should be used to appeal to potential donors, and there is a growing awareness of what some have called 'charity porn', the conscious deployment of maximally emotionally urgent images to increase donations. Some aid charities have very deliberately minimized their use of images of suffering (especially suffering children) so as to avoid this trap, even at the risk of jeopardizing donations. A notable moral quagmire.
63 Ibid., pp.137–9.
64 These are the terms cited by Songhorian, art. cit., p,132. Cf. in the same volume Riana J. Betzler, 'Finding Empathy: How Neuroscientific Measures, Evidence and Conceptualizations Interact', pp.102–22, esp. p.118 on definitions of empathy in recent neuroscientific discussion in terms of 'affective' states that are 'isomorphic' with those of others and stand in a conscious relation of causal dependence to those other states. The word 'affective' is a helpful alternative to 'emotional', allowing something of the broader perspective defended here.
65 'Empathy and First-Personal Imagining', *Proceedings of the Aristotelian Society* 119.1 (April 2019), pp.77–104; cf. Chappell, *Epiphanies*, pp 372–3, on empathy as a 'thought experiment'.
66 Cavell, *Here and There*, p.180.
67 See the essay by Riana Betzler mentioned above (n.111), as well as Paul Bloom's reservations in *Against Empathy*.
68 For a popular and lucid account of this, see Sue Gerhardt, *Why Love Matters. How Affection Shapes a Baby's Brain*, Hove and New York, Brunner-Routledge 2024, ch.2, esp. pp.35–46.
69 Most recently, the two volumes of *The Matter with Things. Our Brains, Our Delusions, and the Unmaking of the World*, London, Perspectiva Press 2021.
70 McGilchrist gives some dramatic examples of three crucial malfunctions in brains whose right hemisphere operations have been inhibited or injured. There may be an inability to connect separate areas of a perceived object that would normally be seen as a whole – notably a human face or body – so that all that the person can

represent visually is a series of physically disjoined items. There may be a discontinuity in the body's experience of itself as a whole, so that individual organs or limbs are not recognized as part of one's own body. And there may be a disjunction as regards awareness of time, an incapacity to experience or construct a continuous narrative of the subject's past.

71 The phenomenon famously and vividly described in the work of Oliver Sacks, especially *A Leg to Stand On* (New York, Harper and Row 1984) and *The Man Who Mistook His Wife For a Hat* (New York, Summit Books 1985).

72 Bourke, *What It Means to Be Human*, p.261. Bourke notes (pp.205–8) some of the contortions that Levinas has to go through in handling the question of whether it is possible to have an ethical relationship (to recognize the face of an ethical other) where an animal is concerned. Levinas relates a moving recollection of a dog in the prison camp where he was a slave labourer, a dog that reacted with excitement and apparent delight to the presence of human beings of all kinds, in stark contrast to the inhumanity of the camp guards. Yet he still considers animality as such to be no more than a struggle for survival, while humanity transcends this in its 'unreasonable' capacity for moral openness to others over and above what is necessary for material security. Levinas's discussion can be found in 'The Name of a Dog; or Natural Rights', in *Difficult Freedom: Essays on Judaism*, London, Athlone Press 1990. As noted in the first chapter, the refusal of moral recognition to the animal world is regularly bound up with the legacy of a philosophy that treated signs of animal 'subjectivity' (including suffering) as seductive invitations to project on to animal life an interiority that could not in fact be present, invitations to a childish anthropomorphism.

CHAPTER 3 THE CLAIMS OF STRANGERS: DEBATING HUMAN RIGHTS

1 Oliver O'Donovan, *The Ways of Judgment*, Grand Rapids, Eerdmans 2005, p.297.
2 Costas Douzinas and Conor Gearty, eds, *The Meanings of Rights: The Philosophy and Social Theory of Human Rights*, Cambridge University Press 2014.

3. Especially *The End of Human Rights: Critical Thought at the Turn of the Century*, London, Hart 2000, *Human Rights and Empire: The Political Philosophy of Cosmopolitanism*, London, Routledge 2007, and *The Radical Philosophy of Rights*, London, Routledge 2019. The main arguments of the first of these are distilled in 'The End(s) of Human Rights', *Melbourne University Law Review* 23 (2003), at https://www5.austlii.edu.au/au/journals/MelbULawRw/2002/23.html, accessed 16/07/2024.
4. In section III of his Melbourne University Law Review digest.
5. On the association between rights and both national sovereignty and cosmopolitan/globalizing politics, see also Samuel Moyn, 'Plural Cosmopolitanisms and the origins of human rights', in Douzinas and Gearty, pp.193–211, as well as his major work, *The Last Utopia: Human Rights in History*, Harvard University Press 2010.
6. See his essay, 'Against Human Rights: Liberty in the Western Tradition', in Douzinas and Gearty, pp.39–70. There is a slightly different text – in which some of the arguments (including a critique of the present writer) are significantly extended, but rather confusingly sharing the same title – in the *Oxford Journal of Law and Religion* i.1.2012, pp.203–34. I shall be referring to both versions in what follows.
7. Thomas Aquinas, *Summa Theologiae* II.ii.58.xii, c.(*iustitia autem laudatur secundum quod virtuous ad alium bene se habet; et sic iustitia quodammodo est bonum alterius*), which draws on Book V of Aristotle's *Nicomachean Ethics*.
8. Douzinas and Gearty, pp.50–1; see Michel Villey, *Le droit et les droits de l'homme*, Paris, PUF 1983. Milbank is defending Villey against the criticisms of Nicholas Wolterstorff, *Justice: Rights and Wrongs*, Princeton University Press 2008.
9. In section I of his Melbourne University Law Review paper.
10. Roger Ruston, *Human Rights and the Image of God*, p.279.
11. Art. cit., Douzinas and Gearty, pp.40–1.
12. Ibid., p.41, and the discussion that immediately follows.
13. 'On a Radical Politics for Human Rights', in Douzinas and Gearty, pp.106–20, especially p.117.
14. *Summa Theologiae* II.ii.66.vii.c
15. Art. cit., section 2.
16. Boethius, *contra Eutychen* 29.1.2; see Thomas Gilby, OP, *Principality and Polity: Aquinas and the Rise of State Theory in the West*, London,

Longmans 1958, p.238, for the identification of this formula and similar phrases in Boethius as a statement of the person's 'inalienable value'.

17 This is close to but not quite identical with the view argued by Brian Tierney, *The Idea of Natural Rights: Studies on Natural Rights, Natural Law and Church Law 1150–1625*, Atlanta GA, Scholars' Press 1997; Milbank (pp.57–9 in Douzinas and Gearty), while acknowledging the weight of Tierney's scholarship on the details of medieval argument, contends that he overstates the degree to which Aquinas can be seen as anticipating something like a doctrine of 'subjective' right and minimizes the scale of the intellectual rupture represented by later medieval approaches like that of Ockham.

18 On this, see B. Brady's lucid and comprehensive article on 'The Evolution of Human Dignity in Catholic Morality', *Journal of Moral Theology* 10.1 (2021), pp.1–25, notably pp.3–7 on the use of *dignitas* in Aquinas, for whom it is something inherent in the human person, yet existing in varying degrees and subject to diminution or suspension as a result of various kinds of circumstance or in order to protect the common good. The *Summa Theologiae* II.11, qu.64 and 65, for example, detail how a legitimate authority may inflict extreme punishment (imprisonment, mutilation or death) that overrides human 'dignity' to avoid grave injury to others. On this question, see also Samuel Moyn, *Christian Human Rights*, and Anna Rowlands, *Towards a Politics of Communion: Catholic Social Teaching in Dark Times*, London, Bloomsbury 2021, e.g. pp.47–57. I am very grateful to my former research student, Patrick McCormick, for insights on this topic.

19 Ernest Fortin, *Classical Christianity and the Political Order: Reflections on the Theologico–Political Problem*, ed. J. Brian Benestad, Lanham MD, Rowman and Littlefield 1996, p.229.

20 Op.cit., p.203. Drucilla Cornell in her essay in Douzinas and Gearty ('Fanon Today', pp.121–36), notes the case of the French revolutionary, Olympe de Gouges, who argued that if women had the 'right' to be guillotined, they must by implication have the right to civic equality. It is a rather unexpected echo of Fortin's point.

21 Nigel Biggar, *What's Wrong with Rights?* Oxford University Press 2020, while arguing against what he terms a 'fundamentalism' of forensically defined rights, and also against pretty well any recognizable version of incommunicable or inalienable natural right, also

helpfully queries some of the more overdrawn contrasts between medieval and modern discourse.
22 Art.cit., Douzinas and Gearty, p.64.
23 Ibid., p.59.
24 For some sympathetic discussion, see *Contemporary Human Rights Challenges: The Universal Declaration of Human Rights and its Continuing Relevance*, ed. Carla Ferstman, Alexander Goldberg, Tony Gray, Liz Ison, Richard Nathan and Michael Newman, London, Routledge 2019.
25 On this subject, the work of Pamela Slotte is particularly illuminating; see especially her '"Blessed Are the Peacemakers": Christian Internationalism, Ecumenical Voices and the Universal Declaration of Human Rights' in Pamela Slotte and Miia Halme-Tuomisaari, eds, *Revisiting the Origins of Human Rights*, Cambridge University Press 2015, and 'Whose Justice, What Political Theology? On Christian and Theological Approaches to Human Rights in the Twentieth and Twenty-First Centuries', in M. Koskenniemi, M. García-Salmones Rovira and P. Amorosa, eds, *International Law and Religion*, Oxford University Press 2017. See also Meghan J. Clark, *The Vision of Catholic Social Thought*, pp.9–10.
26 Rowan Williams, 'Religious Liberties and the Need for Moral Universalism' in *Contemporary Human Rights Challenges*, pp.141–7, quotation from p.146.
27 See Roger Ruston, *Human Rights and the Image of God*, p.287: 'It is… difficult to see how the conclusion of basic human equality could have been arrived at in any other way than through the mediation of a religious conviction'. This whole section of his Conclusion (pp.284–8) is particularly helpful in mapping the unavoidable tensions between what he calls (following Michael Walzer) 'thick' and 'thin' views of the social good in a religiously and culturally plural world – i.e. between models strongly anchored in specific historical communities and models that prescind from this in the name of brokering peace between radically different cultural and moral worlds. Ruston's argument is that the rootedness of a view of natural right in a specific theological culture does not automatically mean that it is incapable of being deployed in a wider and more secular framework; but problems arise when this rootedness is completely obscured.
28 As quoted by Ruston, op. cit., p.286.

29 Art. cit., pp.63–4.
30 *Summa Theologiae* II.ii.104.5. Freedom of religious commitment is also exempt from the authority of the master.
31 For a discussion of the ethics of disobedience in a modern context, with close attention to the Marxist rationale for revolutionary action, see Howard Caygill, *On Resistance: A Philosophy of Defiance*, London, Bloomsbury 2013, esp. chapter 5.
32 Rowan Williams, 'Religious Faith and Human Rights' in Douzinas and Gearty, pp.71–82, quotation from p.74.
33 Milbank in his *Oxford Journal of Law and Religion* text, p.231.
34 Ibid., p.231.
35 Williams, 'Religious Faith and Human Rights', pp.75–7.
36 Milbank, op. cit., p.232.
37 Ibid., pp.232–3.
38 Ibid.
39 For a very helpful and far from reassuring survey of recent instances of this in legal rulings, see Malcolm Evans, 'Human Rights and the Freedom of Religion', in Michael Ipgrave, ed., *Justice and Rights: Christian and Muslim Perspectives*, Washington DC, Georgetown University Press 2009, pp.109–16.
40 The 1904 ruling of the House of Lords in the case of the Free Church of Scotland Appeals is regularly cited as an example of how the legal processes of the state can misconceive the very nature of a voluntary religious body by treating it simply as a legal trust with no intrinsic capacity to adjust or develop its doctrine and practice. There is a well-known discussion of this by the Anglican historian and political theorist, John Neville Figgis, in the first chapter of his *Churches in the Modern State*, London, Longmans, Green and Co. 1913.
41 He writes (Douzinas and Gearty, p.44): 'And while contemporary China may, for the moment, ignore crucial aspects of "human rights", there is nothing in its agenda of over-riding the natural justice of procreation or of consigning masses of people to misery in the name of economic and political progress which is essentially out of keeping with the principles of liberalism, nor its past manifestations in the west in terms of various (subtle as well as unsubtle) eugenicist procedures, besides processes of primary accumulation that have commodified land, labour and value.' See also, the longer version of the article in the *Oxford Journal of Law and Religion*, pp.232–3, on the question of whether a legal sovereign can decide to override religious

rights in order to secure a universal and homogeneous application of the rights of women or gay people, or could support a local congregation against the norms and authorities of its own tradition. He goes on to discuss how the notion of a purely individual and inalienable 'right' can be seen as threatened or violated by *any* notion of collective norms or even the democratically expressed will of a majority, leading to 'post-democratic totalitarian market anarchy'. Prescient words: technocratically obsessed libertarianism has in recent months become a more than academic worry in politics, especially in the USA.

42 Art. cit., section 8.
43 Douzinas and Gearty, pp.119–20; and cf. in the same collection the essays by Drucilla Cornell, Paul Gilroy, Bruce Robbins and Joseph R. Slaughter, which cast light on the 'imaginative' imperative from various standpoints.
44 Ibid., p.119.
45 pp.101–5 of his 'Philosophy and the Right to Resistance' in Douzinas and Gearty.
46 Ibid., pp.103–4.
47 Ibid., p.105 (italics in original).
48 Douzinas in his Melbourne Law Society essay (section 6) is less happy with the word 'communion' or any language that would entail a notion of 'common substance'; as he puts it, there is a difference between 'being in common' and 'common being', with the former as the preferred register for talking about an ethically serious common life. As we shall see later on, the theological senses of 'communion' offer more resources than he allows.

CHAPTER 4 SOLIDARITY: THE MAKING OF A DISCOURSE

1 On the history of the term, see Marie-Claude Blais, *La solidarité; histoire d'une idee*, Paris, Gallimard 2007; and much more briefly but helpfully, the article 'Solidarismus' by Alois Baumgartner in the *Lexikon für Theologie und Kirche*. For an excellent overview of the debates around its meaning in the last 200 years, to which I am heavily indebted, see the article by Andrea Sangiovanni and Juri Viehoff on 'Solidarity in Social and Political Philosophy' in the *Stanford Encyclopaedia of Philosophy* (ed. Edward N. Zalta and Uri Nodelman; https://plato.stanford.edu/archives/sum2023/entries/solidarity/; accessed 29/07/2024). Sangiovanni's monograph on *Solidarity:*

Nature, Grounds and Value was published by Manchester University Press later in 2024.
2. *Solidarité: vue synthétique sur la doctrine de Charles Fourier.*
3. For a telling quotation from the Comtean Pierre Leroux, see p.87 of Jacek Salij, 'On Solidarity, Somewhat Theologically', in *Thinking in Values. The Tischner Institute Journal of Philosophy* 1 (2007), pp.85–95: solidarity is presented as intrinsically less self-oriented than Christian charity. As Salij notes here, this explains the initial lukewarmness of some French Catholic theologians towards the term.
4. See, for example, texts discussed in ch. 4 of Kenneth Allan, *Explorations in Classical Sociological Theory: Seeing the Social World* (1st ed.), Newbury Park CA, Pine Forge Press 2005, esp. pp.107, 110–11.
5. Above, pp.17–19.
6. Sections 1 and 2.5 of Sangiovanni and Viehoff deal extensively and lucidly with these questions in slightly different terms.
7. Avery Kolers, *A Moral Theory of Solidarity*, Oxford University Press 2016.
8. See Reni Eddo-Lodge, *Why I'm No Longer Talking to White People about Race*, esp. chapter 3.
9. Rose, *Judaism and Modernity: Philosophical Essays*, Oxford, Blackwell 1993, pp.8, 218–19, *The Broken Middle*, p.254.
10. Rose, *Judaism and Modernity*, p.8.
11. *Judaism and Modernity*, p.217.
12. See Williams, *Solidarity: Necessary Fiction or Metaphysical Given* for development of this formulation.
13. See Valeria Manzano, 'Fraternalmente americanos: el Movimiento Nueva Solidaridad y la emergencia de una contracultura en la decada de 1960', *Iberamericana* xvii.66 (2017), pp.115–38; pp.120–1 for the Arango quotations (*no es la vieja idiota fraternidad humana*). See also Grethel Domenech Hernández, 'Por una nueva solidaridad; *El Corno Emplumado* y la conformacion de una red de fraternidad intellectual (1962–1969)', *Secuencia* (108) 2020, pp.1–29.
14. Manzano, art. cit., p.118.
15. E.g. ibid., pp.115, 122.
16. *Todos frente a las presiones de sociedades deshumanizantes* ('all those facing the pressures of dehumanizing societies'); the phrase is found in the 1964 meeting's concluding document, *Paz a traves del arte*, 'Peace through Art'; Manzano, art. cit., pp.131–2.

17 Ibid., pp.124, 125; cf. Thomas Merton, *Dancing in the Water of Life: The Journals of Thomas Merton*, vol.5 1963–1968, HarperSanFrancisco 1997, pp.89–90. Merton was at this time regularly in contact with a number of leading Latin American poets and radicals.
18 Manzano, art. cit., p.124.
19 See Martin O'Malley, *Wilhelm Ketteler and the Birth of Modern Catholic Social Thought: A Catholic Manifesto 1848*, Munich, Herbert Utz Verlag 2008, for a helpful overview; also the article, *Solidarismus* by Alois Baumgartner in the *Lexikon für Theologie und Kirche*.
20 Anna Rowlands, *Towards a Politics of Communion: Catholic Social Teaching in Dark Times*, pp.24–5.
21 Freiburg, Herder 1899–1901; translated by Rupert J. Ederer as *Liberalism, Socialism and Christian Social Order* (5 volumes), Lewiston, Queenston and Lampeter, Edwin Mellen Press 2000.
22 Pesch, *Liberalism, Socialism and Christian Order*, vol.1, pp.29–30.
23 Ibid., pp.202–7.
24 Ibid., p.210.
25 Ibid., p.242.
26 Ibid., vol.2, pp.9–15.
27 Ibid., p.9.
28 Ibid., pp.9–10.
29 Ibid., pp.10–11.
30 Ibid., p.12.
31 Ibid., p.123.
32 Freiburg, Herder 1905–1923; translated by Rupert Ederer as *Teaching Guide to Economics*, Lewiston, Queenston and Lampeter, Edwin Mellen Press 2002–3.
33 See William R. Hauk Jr, 'Heinrich Pesch and the Anglo-German Divide in Economics', https://www.haukeconomics.com/pages/working_papers/pesch.pdf (accessed 31/07/2024).
34 As spelled out in Rupert J. Ederer (ed. and tr.), *Heinrich Pesch on Solidarist Economics: Excerpts from the* Lehrbuch der Nationalökonomie, Lanham MD, University Press of America 1998, pp.69–70.
35 See, for example, *Liberalism*...vol.2, pp.236–7; 'The struggle against Godlessness is...identical with the struggle for mankind.'
36 *Towards a Politics of Communion*, p.249.
37 Ibid., pp.250 ff.

38 See #1939 of *The Catechism of the Catholic Church* (1992): Pius speaks of 'the law of human solidarity and charity, dictated and imposed both by our common origin and by the equality in rational nature of all men [sic]'.
39 Pontifical Council for Justice and Peace, *Compendium of the Social Doctrine of the Church*, London and New York, Continuum 2004, #98.
40 Ibid. #96.
41 Rowlands op. cit., pp.255–6. We shall be returning in the next chapter to a fuller discussion of his ideas.
42 *Compendium* #321.
43 See Rowlands, op. cit., p.53, on the critique of 'failed' models of economic development that neglect the fundamental nurturing of human dignity.
44 *Sollicitudo rei socialis* #38. The echo of Dostoevsky in that last phrase must be deliberate.
45 Ibid., #39.
46 Rowlands, op. cit., p.258.
47 *Sollicitudo* #40.
48 In his message to the 33rd World Day for Peace in 2000.
49 Libreria Editrice Vaticana 2008.
50 Rowlands, op. cit. pp.260–1. A point that has sometimes been made about the growing popularity of 'solidarity' in (especially French) nineteenth-century usage is that the word lacked the residual religious connotations of 'fraternity'.
51 *Evangelii gaudium* #188. As Rowlands notes (op. cit., p.262), this lukewarmness about the word appears elsewhere.
52 See, e.g., *Caritas in veritate* 51 for some strong statements about the environment and the common good.
53 See, e.g.,##103–6.
54 Vigo Demant, *Theology and Society*, London, Faber 1938. His first chapter is on 'The Christian Doctrine of Human Solidarity', and is summarized in Kenneth Leech, *The Sky is Red: Discerning the Signs of the Times*, London, Darton, Longman & Todd 1997, p.34.
55 The words are those of the literary scholar and critic, Valerie Pitt, *Old Bottles and New Wine*, published by the Jubilee Group in 1996, quoted by Kenneth Leech, op. cit., p.159.
56 *The Shield of Achilles. War, Peace and the Course of History*, New York, Knopf/ London, Penguin 2002.

CHAPTER 5 THE SOLIDARITY OF THE SHAKEN: JAN PATOČKA AND THE CARE OF THE SOUL

1. The English-speaking world was initially a bit slow to catch up, but several works are now available in translation: *The Selected Writings of Jan Patočka: Care for the Soul*, ed. Ivan Chvatík and Erin Plunkett, tr. Alex Zucker, London, Bloomsbury 2022, is a good place to start (in addition to the works discussed later in this chapter), and has a substantial bibliography as well as an excellent introduction to his life and work by Erin Plunkett. See also the 'Translator's Postscript' in Jan Patočka, *Body, Community, Language, World*, tr. Erazim Kohak, Chicago and La Salle, IL, Open Court 1998, pp.178–83, and the luminous discussion in Chapter 3 of Andrew Shanks, *Civil Society, Civil Religion*, Oxford, Blackwell 1995, to which I acknowledge a great debt; see also Shanks's more recent account in the first chapter of *Apocalyptic Patience: Mystical Theology, Gnosticism, Ethical Phenomenology* London, Bloomsbury 2024, and the brilliant further elaboration of the theme of shakenness in relation to 'catholicity' in the third section of the book.
2. ET by Erazim Kohak, ed. James Dodd, Chicago and La Salle IL, Open Court 1996. The collection was first published in Prague in 1990.
3. Ibid., pp.134–6.
4. Ibid., p.134.
5. Ibid., p.135.
6. Ibid., pp.129–30.
7. These are the lectures published in English as *Body, Community, Language, World*; the text was constructed from students' notes, and circulated privately for many years.
8. *Body, Community...*, p.51.
9. Ibid., p.52.
10. Above, pp.42–7.
11. Ibid., pp.55–7.
12. Ibid., p.59
13. Cf. ibid., p.66: 'The original I gives meaning to everything.'
14. Ibid., pp.60–1.
15. *Body, Community...*, p.139.
16. *The Selected Writings...*p.4.
17. *Body, Community...*, pp.150–1.
18. *The Selected Writings...*, p.4.

19 See, e.g. ibid., p.104, where there is a challenge in the light of all this to a technologically dominated model of education. He is moving on from the more rhetorically ambitious language of his earlier (1938) essay on education (ibid., pp.39–51), while still seeing education as bound up with the risk of losing comfort and security for the sake of a fuller apprehension of truth.

20 *Heretical Essays*, pp.44–5; Heidegger – as a phenomenological thinker – is a good deal more prominent in these texts than Hegel, and Husserl is also a regular interlocutor.

21 Ibid., p.83.

22 See, e.g., *The Selected Writings*, pp.320–1.

23 Patočka liked to describe his work as a 'negative Platonism', the title of a *samizdat* collection of his essays from 1953; the Platonic discipline of detaching the mind from obsession with physical particulars, the *chorismos* between spirit and the world of things, is what we still need – not to arrive at the contemplation of 'higher' or more spiritual objects, however, but to encounter the radical groundlessness of spirit itself. And this distancing ironically takes us back – if we do not learn what dispossession has to teach – to another kind of material obsession, the manipulative dominance of things in the name of human security. See Johann P. Arnason, 'The Idea of Negative Platonism: Jan Patočka's Critique and Recovery of Metaphysics', *Thesis Eleven* 90 (August 2007), pp.6–26; and Marek Drwięga, 'Freiheit zwischen Geschichte und Metaphysik'. Zu den philosophischen Menschenbildern Jan Patočkas und Jozef Tischners, *Orbis Idearum* 4.2 (2016), pp.109–41, especially 124–5 on *chorismos*. My thanks to Andrew Karpinski for pointing me to these discussions.

24 The fourth and fifth of the *Heretical Essays* spell this out.

25 Ibid., p.97.

26 Ibid., pp.97–8.

27 Ibid., pp.99–101. Cf. Andrew Shanks, *Civil Society*, pp.119–20, for a lucid digest.

28 Ibid., p.102.

29 Ibid., p.103.

30 Ibid., pp.67–70.

31 Ibid., p.67.

32 Ibid., pp.68–71; the language of 'nihilism' here is associated with the thinking of another phenomenologically trained (and theologically

literate) philosopher, Karl Löwith, who resisted any accommodation between a philosophy of history based on immanent historical process and a theological guarantee of meaning grounded in the divine freedom.

33 Ibid., pp. 106–12.
34 Ibid., p. 107.
35 Below, pp. 184–6.
36 Ibid., p. 108.
37 It is worth noting the work of Barth's Czech student, Josef Hromadka, who played a very prominent role in introducing Barth's thought to Czech Christian circles and deploying his ideas in Christian–Marxist dialogue. Patočka will not have been unaware of this, given Hromadka's high profile in Czechoslovakia, his public support of the reformists in 1968, and his repudiation of Soviet influence in ecumenical European bodies in the wake of the Soviet invasion of October 1968.
38 Her complex interactions with Augustine's political thinking reflect this; for a brief overview, see Chapter 6 of Rowan Williams, *On Augustine*, London, Bloomsbury 2016.
39 Patočka himself admits (*Heretical Essays*, p.69) that what he has been characterizing as the distinctively Christian approach to 'nature' as simply the alien object of the soul is strictly something that has prevailed 'since the age of nominalism' (i.e. the fourteenth century onwards) – a rather substantial qualification of his account of cultural history.
40 As we have seen, this doesn't mean that Patočka is dismissive of Christianity, which for him plays a key role in the dialectical movement of self towards soul. In another tantalizingly brief comment in his lectures, Patočka contrasts Christianity and Buddhism as two responses to 'the domination of the Earth within us' – i.e. our bondage to the demands of 'living'. Where Buddhism sees the central problem as 'the domination of thirst', the desire to fill the void within, Christianity sees it as a self-enclosure, an obsessive concern with the self in isolation from other selves and from wider reality. Buddhism, Patočka argues, seeks to annihilate need, but in doing so also annihilates the dynamic of *understanding*; Christianity conserves the reality and validity of 'the world as world', and so affirms the significance of understanding. It is virtually a throwaway remark, but it reflects another significant

aspect in his engagement with Christian discourse. As an account of Buddhist thought or practice, it is as eccentric as his version of Christianity in the *Heretical Essays*: it is not in fact very helpful or accurate to imagine Buddhist enlightenment as the simple negation of 'understanding' or 'comprehending individual existence'. Given the emphasis (in Mahayana Buddhism especially) on the need for a comprehensive revolution in how we think about knowledge itself, enlightenment is better thought of as the recognition that the knowing self is itself a contingent and transient moment of relation, not an independent substance – a picture that in fact has something in common with Patočka's own analysis of the emergence of soul in moments of responsibility. And the contrast drawn between the Buddhist and Christian diagnoses of our unfreedom is far too sharp: Christian teaching sees passionate/reactive craving as the root of our trouble, Buddhism identifies the mythologized and isolated self as the prime illusion to be overcome. The overlaps and convergences are clear.

41 On boredom, see *Heretical Essays*, pp.114–15.
42 Ibid., p.42.
43 This appears as fr.62 in John Burnet's English version, *Early Greek Philosophy*, London, A & C Black 1920 (3rd edn), p.137: 'We must know that war is common to all and strife is justice and that all things come into being and pass away through strife'; cf. fr. 44, 'War is the father of all and the king of all' (p.136).
44 *Heretical Essays*, p.43.
45 Ibid., p.116.
46 Ibid., pp.120 ff.
47 Ibid., p.132.
48 Ibid., p.125.
49 Ibid., p.129.
50 Ibid., p.131.
51 Ibid., p.134.
52 For some lucid discussion, see Michaela Belejkanicova, 'Solidarity of the Shaken: from the Experience (Erlebnis) to History', *Studies in East European Thought*, 2021 (73), pp.287–307, and James Dodd, 'The Twentieth Century as War', in Erika Abrams and Ivan Chvatík, ed., *Jan Patočka and the Heritage of Phenomenology*, Dordrecht, Springer 2010, pp.203–14.
53 *Heretical Essays*, pp.136–7.

54 See Marek Drwięga, 'Freiheit zwischen Geschichte und Metaphysik', p. 125, on the 'heroic and tragic' dimension of Patočka's scheme.
55 Ibid., p.136.
56 Shanks, *Civil Society*, p.126. I suspect he may be just a little too sanguine about Patočka's openness to a distinctively Christian resolution for this, and a little reluctant to challenge Patočka's focus on the exceptional character of the 'shaken'. But in his most recent discussion (in *Apocalyptic Patience: Mystical Theology/Gnosticism/Ethical Phenomenology*, London, Bloomsbury 2024, pp.24–6), Shanks makes a good case for seeing the emergence of the Charter 77 movement, deeply inspired by Patočka, as supplying the context for an 'all-encompassing' solidarity that is not simply the solidarity of philosophers.
57 *Heretical Essays*, pp.136–7.
58 Ibid., pp.132–3.
59 See for example, in addition to *Heretical Essays*, pp.129–30, *The Selected Writings*, pp.288–92. Those who undertake self-sacrifice embody the most radical kind of protest against a functionalist civilization, but they are most clearly embodying such a protest when 'they dedicate themselves to that of which it cannot be said that it "is" something, or something objective' (p.291, from a lecture of 1973). Sacrifice simply declares the basic relation of humanity to the real, to Being, and so is fully what it is when it is not made for the sake of any particular end or determinate value.
60 E.g. *Heretical Essays*, pp.15 ff.
61 'Mobilization' in the sense that every citizen in modern warfare is judged to be a legitimate target for the enemy's violence, notionally on the grounds that in a complex modern society practising universal suffrage and existing on the basis of tightly interlocking fiscal and economic practices, all citizens are implicated in all acts of a state or quasi-state administration. In the first weeks of the conflict between Israel and the Hamas network in late 2023, both sides actively promoted the idea that there were 'no civilians' among the enemy.

CHAPTER 6 SOLIDARITY WITHOUT ENEMIES: JOZEF TISCHNER AND THE CONVERSATION OF HUMAN LABOUR

1 A useful historical overview can be found in William D. Perdue, *Paradox of Change: The Rise and Fall of Solidarity in the New Poland*, Westport CT, Praeger 1995.

2   There is a short biographical sketch by Mirosław Pawliszyn in *The Polish Christian Philosophy in the Twentieth Century: Jozef Tischner*, ed. Jarosław Jagiełło, Krakow, Ignatianum University Press 2020, pp.11–20. Once again, my thanks to Andrew Karpinski for this reference.
3   *Etyka Solidarności (The Ethics of Solidarity)*, Paris, Editions Spotkania 1982); ET by Marek B. Zaleski and Benjamin Fiore SJ, *The Spirit of Solidarity*, San Francisco, Harper and Row 1984.
4   ET, 'The Ethics of Solidarity Years Later', pp.52–67 in *Thinking in Values. The Tischner Institute Journal of Philosophy* 1 (2007) – an exceptionally valuable collection both of texts by Tischner and of critical discussion, mostly from Polish commentators.
5   *The Spirit of Solidarity*, p.5.
6   Ibid., p.3.
7   Ibid., p.6.
8   Ibid., p.23.
9   Ibid., p.9.
10 Above, pp.101–02.
11 E.g. *The Spirit...*, pp.32–4, 86.
12 Ibid., p.17.
13 Ibid., p.24.
14 Ibid., p.86.
15 Ibid., p.14.
16 Ibid., p.15.
17 Tischner was familiar with at least some of Patočka's work, mentioning him briefly in his significant late work, *The Philosophy of Drama* (1989; ET by Artur Rosman, University of Notre Dame Press 2024), but there is no evidence that he engaged with Patočka's specific treatment of solidarity. Cyril O'Regan, introducing the English translation of Tischner's book, touches on the convergences and differences between the two (p.xii). See also above, chapter 5, n.54, for reference to Marek Drwięga's article on the two philosophers.
18 A recurring theme in the first two pieces in *The Spirit...*
19 Ibid., p.92.
20 Ibid., p.67.
21 Ibid., p.95.
22 Ibid., p.12.

23 Ibid., pp.10–13.
24 Ibid., p.23.
25 On this point in Tischner's writing, see pp.15–16 of Aleksandr Bobko, 'Philosophical Anthropology as the Main Thread of Tischner's Work', in *Thinking in Values* I, pp.11–27. See also Tischner's essay, 'The Ethics of Solidarity Years Later', pp.52–67 in the same volume, especially pp.65–6 on the effects of a 'refusal of heroism' in the wake of the original workers' movement of the 1980s: the unwelcome call to a recovery of truthfulness in working relationships has led to the revival of a partisan and reductively materialist kind of socialism: 'Consumerism essentially consists in the refusal of heroism' (p.66), and renders sacrifice unimaginable.
26 See Tischner's 1985 essay, 'Perspectives of the New Ethos of Work', in *Thinking in Values* I, pp.28–36, especially pp.34–5 on 'common openness' and the struggle for meaningful labour and truthful communication as sources for fidelity.
27 Levinas and Rosenzweig are extensively cited and discussed in the opening chapters of *The Philosophy of Drama*. On this background, Drwięga's article on Tischner and Patočka (above, chapter 5, n.54) is invaluable; see also the overviews and extracts in *The Polish Christian Philosophy in the Twentieth Century*. Tischner's sympathetic use of two major Jewish thinkers is unsurprising in view of his consistent opposition to the antisemitic strands in Polish nationalism, not least in its post-*Solidarność* phase.
28 See especially chapter 2 of *The Philosophy of Drama*, e.g. p.57: 'The I as a subject is relative to the object; the I as a totality is relative to the parts that go into its composition' – that is, the I as more-than-subject, as the ensemble of attitudes, capacities and so on, emerges to view not as the knowing agent but as the addressed, engaged, invested partner in a reciprocal process of manifestation and interaction.
29 Tischner's essay on 'Axiological Impressions' (*Impresje aksjologiczne*), in his important early collection of pieces from 1966 to 1975, *Świat ludzkiej nadziei: wybór szkiców filosoicznych* (*The World of Human Hope. A Selection of Philosophical Sketches*), Krakow, Znak 1975, sets out the basics; see Drwięga, art. cit., pp.135–6.
30 Tischner's *Philosophy of Drama*, published in Polish in 1998, is now available in English translation (South Bend, University of Notre Dame Press 2024). Also published in 1998, but not yet translated,

is his *Spor o istnenie człowieka* (*The Struggle for Human Existence*, a title deliberately echoing a classic work by Ingarden, developing his critique of Husserl), which contains some parallel discussion. See Drwięga, art. cit., pp.137–40.
31 Drwięga, art. cit., p.138 (*biblisch dramatisierten Platonismus*).
32 *The Spirit...* p.3.
33 *Thinking in Values* 1, pp.54–9.
34 Ibid., pp.62–7.
35 *Polski kstadt dialogu* (*A Polish City of Dialogue*), Paris, Spotkania 1981, p.185. See Krzystof Wieczorek, 'Tischner as a Metapolitician', *Studies in Eastern European Thought* 2019, pp.345–60.
36 'Several Reflections on the Theme of Solidarity,' *Thinking in Values* 1, pp.68–77.
37 Ibid., p.69.
38 'Solidarity Without Solidarity', *Thinking in Values* I, pp.96–106.
39 Ibid., pp.98–9, 104–6.
40 Ibid., pp.102–3.
41 Tischner, 'The Ethics of Solidarity Years Later', p.61.
42 See the sharply polemical discussion by Chantal Millon-Delsol, 'Solidarity and Barbarity', pp.78–84 in *Thinking in Values* 1, where she castigates some popular forms of moral universalism that appeal to sheer animal 'solidarity' as showing a yearning for 'ethics without mediation' (p.81). The suspicion of 'animal' empathy or mutuality is dramatically overstated here, though the point about the ambivalence of unmediated mutuality and common interest is a serious one.
43 Above, p.76.
44 *The Spirit...* p.53.
45 On this, see Rowan Williams, 'Tradition, Traditionalism and Culture Wars', pp.5–24 in Hans-Peter Grosshans (ed.), *Religion and Change*, Berlin, de Gruyter 2023.
46 See ch.3 of Reni Eddo-Lodge, *Why I'm No Longer Talking to White People about Race*, esp. pp.88–98.
47 *The Spirit...*, p.14.
48 It would be intriguing to imagine in the light of this how Tischner would comment on the opening sections of Wittgenstein's *Philosophical Investigations*, with their celebrated thought-experiment about language in the context of the builders' yard.

CHAPTER 7 SOLIDARITY, RESPONSIBILITY, GUILT: DIETRICH BONHOEFFER'S HELPLESSNESS

1 Dietrich Bonhoeffer, *Ethics* (*Dietrich Bonhoeffer Works, Volume 6*), tr. Reinhard Krauss, Charles C. West, Douglas W. Scott, ed. Clifford J. Green, Minneapolis, Fortress Press 2005, p.233.

2 As we shall see, what Bonhoeffer has in mind here is not some kind of romantic and tragic picture of the 'necessity' of evil actions, nor is it even a real departure from his principled pacifism. The use of the guilt-and-responsibility trope as a theoretical justification of violent action in certain situations – a version of Bonhoeffer that has (bizarrely) become popular in some conservative Christian quarters in the USA – is a drastic oversimplification. On this, see Christine Schliesser, *Everyone Who Acts Responsibly Becomes Guilty: Bonhoeffer's Concept of Accepting Guilt*, Louisville, Westminster John Knox, 2008, and '"Everyone Who Acts Responsibly Becomes Guilty": Contested Themes in *Ethics*', pp.188–220 in Mark Thiessen Nation, Anthony G. Siegrist and Daniel P. Umbel, *Bonhoeffer the Assassin? Challenging the Myth, Recovering His Call to Peacemaking*, Grand Rapids, Baker Academic 2013, esp. pp.205–9. Jens Zimmermann, *Dietrich Bonhoeffer's Christian Humanism*, Oxford University Press 2019, ch.6, is an excellent discussion of the language of responsibility and guilt.

3 Cf. Peter Brown, *Augustine of Hippo: A Biography*, London, Faber & Faber 1967, p.365: 'The Pelagian man was essentially a separate individual: the man of Augustine is always about to be engulfed in vast, mysterious solidarities.' Karl Barth's classic commentary on *The Epistle to the Romans* (ET from the sixth German edition by Edwyn Hoskyns, Oxford University Press) contains a section entitled 'Solidarity' (pp.330–9), reflecting on Paul's affirmation of his continuing membership of the people of Israel as a sign of the believer's unbroken fellowship with the non-believer in virtue of the universal failure of humanity to achieve reconciliation with God. 'It is the lack of the glory of God which creates fellowship and solidarity among men' (p.335).

4 As in *Brothers Karamazov*, Book 6, ch.2, Book 11, ch.4. See George Pattison, *Conversations with Dostoevsky: on God, Russia, Literature, and Life*, Oxford University Press 2024, pp.215–18, especially p.218, for Dostoevsky, 'Accepting our guilt reveals what the Anglican writer Charles Williams called our coinherence and, thus understood,

opens us up to new levels of relatedness.' More on Charles Williams in the next chapter.
5   Above, p.101.
6   *Ethics*, p.220.
7   Ibid., p.221; Bonhoeffer's example – good patriarchal North German Protestant as he was – is being the father of a family.
8   Ibid., pp.222–9.
9   Ibid., p.232.
10 pp.108–09 on Rose; and cf. the perhaps slightly over-sanguine reading of Bonhoeffer's earlier sketch of these issues argued for by Amy Marga in 'The Robust Female Self: Feminist Theology in Dialogue with *Sanctorum Communio*', *Dietrich Bonhoeffer in einer globalen Zeit/in a Global Era: Christliche Glaube, Zeugnis, Dienst/Christian Faith, Witness, Service*, ed. Christoph Ramstein, Christiane Tietz, Philip G. Ziegler, Gottingen, Vandenhoeck & Ruprecht 2023, pp.405–21.
11 Ibid., p.237; cf. above, n.324.
12 Above, n.336.
13 Notably his doctoral thesis, *Sanctorum Communio*, published in 1930 (ET in vol. 1 of *Dietrich Bonhoeffer Works*, ed. Clifford J. Green, tr. Reinhard Krauss and Nancy Lukens, Minneapolis, Fortress Press 1998.
14 Ibid., pp.151–3.
15 Ibid., p.152.
16 Ibid.
17 Ibid., pp.153–4.
18 For an acute study of this, see Brian Walters, *The Deaths of the Republic: Imagery of the Body Politic in Ciceronian Rome*, Oxford University Press 2020; it is anecdotally associated with the figure of Menenius Agrippa in Livy's History (II.16), and is familiar to many through Shakespeare's reworking of this story in *Coriolanus*.
19 Above, p.159.
20 Esp. pp.56–61.
21 Tischner, *The Philosophy of Drama*, p.61.
22 Cf. his well-known comment in the letter to his godson of May 1944 that 'Our church, which has been fighting in these years only for its self-preservation,…is incapable of taking the word of reconciliation and redemption to…the world' (*Letters and Papers from Prison. The Enlarged Edition*, London, SCM Press 1971, p.300).

23 Recently explored in relation to the idea of an 'unconscious' Christianity in Eleanor McLaughlin's fine study, *Unconscious Christianity in Dietrich Bonhoeffer's Late Theology: Encounters with the Unknown Christ*, London, Lexington Books/Fortress Academic 2020.
24 But see the essays on 'Bonhoefferian Inspiration for an Eco-Theology and an Eco-Ethics' (by Carlos Caldas) and 'Bonhoeffer's Theology of the Body and the responsibility for the Earth' (by Gregor Etzelmüller) in Robert Vosloo, Teddy Sakupapa, Ashwin Thyssen and Karola Radler, eds, *Bonhoeffer and the Responsibility for a Coming Generation: Doing Theology in a Time Out of Joint*, London, T. & T. Clark 2024, pp.89–98 and 99–109, for a thoughtful extrapolation of Bonhoeffer's arguments.
25 Most familiarly in Rom.8, where the inextricability of human healing and the restoration of some new and necessary depth in the entire material world is strongly asserted.
26 For a further reflection on this, see Rowan Williams, 'Has secularism failed?', pp.11–22 in Rowan Williams, *Faith in the Public Square*, London, Bloomsbury 2012, especially pp.13–18.
27 Among the vast literature of recent years on Maximus, the essays in Antoine Lévy, Pauli Annala, Olli Hallamaa and Tuomo Lankila (eds), *The Architecture of the Cosmos. St Maximus the Confessor: New Perspectives*, Helsinki, Luther-Agricola Society 2015, are especially helpful, especially the formidable concluding essay by Alexei Nesteruk on the interface between this theological tradition and contemporary scientific thought.
28 A fresh and lucid overview in Michael Fishbane, *Sacred Attunement: A Jewish Theology*, Chicago and London, University of Chicago Press 2008.
29 See, for example, Muhammad Yaseen Gada, *Islam and Environmental Ethics*, Cambridge University Press 2024.
30 Not just a courtesy reference: her posthumously published magnum opus on philosophy and theology, *Finite and Eternal Being. An Attempt at an Ascent to the Meaning of Being*, tr. Kurt F. Reinhardt, Washington DC, Institute of Carmelite Studies 2002, outlines an ontology in which finite substance in general is analysed in these terms of actualization and generation.
31 Cf. Raimond Gaita, *A Common Humanity*, p.24, discussing the ways in which we establish the 'sacredness', the unconditional value of the

person: whether we own to any active faith or not, we find ourselves to some degree or another being parasitic upon 'the unashamedly anthropomorphic claim that we are sacred because God loves us, his children'. Gaita is speaking of the value of human subjects, and wants to say that the person's claim on us represents a unique limit to the right and power of the human will ('as does nothing else in nature', p.23). But as with Bonhoeffer, it is not difficult to extend the principle without compromising the distinctive place of the human in the world.

32 This theme is developed by Bruno Latour in some of his last writings, where he cautions against an ecological ethic that argues for a virtually total withdrawal from the responsible use of technology: see, for example, *Politics of Nature: How to Bring the Sciences into Democracy*, tr. Catherine Porter, 2004, and chapter 4 of *If We Lose the Earth, We Lose Our Souls*, tr. Catherine Porter and Sam Ferguson, Cambridge, Polity Press 2024.

33 Columba Stewart OSB, *'Working the Earth of the Heart': The Messalian Controversy in History, Texts, and Language to AD 431*, Oxford, Clarendon Press 2011.

34 Above, p.28.

CHAPTER 8 SOLIDARITY, CO-INHERENCE, COMMUNION

1 Grevel Lindop's biography, *Charles Williams: The Third Inkling*, Oxford University Press 2015, is an exemplary study.

2 London, Faber & Faber 1939.

3 Ibid., p.28; the reference is to the *Passio Perpetuae*, one of the most important early martyrological texts, incorporating first-person material from Perpetua.

4 Ibid. pp.36–7.

5 Ibid., pp.54–5.

6 Paul Fiddes, *Charles Williams and C. S. Lewis: Friends in Co-inherence*, Oxford University Press 2021, p.89. As Fiddes notes, this text is from a seventh-century Syriac collection of monastic maxims, translated as *The Paradise or Garden of the Holy Fathers* by E. A. Wallis Budge (London, Chatto & Windus 1907). Fiddes points out that the 'double man' image reappears in W. H. Auden's work; Auden's return to Christian faith had much to do with his contact with and reading of Williams.

7 Williams, *Descent*, p.46; the earliest version of this is in the fifth-century 'alphabetical collection' of the *Sayings of the Desert Fathers*, translated by Benedicta Ward SLG, London, Mowbray, 1975, p.4. The passage continues, 'If we gain our brother we have gained God, but if we scandalise our brother, we have sinned against Christ.'

8 Fiddes, op.cit., provides an authoritative overview of the development of the idea in Williams (see especially chapter 4). I have chosen to follow Williams himself as well as Fiddes in spelling the word with a hyphen, though usage has varied in theological literature.

9 Dante, *Paradiso* IX.73–9, translated by Robin Kirkpatrick, London, Penguin, 2007, p.85.

10 On Dante's remarkable readiness to do bizarre things with Italian verbs, especially where the transforming effect of grace is concerned, see most recently Joseph Luzzi, *Dante's Divine Comedy: A Biography*, Princeton and Oxford, Princeton University Press 2024, p.75.

11 Williams, *Descent*, p.138. This is elaborated in full in Williams' *The Figure of Beatrice*, London, Faber 1943, where he writes (p.51) of the 'in-othering' and 'in-Godding' implicit in Dante's account of Beatrice's love and in the famous phrase in the *Paradiso* (XXXIII.1) describing the Virgin Mary as *figlia del tuo Figlio*, 'daughter of your Son'. The theological point is that we as human subjects/agents of love are both generated by and generative of the generative life of the other as a result of the pattern of divine generative love in the eternal Trinity.

12 Oxford University Press 1938.

13 *Descent Into Hell*, London, Faber 1937, p.98.

14 Ibid., p.99.

15 London, Faber & Faber 1945.

16 London, Heinemann 1938.

17 Fiddes, op. cit., pp.108–10, and chapter 12 for a particularly careful and illuminating survey of the last novels.

18 For detail and discussion, see Lindop, op. cit., esp. pp.139–41, 241–2, 385–7.

19 Lindop, op. cit., chapter 16 (pp.281–99) is an invaluable overview; for Williams' principles for the 'Order', see pp.291–2.

20 Op. cit., p.307.

ENDNOTES

21 p.203.
22 Above, p.28.
23 Bourke, *What It Means To Be Human*, p.385.
24 Ibid.
25 Shanks, *Apocalyptic Patience*, p.212.
26 Cambridge, Mass. and London, The Bellknap Press of Harvard University Press 2007, p.278.
27 Bourke, op. cit., p.385.
28 Above, e.g. pp.157–9, 163–6.
29 *The Philosophy of Drama*, p.61.
30 Ibid.
31 Above, p.213.
32 London, Serpent's Tail 2018.
33 There is an edition in Penguin Classics, most recently reprinted in 2000.
34 Perry, *Melmoth*, p.265.
35 Ibid., p.271.
36 See especially their *Frames of War: When is Life Grievable?*, 2nd ed. London, Verso Books 2016. I must also acknowledge my debt to a shared discussion online of these and related issues with Judith Butler and J. Kameron Carter in October 2024, in which the pertinence of the question to the grievability of the non-human world was explored as well.

CONCLUSION

1 *Together*, p.115.
2 See esp. ibid., chapters 5 and 6.
3 Ibid., p.279.
4 Cf. Williams, 'Tradition, Traditionalism and Culture Wars' for further reflections on this; and also James Davison Hunter, *Democracy and Solidarity*, chapters 10 (containing a good analysis of Richard Rorty's post-metaphysical approach to solidarity) and 11 (discussing the pressure to *emotional* solidarity in the absence of any more durable foundations).
5 See also his significant essay on *The Craftsman*, New Haven and London, Yale University Press 2009.
6 John Hughes, *The End of Work: Theological Critiques of Capitalism*, Malden MA, Blackwell 2007.

7. On this, see Lucy Easthope's outstanding memoir, *When the Dust Settles: Stories of Love, Loss and Hope from an Expert in Disaster*, London, Hodder & Stoughton 2022.
8. And John Hughes' book (above, n.6) says a great deal of it admirably.
9. *Together*, pp.93–5.
10. For some discussion of this, see the first chapter of Rowan Williams, *Lost Icons: Reflections on Cultural Bereavement*, London, T. & T. Clark 2000.
11. See Ewan Fernie, ed., *Redcrosse: Religious Poetry for Today's World*, London, Bloomsbury 2012.
12. In discussion of this in a seminar at Stellenbosch University in November 2024, a participant very perceptively noted the dominance of visual terminology in what I and others were saying about justice; he proposed that we think also about hearing and touching 'justly'. Point taken; there is more than one way of sensing adequately or aptly.
13. Lamorna Ash, *Don't Forget We're Here Forever: A New Generation's Search for Religion*, London, Bloomsbury 2025, p.135.

INDEX

abjection, 107, 109, 197, 232
Aboriginal Australians, 23, 27
abortion, 44, 93
accountability, 117, 121, 157, 215
advertising, 272
'affective' (the word), 272
aftotes, 22
agathology, 164–5, 167, 171–4, 177, 242
Agee, James, 58
allyship, 12, 54–5
animals, 24, 26–30, 33–4, 36–7, 46–7, 63, 92, 132–3, 159, 198, 224, 235, 237, 266, 273, 289
see also non-human life
anomie, 103, 142
anthropomorphism, 29, 228, 273, 293
Aquinas, Thomas, 79–82, 88, 99, 232, 275
Arango, Gonzalo, 110
Arendt, Hannah, 140, 146, 152, 159, 246
Aristotle, 232
artificial intelligence, 30, 33–5, 47
Ash, Lamorna, 258
Asperger's Syndrome, 51
assisted dying, 89
atomocentrism, 92
Auden, W. H., 209, 293
Auschwitz, 60

authenticity, 24–5, 28, 31, 132–3, 135–6, 143–4, 150, 152, 174
autism, 29, 51–2, 267
axiology, 67, 160, 162–7, 171, 177, 271

Baghdad, 147
Bakhtin, Mikhail, 244
baptism, 26, 122, 216
Baron-Cohen, Simon, 51–5, 72
Barth, Karl, 139–40, 189, 290
Bataclan Concert Hall, 261
bees, 30
Benedict XVI, Pope, 120–1
Bereaved Families' Forum, 54
Bismarck, Otto von, 102
Black Lives Matter, 12, 261
Black Mountain poets, 110
Bloom, Paul, 67–8, 271–2
Bobbitt, Philip, 126, 167
Boethius, 80
Bonhoeffer, Dietrich, 183–207, 209, 215, 217–18, 221, 224, 238–43, 253, 290–1
Bourgeois, Léon, 102–3, 111
Bourke, Joanna, 24–30, 32–3, 42, 44–5, 73–4, 99, 205, 218–20, 224, 245, 268
brains, 51–2, 70–2, 272–3
  amygdala, 52
  empathy circuits, 52, 59, 70
  mirror neurons, 52, 59, 267
  orbitofrontal cortex, 70
  temporoparietal junction, 52

Buddhism, 284–5
Butler, Judith, 231, 233

Canadian First Nations, 56
capitalism, 12–14, 112, 114, 244
Catholic Church, 16, 60, 93
  Catholic Social Teaching, 5, 16, 19, 73, 100, 126, 155–6, 220, 237
  political advocacy, 103, 237
  teachings on solidarity, 111–26
Cavell, Stanley, 42–4, 48–9, 68–9, 71, 131, 267
charity campaigning, 68, 272
Charlie Hebdo, 9, 104
Charter 77, 129
Chesterton, G. K., 116
child abuse, 33
Civil Rights movement, 111
Clark, Meghan, 116
Claver, Peter, 119
Clement of Alexandria, 210
Coleridge, Samuel Taylor, 148
collectivism, 101–2, 114, 146, 219, 234
colonialism, 27, 84, 235
communion, 28, 74, 99–100, 158–9, 190, 205, 211, 218–20, 224, 227, 229, 231–2, 239–40, 258, 264, 278
  Communion of Saints, 222
Communism, 16, 155–6, 158, 171
communitarianism, 13, 16, 101, 103, 114, 119
Company (Order) of the Co-inherence, 213–15, 227
Comte, Auguste, 102, 158
Confessing Church, 197
conscience, 12, 49, 114, 156–61, 165–7, 175, 238, 242–3
consciousness, 32, 35–6, 41, 62, 73, 89, 91, 98, 108, 125, 130, 157, 161
  dialogic formation of, 66
  see also historical consciousness

consumerism, 142, 288
conversational labour, 220, 250, 254
co-operation, 3, 12–13, 112, 125, 132, 155, 169, 226, 244–8, 253–5
co-production, 247
Covid-19 pandemic, 7, 233, 251–2
Cuban revolution, 111
cultural covenant, 122
culture wars, 94, 262
Czechoslovakia, 16, 127, 129, 284

D'Souza, Aruna, 55–8, 68, 219–20, 224, 243, 252, 268–9
Dante, 209–11, 294
decadence, 136, 138, 141, 144
'deficient' humans, 44, 235, 263
Dennett, Daniel, 265
Derrida, Jacques, 95
Descartes, René, 33, 47
Desert Fathers, 210
dialogism, 66, 168–9, 171–2, 174, 226, 244
Diamond, Cora, 45
Dickens, Charles, 24, 34
Dionysiac transcendence, 136
disability, 44, 198
disobedience, 85, 88, 277
displacement, 193, 195, 202, 207
displacement of populations, 152, 249
Distributists, 116
Donne, John, 224
Dostoevsky, Fyodor, 184, 224
Douzinas, Costas, 75–80, 86–7, 92, 94–7
Down's Syndrome, 44
dreaming, 40
Dresden, 147
drone warfare, 147
drugs, 97

INDEX

Durcharbeiten, 262
Durkheim, Émile, 15, 19, 102–3, 105, 111–13, 124

Eddo-Lodge, Reni, 12, 108
egalitarianism, 221, 238, 254
ego, 32, 37, 56, 58, 163, 165–6, 190, 202, 220, 225–6, 242, 250, 258
El Corno Emplumado, 110
Eliot, T. S., 209, 211
embodiment, 21, 81, 122, 160, 192, 212, 254, 266
empathy, 5, 17, 19, 45, 50–74, 109, 114, 214, 218, 228, 235, 241
  'animal' empathy, 289
  brain empathy circuits, 52, 59, 70
  distinct from sympathy, 66
  empathic harmony, 132–3
  geistlich relationship, 64–5
  and interrogated sentimentality, 59
  and moral decision-making, 67–8
  and opacity, 56, 58–9
  and pain, 52–3, 57–60
  performative empathy, 228
  and primordiality, 60–1, 63, 65
  and torture, 53–4
Enlightenment, 80, 91, 221
enslavement, 26, 54, 88–9, 93, 105, 139, 209, 227, 235, 264
environmental crisis, 248–9
EU referendum, 261
European Court of Human Rights, 74
European imagination, 134–6
Evelyn, John, 24
evolution, 28–9, 34, 37, 40, 113
'expectation of the face', 30–1, 44–5, 73–4

faithfulness, 156, 158–60, 178, 202, 238, 245, 254, 256
Felicitas, 209–10
Fiddes, Paul, 212, 216, 241

fidelity, 43, 158–61, 165–7, 170–3, 175–6, 185–6, 238–9, 242, 253–4, 288
First World War, 144
first-person presence/perspective, 24, 26, 29, 31, 33–6, 38, 40, 45, 47–8, 163
Fortin, Ernest, 81–2
Fourier, Charles, 15, 19, 101
Francis, Pope, 120–2, 237
Free Church of Scotland, 277
free markets, 112–13, 115
free speech, 90–1
French Third Republic, 111–12
Freud, Sigmund, 95
friendly societies, 114
Fronterlebnis, 145–6, 151–2

Gaita, Raimond, 23–4, 41, 45–6, 292–3
Gandhi, Mahatma, 183
gay rights, 92, 236, 278
Gaza, 10, 104
gender identity, 178, 221
gender inequality, 90
Ginsberg, Allen, 110
Glissant Édouard, 268
Good Samaritan, 157, 170–1, 221
grace, 20, 122, 141, 171, 191, 196, 203, 213, 216, 220, 242–3, 254, 294
Gregory of Nyssa, 140
grievability, 231–3, 295
groundlessness, 43–4, 150–1, 283
gun ownership, 88

Habermas, Jürgen, 170
Haiti, 25–6
Hamas, 10, 286
Havel, Václav, 129
Hegel, G. W. F., 134, 142, 283
Heidegger, Martin, 132, 134–5, 163, 283

Heraclitus, 143, 146, 211, 240
heroism, 110, 150, 153, 161, 168, 189, 214, 288
Hiroshima, 144, 147
historical consciousness, 134–5, 150, 152, 155
Hitler, Adolf, 183, 190
HIV/AIDS, 231
Hofstadter, Douglas, 36
Holy Spirit, 123, 193–4, 213, 242
Holy Trinity, 212–13
homelessness, 97, 231, 262
Honneth, Axel, 24, 263
Houthis, 10
Hromadka, Josef, 284
Hughes, John, 246
human agents, 102, 115, 120, 125, 162, 175, 218, 228, 241, 246, 248
  and first-person presence, 26, 29, 34, 36, 40, 45
  and hierarchy of characteristics, 24–31
human dignity, 18, 84, 95, 118, 166, 231, 254, 281
human rights, 5, 19, 21, 26, 69, 74–100, 167, 174, 236–7, 261, 277
  and China, 277–8
  'fundamentalism', 275–6
  inalienable, 78, 84, 92, 94
  incommunicable, 80–2, 275
  as liberties, 79, 85, 88, 92–3
  and moral maximalism, 86
  and religious freedom, 92–4, 277–8
  'right to be loved', 95
  and will, 96–7
humanism, 1, 17, 26, 117, 124, 134, 146
Husserl, Edmund, 60, 129, 152, 162

Illich, Ivan, 221
India, postcolonial, 2
indigenous peoples, 26, 56, 84, 263
individualism, 16–17, 74, 83, 85, 88, 94, 99, 103, 127, 186, 237, 242
infant mortality, 23
Ingarden, Roman, 156, 162, 289
injustice, 3–4, 10–11, 14, 97, 105, 158, 167, 239, 246, 250
  ecological, 122
  racial 107–8
introspection, 66, 72, 271
Iraq, 76
Israel–Palestine conflict, 10, 54, 286
ius and *iustitia*, 76–7, 79–83, 87, 90, 92–3, 99, 109, 111

Jacobson, Howard, 12, 49
Jamison, Leslie, 57–9, 220
Jesus Christ, 80, 119, 187–8, 190, 200, 206, 239, 241–2, 294
  Body of Christ, 192–5, 211, 224, 239
  God in Christ, 196, 198
  incarnation, 138, 140, 142, 190, 196–7, 201, 203, 212, 216, 221, 238, 243
  resurrection, 191, 221, 230
John XXIII, Pope, 116
John Paul II, Pope, 16, 117–23, 151, 155–6, 237
Jubilee of Workers, 118
Judaism, 20, 140
Jünger, Ernst, 145–7, 149
justice, 6, 18, 76–7, 83, 90, 96, 112, 119, 176, 188, 200–1, 232, 256, 263, 285, 296

Kabbala, 200
Kant, Immanuel, 25
Kenya, terrorist attacks, 261

INDEX

Ketteler, Bishop Wilhelm von, 111–12
koinonia, 206
Kolbe, Maksimilian, 119
Kolers, Avery, 105, 107
Kot, Dobrosław, 171–2, 180

landscapes, personified, 29
Langton, Rae, 69
Lanzoni, Susan, 52, 57, 59
Las Casas, Bartolomé de, 26
Latour, Bruno, 293
Leibniz, Gottfried Wilhelm, 113
Leo XIII, Pope, 112
Levinas, Emmanuel, 74, 109, 162, 165, 273
Lewis, C. S., 209
lex naturae, 140
liberation theology, 2, 119
libertarianism, 234, 278
lifestyle choices, 96
liturgy, 254–7
Locke, John, 26, 113
Logos, 200
Lost Icons, 4
Löwith, Karl, 139, 284

McGilchrist, Iain, 71
Mandela, Nelson, 1, 4
Marius Victorinus, 140
market society, 126, 167
Marx, Karl, 95, 114
Marxism, 16, 97, 119, 167, 246, 284
Marxist-Leninism, 114
Matrix, The, 40, 265
Maturin, Charles, 230
Maximus the Confessor, 140, 200–1
Mboti, Nyasha, 3
Menenius Agrippa, 291
Merleau-Ponty, Maurice, 60, 63
Merton, Thomas, 110

Miedaner, Terre, *The Soul of Anna Klane*, 35–9, 42
migration, 13–14, 231, 261
Milbank, John, 76–9, 83–4, 87, 91–4, 112
Millon-Delsol, Chantal, 289
Milton, John, 78
mimetic theory, 37
mobilization, 145, 147–8, 151–2, 286
Möhler, Johann Adam, 111
mourning, 233
Muhammad, Prophet, 9
mutual exposure, 46, 54
mutuality, 1, 3, 19–20, 49, 90, 107, 110, 112–14, 116, 119, 121, 152, 165, 171–2, 180, 186, 203, 205, 219, 227, 233, 236, 242, 244, 249, 256, 289
mystery plays, 255

Nagasaki, 144
Napoleonic Code, 101
negative theology, 27
Nietzsche, Friedrich, 95, 150
nihilism, 138, 283–4
Noh drama, 266
non-human life, 7, 32, 35, 198–9, 202, 204–5, 227, 231, 233, 249, 257, 262, 263, 295
Nueva Solidaridad, 110–11, 123
Nygren, Anders, 140

Occupy movement, 97
ontology, 125, 165, 171–2, 206, 292
opacity, 56, 58–9, 219, 224
orientation, 17, 33, 60–3, 68–9, 71, 74, 108, 135, 162, 193, 201, 220, 232
Origen, 140
original sin, 184
Orthodox Christianity, 17, 22, 136
Orwell, George, 53

pain, 24, 33–4, 37–9, 41, 153, 157–8, 173, 177, 189, 238, 243, 265–6, 270
   and empathy, 52–3, 57–60
   in Charles Williams' theology, 210, 214–17, 225, 228
Palestine, 10
Patočka, Jan, 16, 19–20, 103, 129–53, 159, 162, 169, 206, 237–8, 246, 284–6
Paul VI, Pope, 117
performativity, 9, 11–12, 14, 19, 55, 228–9, 261
Perry, Sarah, 229–30, 233
Pesch, Heinrich, 112–16, 119, 123, 125
phenomenology, 7, 60, 71–3, 92, 125–6, 129, 152, 156, 162–3, 173, 237
philaftia, 22
Phillips, D. Z., 45–6
Pius XI, Pope, 116
Pius XII, Pope, 116, 281
Platonism, 137–8, 164, 173, 176
   'negative', 283
Plunkett, Erin, 132
Poland, 16, 117, 127, 155–6, 168, 171, 176, 238
   see also Solidarność
polemos, 143, 146
polis, 136–9, 141, 143, 148
Pontifical Academy of Social Sciences, 120
Port Talbot, 255
postmodernity, 96
Prague Spring, 129–30
projection, 29, 37, 41, 194, 256

Qur'an, 200

racial inequality, 90, 106–8
racism, 27, 34, 54, 178–9
rape, 39, 97, 262

recognizability, 21, 25–6, 30–4, 45–7, 165, 202, 221, 235, 257
redemption, 137, 186, 194, 256, 291
Renaud, Hippolyte, 101–2
Ricard, Matthieu, 58–9, 68
Robinson, Dylan, 56
robots, 40, 266
rock concerts, and inclusivity, 255
Roma, 198
Romanticism, 43, 45, 48, 112, 148, 153, 267
Rorty, Richard, 15, 43, 267
Rose, Gillian, 5, 21, 27, 66, 69, 107–9, 169, 188, 197, 219–20, 232
Rosenzweig, Franz, 162
Rowlands, Anna, 116, 118, 121, 123, 220, 222
Ruston, Roger, 77, 276

sacredness, 292–3
St Antony the Great, 210
St Augustine, 140, 144, 185, 232
St George's Day, 255
St Paul, 80, 157, 184–5, 192–3, 198
Sartre, Jean-Paul, 163
Sayers, Dorothy, 209
scepticism, 26, 30–1, 33, 42–3, 48, 72, 267
Second World War, 104, 209
self-appropriation, 63
self-awareness, 131–2, 135, 162, 236, 258
self-dispossession, 186
self-estrangement, 58, 135–6
self-expression, 92, 236
self-formation, 241–2
self-interest, 84, 107, 168, 226, 232, 243
self-ownership, 78, 85
self-perception, 62–3, 188, 236
self-preservation, 88–9
self-representation, 33, 133, 254

INDEX

self-repugnance, 185
self-scrutiny, 72, 226, 229
self-transcendence, 122
selfhood, 22, 43, 69, 71, 74, 98, 100, 124, 131, 135, 185–6, 188, 207, 215, 220, 236, 258
   erasure of, 108–9
Sennett, Richard, 12–13, 244–8, 255
sentience, 42, 47
sexual partnerships, 88
shakenness, 130, 141, 143, 146–51, 162, 238, 286
Shakespeare, William
   Othello, 48
   Titus Andronicus, 39
Shanks, Andrew, 147, 220, 257
Sheen, Michael, 255
Skobtsova, Mother Maria, 104
Smith Adam, 269–70
Social Darwinism, 113
social market, 115
socialization, 29–30, 49, 125
solidarisme, 102, 112
Solidarismus, 112, 125
'Solidarity forever', 14
Solidarność, 11, 15–16, 117, 155–6, 171
soul, 36, 77, 132–47, 210, 230, 237, 284–5
South Africa, 1–6
Spencer, Herbert, 113
Stein, Edith, 59–69, 71, 73, 81, 129–30, 133, 152, 156, 169, 193, 201, 206, 220
stereotypes, 25, 46, 178
subsidiarity, 16, 112, 115–16, 123, 126
substitution, 107–9, 211–14, 216–18, 222, 224, 228, 233, 238–40, 240, 243
   'substituted love', 211, 216, 218, 240, 243

taxation, 102, 105
Taylor, Charles, 170–1, 220, 222, 224, 237
Teilhard de Chardin, Pierre, 145–7, 149
theory of mind, 32, 267
Third Reich, 139, 183, 195
Tierney, Brian, 275
Tillich, Paul, 149
Tischner, Józef, 16, 20, 117, 155–81, 193–4, 196, 198, 202, 206, 220, 225–6, 228, 238, 240, 242–3, 245–7, 253, 271, 288–9
torture, 53–4
total war, 145
totalitarianism, 116, 127, 134, 162, 168, 198, 237–8, 278
toys, 30–1, 35–7
trade unions, 11, 14–16, 104, 114, 155, 170
transcendence, 136, 206
Trump, Donald, 13, 261
Tutu, Archbishop Desmond, 1, 4

ubuntu, 1–4, 6
unemployment, 97
Universal Declaration of Human Rights, 84–6, 99
universalism, 80, 94, 180, 289

Valladolid Disputation, 26
Vatican Council, 117
Villey, Michel, 77
virtue-signalling, 11
vivisection, 26

Wall, Illan Rua, 78–9, 96, 110
Walzer, Michael, 86, 276
Weber, Max, 95
Weil, Simone, 104, 109

303

West Germany, 115
'white guilt', 12, 108
'white saviour' mentality, 107
'white victimhood', 106, 179
'will to feel innocent', 220, 222, 257
Williams, Charles, 209–18, 222–5, 227–9, 233, 239–41, 290–1, 293–4

witness, 2, 4, 22, 54, 168, 191, 222, 229–30, 238, 241
Wittgenstein, Ludwig, 5, 39, 95, 265–6, 289
women's rights, 92–3, 106, 278

'zero point of orientation', 61–3, 66–7, 71, 81, 232, 270
'zoelogy', 27